POKER, SEX & DYING

INSIDE THE MIND OF A GAMBLER

JUEL E. ANDERSON

MARKETPLACE BOOKS
ELLICOTT CITY, MARYLAND

ISBN 1-59280-055-6

Printed in the United States of America.
1 2 3 4 5 6 7 8 9 0

CONTENTS

POKER, SEX & DYING

BY
JUEL E. ANDERSON

GAMBLERS I'VE KNOWN

"Just how good are you?" I ask.

She replied, "Twice as good as most but only half as good as I think I am."

"What is your name?" I ask.

She said, "Treli, that's Greek for crazy."

It was an ordinary game till about half past midnight. As usual, my stack was a little limp, considerably shorter than just a few hours earlier. Then Lady Luck walked in and sat down next to me. Wearing a red dress and silk stockings, she leaned over and whispered, "Why don't we raise it up?" "You gotta be crazy I screamed, all I got is a pair of fives!" "Trust me, sit back, relax, let me play for you awhile" she said, as her hand moved over to encircle what was left of my stack. She ran her fingers up and down the stack caressing it as if it might hold possibilities. Slowly she began to grind. Took care of the third seat first. Then she lured in the chump at the end of the table. The fourth seat was next, cracked his nuts with a sledgehammer. The poor bastard. Suddenly I realized my stack had grown to an enormous size. I grabbed it away from her and said, "Let me help you, let's get it all in, they don't know how good you are, hell, I don't know how good you are..."

Watched the waves roll in the next day. Lady Luck had blown it, deserted me just hours after she had arrived. The huge stack of a few hours earlier was also gone, dust in the wind.

The next night I waited for Lady Luck to arrive. She never did. The fat slob at the end of the table, the one with dirty fingernails and all my chips, said she was across town playing 7-stud with some Australian who had Robert Mitchum eyes, choir boy scruples and priestly intentions. It sounded just like every stud player I'd ever known. I vowed to quit gambling. . . soon, someday soon.

Son, if you ain't been broke, it just means one thing, you ain't been gambling enough. And if you ain't been rich, it means the same thing. The only difference between $3,000 and $300,000 is attitude. But, most people have got the attitude backward. If you ain't got the right attitude, that $300,000 you're guarding and squeezing is liable to be dust tomorrow. Likewise, that $3,000, if you got the right attitude, is liable to catch fire and you're gonna have to have a Brink's truck to haul it all away. People that ain't got no money got that way cause they're afraid to gamble. They keep believing that crap about a bird in the hand is worth more than two in the bush. I can always spot 'em a mile away. They always got bird shit in their hand, and a worried look on their face. But, I love 'em. Every time I raise "em, I see their pulse go pitty patter and I know it ain't gonna be long till I've ground that 300 grand to dust.

Discipline, it's the only God that wealth and power bow to. To the majority, it resembles a ball and chain that shackles; to the minority, it's a throne. To most, it's as elusive as a disappearing mist; to a few, it's their finest outer garment. The forefather of discipline is pain, adversity and failure. It's lessons learned and experiences that taught. It flies on wings of steel, an unalterable course that gives full meaning to that destination called life. Its pathways are as straight as an arrow; its impact is as sure as an arrow to the heart.

At its dawning, discipline is rooted in pain; yet, by the evening its reward is pleasure. Those who reject discipline, accept the momentary pleasure of being undisciplined, while not knowing that their pain arrives in the evening, remaining there as a constant companion.

Before you decide to gamble, go make an unassailable covenant with discipline. To do so will make you an unbeatable foe; the hunter, not the hunted; the stalker, not the prey. Come... show me the man, the institution or the blinding thought that can wrestle successfully; the one who is fully armed with patience, persistence, perseverance and commitment. At twilight, your enemies will be weary, full of compromise, begging for the negotiated settlement. Because your covenant was borne of fire and steel, it's superior to the covenants of those without discipline. Look closely! Their supposed fortress is but a mere raggedy-ass tent pitched in the desert. Know this! Bravado in the heart of a gambler without discipline is nothing more than an application for slavery, a resume submitted by the foolish. The only thing left to negotiate is mercy. Know this, also! Mercy springs forth from God and from man's conscience. Discipline has no prisoner of war camps. Do not give the foolish a second chance. Discipline demands that you have no opponents who can arise from the dust to attack while you sleep peacefully.

Pulse. Every poker game, every market, every sporting event has a pulse. To gamble and win successfully, you have to find and understand the pulse of the event in question. To many, gamblers are post-mortem pulse takers. They chunk down the money, oblivious to the actuality of the situation. The end result is akin to trying to find the pulse of a corpse. The most important reason for understanding the pulse of an event is so you can accurately predict the future. There is no value in gambling if you cannot predict future trends before they become a reality. Value comes from betting on that which is yet to occur, not on what is transpiring at the moment. If you can't predict courses, trends and probable action, all that you will accomplish is the paying of the Vigorish on someone else's bet. By the time your money arrives, ready for action, the value is gone. The smarter money has already depleted the value. The biggest money burner I've ever known is called "public opinion." If its money arrives before yours, then the majority of time, it will mean only one thing: your bet is a losing proposition.

"Mister, you ain't running me out of any of these pots tonight, 'cause I got balls as big as a brass monkey. I raise."

"Sir, I don't know what to say except I've never seen a brass monkey and I love you guys that sit at poker tables and mentally masturbate. Every dollar you ever owned has a hard on and is always looking for a new home. I raise."

The most valuable lesson you can learn (it's not taught in physiology class), about the human anatomy is this: God, in His infinite wisdom, constructed us in such a way that we can kiss everyone's ass except our own. This lesson, in and of itself, should be cause enough for a man to be willing to engage in risk-taking, or at the very least, to take a moment and ponder the direction of his life. The saddest epitaph you will ever read is this: "Here lies a man who never took a chance. . .He died anyway." Don't think it an unusual epitaph. It's chiseled in invisible stone on the tombs of millions of men; the final indignity imposed on men by the Grim Reaper. Come. . .let us gamble this very night; tomorrow we may die.

If you want to be a better-than-average poker player, you must sell hope to those who are less skillful than you. Conversely, you must sell fear to the mind of the opponent who is more skillful than you. Hope and fear are the driving emotions in gambling.

It's wise to remember that in gambling, the wolves always arrive before the sheep. The confusion on this issue is caused because the sheep can't believe that the wolves often arrive in sheepskin. Where gambling and money are involved, always assume it's Halloween and every sheep present is a wolf in drag, until proven different.

It's from the lowly weed that life and success are best understood. The weed is ugly, despised, an object that the multitudes
constantly try to eradicate. The fools covet grass, lusting after its
lushness, its softness, its manicured perfection. Yet, character, will
power and the overwhelming desire to survive springs from the
root of the weed and not from the blade of the grass. In the desert
wilderness, the grass withers under the scorching sun; it surrenders
without a fight when the land becomes parched; it starves without
constant attention and perfect conditions. In contrast, the weed
flourishes and survives regardless of the conditions imposed upon
it. Adversity is its fertilizer, struggle is its joy, its roots are embedded with the will to live, to fight, to survive. Likewise are the
hearts of men. I shall hire my help, choose my friends and keep
my company only with those men whose spirit resembles that of
the weed. Life gives its rewards in direct proportion to those who
understand that life's first command is: "Fight for it."

One of the dictates that life enforces is this: "You have to do
the things you don't like in order to do some of the things you do
like." It's the vig or commission that life extracts as a payment for
living. Don't be fooled as to the ratio. It's not an even-money bet.
Nor is it 6/5, 3/2, or even 2/1. In reality, the ratio is closer to 5/1.
You do five things of labor, and life, in turn, gives you one event,
one luxury, one ecstacy. It's neither fair nor unfair. It's simply the
mathematics of life. The understanding of this law will dictate
both the amount and speed with which you realize happiness. The
foolish and the ignorant are forever trying to cheat life out of its
vig. The result is a stacked deck against you as you compound
poverty and unhappiness to the hand you've dealt yourself. Not
one man has ever changed one letter of the laws that enforce life as
we know it.

One part maniacal, one part crazy; one part heart, one part
courage; one part robot, one part passion; one part charity, two
part Robber Baron. . . A Gambler.

I've been criticized, ostracized and patronized. I've yet to be
eulogized, idolized or canonized. I still have the sweet breath of

life and the willingness to gamble on myself, on you, and every-thing in between. Should we meet by chance, I wish you good for-tune. Should we meet at the Gentleman's Gambling Emporium, I hope I cut your fucking heart out. If the tables are turned, please leave me cab fare at the door.

The real secret of gambling (sports betting) has its roots in chaos, anarchy, randomness... aberrations in the law of normal dis-tribution. It's the very same law that keeps the theoretical physi-cists scrambling to explain the universe. It's luck, but it's not dumb luck. It takes discipline and some intellect to position your-self on the right side of luck. Most individuals can't because they think. It's a fatal flaw as it renders the individual impotent to understand, thus use the above-revealed secret. If you want to make The Big Score, a quick million (in and out the door before the paint dried), read the above again and again. Lady Luck is demanding, a bitch in heat. She wants to be serviced, not chal-lenged. Unless you're dropping 40 or 50 grand on a game, proba-bility is nothing more than a hot-sucker bet, an 11 to 10 vig bet that guarantees the hearse will arrive before the Brink's truck. Lady Luck is a 850 to 1 prop bet that shines on a chosen few. The quick score has two dictates:

A. Bet a little on a chance to win a lot, and

B. You have to parlay, win to win and money to money.

The wise guys can't understand it because they are always moaning about the vig charge while not knowing that the real vigorish is extracted by that which can't be controlled. Gambling and probability are doctrines that conflict. Gambling and luck are axiomatic truths without conflict. Lady Luck pisses all over gamblers because they never extend their hands without first violating the laws that govern luck.

Reality is a contradiction of a contradiction.

It's nut cutting time!

"THE JEWELL"

WELCOME

If you're a million miles out in space, looking at planet Earth, it would appear as little more than a dot of light. However, if you are standing on the face of the Earth, your perspective is totally different. Oftentimes what we see and understand is determined by how broad or limited our perspective is on the subject matter. If we can see a problem from a different angle than normal, then the possibility exists that a better or different solution will be found. This book, *Poker, Sex and Dying* is intended to give sales and marketing people a different perspective. Hopefully, it will expand your understanding of those individuals you deal with in your chosen profession.

I've spent the last 25 years in sales and sales management. I've owned companies that had some of the best selling agents in the country. In that time, I've sold just about everything that was in the marketplace. I've trained selling agents who have earned over $1 million per year in sales commissions. I've also trained those individuals who didn't have enough ability to sell themselves on getting out of bed in the morning. Looking back over the last 25 years from the perspective that I now have gives me three concrete beliefs regarding selling or any other profession. Those beliefs are:

♠ Products and services are all the same

♠ People, not things, are what count

♠ People skills result in winners and champions

You can have the greatest product or service in the world, yet it will be of little value unless you can understand the needs, desires, and motivating impulses of the buyers you're dealing with. More than likely, your product or service is going to be just about the same as ten thousand of your competitors'. Today all products and services have the same numbing advertising claims. They are all bigger, brighter, faster, shinier. Therein the buyer's mind is hypnotized to the point that they cannot distinguish a difference. Therefore, the difference will have to be you, the selling agent, and your skill at getting inside the mind of the buyer. If you really want to get inside an individual's mind, then you must understand their dominant personality trait. It is the key that unlocks their minds and gives you access to their values, beliefs, needs, desires, fears and hopes. If you cannot understand these things in an individual, then the best you can hope for is that some of the mud you throw on the wall sticks.

This book is about the 13 different dominant personality traits that comprise the range and scope of our fellow human beings. You have a dominant personality trait, I have one, your best friend has one. If I want to keenly understand you and your uniqueness, the best place I can start is by knowing the trait of personality that controls your behavior and actions. Once I have that understanding, I then have a base from which I can accurately predict what you need, want and desire and the manner in which these results can best be accomplished. In other words, I can sell you in language, action and behavior that is familiar and comfortable to you. If I understand your dominant personality trait it means I have the combination to the safe. I don't need to endlessly twist the dial hoping to get lucky. I'll let the competition twist your dial; I prefer to already be inside your mind, working with you. The bottom line is, selling can be as easy or as difficult as you make it. The choice is yours.

I guess the next logical question is, "What does poker, poker games and poker players have to do with sales and marketing?" The answer is, "everything." In many respects, poker games are the ultimate selling game. Just as products and services are secondary to buyers and sellers; likewise, the cards a poker player holds are secondary to him and his opponent. In poker, the only thing being sold is the player and his/her image. In a poker game there are no products or services. It's one individual testing another individual in the hope of winning the money. Poker is an intense emotional game. More than any other endeavor, it exposes the different personality traits in individuals. Because the stakes are high and the risk great, personality and emotions are magnified. Poker players are extremely good sales people. After all, it's the only asset that they bring to the game. Since they have no product or service to fall back on, poker players live in a world of constant "do or die." Results are measured with each turn of a card.

Even if you've never played poker or know nothing about the game, this book will help you become a better selling professional. The 13 personality types are exposed in two different formats. They are first exposed in how they act and react in a poker game. Next, they are revealed in how they act and react as buyers. It's my belief that the broader perspective you have of how an individual acts, thinks, reacts, etc. can only serve to put you one step up the ladder. I've taken two perspectives, poker and selling, to use as vehicles that can provide you information that can be converted into usable selling skills.

I chose poker players and the selling industry as the profession for looking at the 13 different personality traits. I could just have easily chosen to use doctors, lawyers, commodity traders, engineers, etc. It's my belief that the information in this book is useful regardless of the profession that you are trained in. At the risk of being redundant, I'll state once more that the biggest asset that planet Earth has is people, not things. "Things" are the by-product of people. We don't get "things" from "things," we get "things" from people, and most times we get them in direct proportion to our people skills.

Information is valuable only to the extent that it helps and improves yourself. I have a desk top full of information that was unsolicited and that I find neither useful nor valuable. This is not to say that it's not useful or valuable to others, it's just not useful to me. If it's not useful or valuable, then I have to classify it as gossip, propaganda, etc. It's my belief that the beginning and the continuation of all success comes when an individual first knows of the self. To know thyself is more valuable than gold. When you know yourself thoroughly, then you can begin to know others. It's been my observation over the past 25 years that the biggest reason for failure was that individuals self-destructed. And the tragic part was that they didn't realize that it was their own habits and actions that was leading to this destruction. In reading this book, your first goal should be to find and identify yourself within the 13 personality traits. From that point forward, perhaps you can start to understand and identify others along with their motivating needs, wants and desires. *Best Wishes.*

> The following information will briefly
> explain poker terminology and the poker
> game of Hold'em. Familiarize yourself with
> the overall concept of the game, then
> precede with the rest of the book.

The game of Texas Hold'em is usually played with seven to ten players. As the game begins, the dealer, starting at his left, deals each player two cards face down. The dealing always moves left to right. In casino games, there is a house dealer, so a rotating button or puck is put in front of a player to indicate that he is the dealer for that hand. Whoever has the button is the last to receive cards and gets to act last in the betting round. There is one round of betting on these first two cards. You may call, check, raise, re-raise, fold, etc. When the betting is completed, the dealer deals three consecutive cards face up in the middle of the table. These cards are called the flop. These are community cards that can be used by all the players still in the hand. There is now a second round of betting. The dealer then deals a fourth card face up. Another round of betting takes place, then the dealer deals the fifth and final card face up and the final round of betting takes place. The player with the best poker hand using the best five out of seven cards (his original two cards plus the five community cards) wins the pot. The button then moves one player to the left and the next hand begins. If the game is Limit Hold'em you can bet only in increments that conform to the limit structure such as $20-$40 or $30-$60. If the game is no limit you may bet any amount of the chips or money that you have in front of you. It may be $100 or $1 million.

Poker Terminology

Back Door Flush (or Straight) - A player is said to make a back door flush when the last two cards make his hand even though he played on the flop for some other reason (like a pair or four straight).

Bad Beat - When you get a big hand beaten by someone who makes a long shot draw.

Big Blind - The forced bet in second position before the flop used in many games. Also, the person who makes this bet. Usually, this is a live blind which means that the player in this position can raise if no one else has.

Big Slick - Ace-King.

Blank - A card that comes on either fourth or fifth street and is obviously not of any value to any player's hand.

Board - The five cards that are dealt face up.

Button - Something that signifies the player who is in last position when there is a house dealer.

Calling Cold - Calling a bet and raise all at once as opposed to being in for the original bet and now calling a raise.

Drawing Dead - Having a position where the cards that you are hoping to catch will still give you the second-best hand.

Family Pot - A pot in which most of the players at the table are involved.

Fifth Street - The fourth and last round of betting on the last card.

Flop - The first three cards on the table. They are turned up all at once and start the second round of betting.

Fourth Street - The fourth card on board, the third round of betting.

Freeroll - A situation where two players have the same hand except one of them has a chance to make a better hand.

Gut-Shot - A draw to an inside straight.

Kicker - The side card.

Limp In - To call a bet rather then raise. (Usually applies only to the first round of betting.)

Nuts - An unbeatable hand.

Offsuit - Two different suits, used to describe the first two cards.

Offsuited - Two different suits, used to describe the first two cards.

On The Come - A hand that is drawing to a straight or flush.

Outs - The number of cards left in the deck that should produce the best hand.

Overcard - A card on board higher than your pair.

Overpair - A wired pair higher than any card on board.

Put Him On - To guess an opponent's hand and play accordingly. To put someone on a pair of Kings is to read him for a pair of Kings.

River - The fifth street card.

Running Pair - This occurs when the last and the next to last card have the same value (but different value from any of the other cards on board).

Second Pair (Third Pair) - Pairing the second (third) highest card on board.

Set - Three-of-a kind. (Usually means a pair in your hand and a matching card on board.)

Slow Play - To play a very strong hand weakly.

Suited - The same suit, used to describe the first two cards.

Tell - A mannerism which a player has which may give away his hand.

Trips - Three cards of the same rank (777).

Top Pair - Pairing the highest card on board.

Turn - The fourth street card.

Vigioris (vig) - The commission the casino charges you to play

Wired Pair - A pair in your hand.

Rank and Examples of Hands

Royal Flush - A-K-Q-J-10 same suit.

Straight Flush - (Five suited cards in sequence), 7-8-9-10-J.

4-OF-A-Kind - K-K-K-K, 3-3-3-3. etc.

Full House - 6-6-8-8-8, J-J-J-10-10.

Flush - Five suited cards in any sequence, A-10-5-8-7 of Diamonds.

Straight - Five unsuited, but connected cards, 5-6-7-8-9.

Trips - Three-of-a-kind, 4-4-4.

Two Pair - J-J-Q-Q.

One Pair - 9-9.

Highcard - Highest rank card that player holds.

INTRODUCTION

POKER, SEX AND DYING. You may think it's a strange title for a book on human personality traits. It's really not. When we talk about personality traits, we're really talking about discovering just what it is that makes all of us act, think, react, take chances, gamble, laugh, cry, play, become angry, bluff, give, take and hundreds of other things that we do daily as we play out our lives. In my lifetime, poker, sex and dying were the vehicles that put the traits under a magnifying glass, a literal way of watching mole hills become mountains.

Our traits of personality are like the clothing we wear. They cover us, they protect us, they give us comfort. If the clothing is stripped away we're left naked and exposed. When we start understanding the driving dominant personality trait in an individual we are then in the process of stripping the individual bare. Their motives, actions, fears and strengths then become naked and exposed. An individual who is naked and exposed is vulnerable, susceptible to his enemies. He can't worry enough about you! He can't attack well because you already know the battle plan and the weapons he uses.

I've been fortunate in my lifetime in that I've been involved in three professions where all the individuals involved were forced to become naked and exposed, either willingly or unwillingly. It's from these three professional endeavors that I began to learn about people and their motives, desires, fears, needs and wants. I quickly learned that people, not things, were the keys to succeeding. Things don't matter, they were nothing more than the by-product of what really mattered. . .people and the motivation that caused the action that resulted in things being produced.

The three professions that taught me the most about people and what caused them to act or react the way they did were:

A. THE DATING SERVICE BUSINESS
(the business of sex)

B. THE CALIFORNIA CREMATION SERVICE
TRUST COMPANY
(death and dying, the ultimate exposure)

C. GAMBLING: SPORTS BETTING
AND PLAYING POKER
(the harsh realities of being naked, exposed and alone)

Almost 20 years ago in Kansas City, Missouri, I met a man who was at the forefront of the computer date matching business, first in Ohio, then in Missouri. I needed a job and he needed a sales organization put together. The first day I met him in his office was like sitting across the desk from Clark Gable. He was the spitting image in looks, voice and mannerisms. He took one look at me and said, "We'll make a fortune. The men will hate you and buy out of resentment. The women will love you and buy because their heart always writes the check." He was right and wrong. I could sell but I couldn't make a fortune because all the money I made him went up his nose or to his bookie. I assumed that those who came through the door to spend $800 to get five dates would be those who couldn't otherwise get a date. While there were plenty of that type, there were many more of the type who could get all the dates they wanted.

The magic word was computer. It was the magical instrument that would fulfill fantasies and eliminate problems. In a few short months they all came through the doors. The rich and powerful, the beautiful, the hopeful, those with images and those hoping to create an image. When I asked them about the characteristics they wanted their dates to have, the answers were almost always the same. Warm, caring, thoughtful, nice, honest. However, a strange thing happened on the clients' way to date bliss. I soon learned that the federal judge who sat across my desk and said he wanted a strong woman, as he casually filed his nails, really wanted something more than what his words were saying. The next afternoon he was on the phone screaming that we were stupid sons-of-bitches. It didn't take me long to figure out that when he said strong what he was really saying is he wanted a woman with five-inch spikes who would leave track marks up his stomach and call him a worthless piece of crap. The computer couldn't be magical because the clients lied, either deliberately or because they failed to really know themselves, or refused to accept the reality of what they were or what they were wanting.

After about two weeks, I realized that it was ego walking through the door. I also realized that if they led with the ego I could snap them left and right and they would sit there and take any kind of punishment I wanted to play around with. I started ripping away at the masks they wore, so much so that a highly aggressive and powerful mafioso type ripped off his coat and said, "I'm gonna tear your f'____ing nose off your face." This was after he had coyly tried for a half hour to appear nonchalant, even disinterested. I had the distinct feeling that he was capable of doing just that.

My all-time favorite though, was a woman in her 50s who arrived in a chauffeur-driven limousine and after about ten minutes abruptly interrupted me and coldly said, "I've got $5000 in my purse, what will that get me?" I stared back at her just as coldly and said, "not much." Her eyes narrowed slightly, her lips drew tighter and she nodded her head slightly and said, "Young man, at least you know the correct answers." She never looked back as she walked out the door. I told Clark Gable the story and he looked like he'd just got run over by a train pulling a boxcar full of cocaine.

The more I ripped at the masks, the more naked, vulnerable and exposed they became. Their insecurities and defenses became more pronounced. I began to notice that certain types, when pressured, nervous or stressed, always reacted in a similar manner. The Aggressive type respected aggression, the Emotional would become betrayed by their intense feelings, the egotistical would try to cover their rear, etc. It was a bittersweet experience. I never received monetary value, but in hindsight, I received a valuable lesson in human personalities and what drove people in the intense arena of dating and sex.

In 1984, I formed the California Cremation Service Trust Company. My friends were amused. They keep asking what individual in their right mind would spend a $1000, years before they were dead, just so they could get a piece of paper that said when they died there wouldn't be anything to worry about. I perceived the situation differently. I believed that the single toughest issue that any human being would ever face was their own mortality, because it was an explosive, emotional issue. I believed the advantage was mine.

Emotions, not logic, move the world. Emotion sells, logic stalls the process. Furthermore, I was willing to gamble that psychologically, cremation was more acceptable to the human mind than the grim pomp and ceremony of the traditional funeral and burial. I was right. We didn't sell death. We sold love, peace of mind, the right of individual destiny. We sold the clients' mind not on death, but rather on the subtle suggestion that cremated remains that were scattered at sea or tossed to the wind was actually not death, but freedom, an endless journey into an eternal sunset.

In just a few short years, the Trust Plan became the single biggest seller in the trust industry. We did more than all our competitors combined. We sold tens of thousands of individuals millions of dollars of trust paper. It became so hugely popular that the national media began to refer to it as the Hollywood way of dying, as many world famous celebrities became members of the Society.

It was here, within this arena, that I really began to understand some very basic and fundamental workings of the mind and how different personality types responded to pressure. Death is not an easy subject. When we're dealing with our own future demise, it becomes an even tougher subject. It makes the hardest of individuals become sober. It makes tough men ponder their future and weak men seek shelter. It strips away masks, pretenses, bravado and machismo and replaces it with stark reality. In short order, when our own death is the subject matter, we all tend to deal with it in the manner that best defines our dominant individual personality trait.

Selling is closely akin to poker. Selling agents and the buying public are natural adversaries. One is the hunter, one is the hunted. Selling is a game of perception, intuitiveness, motivation, position, give in order to take, manipulation, image, and often a contest of wills. So is poker.

When you hire and train 5000 selling agents, one thing soon becomes obvious. They are all different. You start noticing that they divide into groups. The difference in the individuals is their personality makeup. All 5000 have the same job and same objective, (to make a sale). The different way in which they went about accomplishing this task was interesting, enlightening and sometimes frustrating. Furthermore, no amount of training could change them. They all had a certain personality style and when the pressure was on, they always reverted back to using the part of their personality that dominated them. Whether it was successful or not didn't matter! Even the most talented and brilliant of individuals was a helpless slave to that dominating part of their personality.

The Aggressive Selling Agent was tough, demanding and would run over the buying public. The I-Dominant was smooth, driven and the giver of confidence. The Eccentric was mystical, always trying to expand the public's mind about beliefs. The Worker Moralist showed up for work every day. A precise individual who could only sell through a mechanical, methodical, plodding style, yet day after day they ground down the opposition. On the other side of the fence was the buying public. The Aggressive Dominant Buyer was gruff, irritable, straight to the point. The type of person whose only objective was to get it over with. The powerful I-Dominant Personality would become introspective when the subject was his own death. They would reveal hypochondriac tendencies. They wanted to know the average life expectancy. One could see the calculator in their head as they tried to subtract the years they had left. The Theatrical Dominant Buyer was always concerned with the show. How to make one final splash, how big was the yacht, how many of their friends could attend the memorial service. The Reflective was practical, somber and most concerned that those they loved the most, be protected, spared any hurt. The Co-Dependent was a predictable robot. They always deferred the decision to someone else. It was always, "Whatever you think, whatever you want, dear."

Then there were the personality clashes. The Aggressive Seller couldn't sell to the Eccentric or Emotional Buyer. The Adventurer Dominant Seller couldn't sell the Worker Moralist Buyer. The Emotional Seller couldn't sell the Vigilant or the Loner Buyer. The I-Dominant could sell anyone; however, the complaints would roll in after the sale as the buyer became remorseful, suspecting that somehow they had been manipulated. The Underachiever sold deals that wouldn't stand up. They would try to cut corners, take short cuts to success.

For the first 90 days, the only selling agent I had was myself. I quickly observed that to make a sale I had to understand each individual's decision-making process. I had to find and understand their dominant personality trait because it was the weapon they used as both an offense and defensive tool to protect themselves and their position. Once I understood their dominant personality trait, I would then know the tactics they would use, how they would try to negotiate, the objections that would confuse or stall their mind. When I knew the dominant personality trait of the individual, I could always lead, always be one step ahead of their next move. I quickly learned about those who came straight at me, those who would try to confuse the issue, those who wanted to bluff and those who wanted to bargain. I learned that if a man sat back, he was negative, he needed more reasons to take action. When he moved forward I owned him, he was surrendering without even knowing it. I learned that if I could make a man cross his arms and stare at his shoes I could verbally punish him, berate him for shirking his family responsibilities.

Above all else, I learned a deep respect for the courage and strength that many human beings have. The one individual I remember most was a powerful rancher who owned tens of thousands of acres of land and was instrumental in the election of two presidents and untold governors. He was a rough, tough, no-nonsense type guy. After an hour of wrestling, shouting and arguing with him, I finally just shut up and stared at him. After a good ten minutes of staring back, he got up, walked to the window and stared out for a moment, then returned. He said in a soft voice, "This is the toughest thing I've ever had to do. I'd rather take a beating." He then picked up the pen and with a shaky hand signed the document. He walked me to the door where his final words were spoken, which I've never forgotten, "Sometimes it's tough to be a man, I hope dying is not as hard."

Most of what I know I learned through trial and error, observation and application. In 1983, I had the good fortune of meeting psychologist Dr. Milt Cotter. This very wise, soft-spoken man owned a company that did personality testing. It was from Dr. Cotter that I learned much of what I know about the different personality traits that drives our being. In many respects, this man was a genius to whom I'm deeply indebted.

In the 1970s I began playing around with sports betting. By the 1980s I was seriously involved. In the late 1970s and 1980s I began playing poker with my managers and business associates, friendly games that often turned unfriendly. In the early 1990s I began to play sporadically in public card rooms in California and Nevada.

Gambling is difficult. In some respects, it's the most difficult of all endeavors. To succeed takes enormous conviction and commitment. Most individuals don't succeed because of the inability to know themselves and/or the inability to control their own actions. In gambling, the only asset you have is yourself. The majority of individuals simply don't have the capacity to be able to depend solely on nothing more than themselves. The reasons are many, but the main one is the self-developed habits or traits that undermine the very structure you're dependent on. If you work for IBM, the company has guidelines and rules that protect the company. These same guidelines and rules also enforce a state of discipline on you that will protect you from yourself. In gambling, you set the guidelines and make the rules. In effect, you become God. When you're God, it's easy to change the rules. You simply say, "Well they don't really apply to me." As an example, in sports betting the enemy is not the line maker, its you! The line maker is wrong more than he's ever right, however, he's right by default because the public and so-called wise-guys are even more wrong than the line maker.

At the crux of the matter is a biased opinion. Gamblers always have biased opinions. It doesn't matter if the opinion is right or wrong. What matters is, it's biased. The line maker never has a biased opinion. He doesn't have to. He can make a fortune off the biases of others. In the early 1980s, I became acquainted with a sports bettor named Lem Banker. If I had to cast one vote for who I think is the most successful gambler I've ever known, Lem would get the vote, hands down. We used to get together once in awhile and compare our lines. I always thought my line was superior to his, more refined, more closely correlated to what the actual outcome would be. I still feel that way (a biased opinion). When Lem talked about winning or losing it sounded mundane, little bits about discipline, control or some statement about being able to play tomorrow. It took me a long time to appreciate his true greatness. I could never be as good as he was because what I considered important wasn't nearly as important as the things he attached importance to. Lem never undermined the only thing he had that he could depend on; namely, himself. All of his actions were designed to strengthen his support system. I, on the other hand, always had to fight both the line maker and myself. I could usually whip the line maker, but handling myself was a constant battle.

There are more opportunities to make money in sports betting than there are in poker; however, you'll make more money, on average, playing poker than you will betting sports. There are several reasons. First, it's easier to get out of a poker hand than off a football game. If you have A-K and the flop comes Q-Q-Q, even an idiot will cut their losses and throw away the hand if the action before or after their position warrants it. If you bet the Raiders and they're losing 35-7 at the half, you're going to eat the whole bet. Second, almost every sport bettor I know has a fatal flaw. I call it the can't lose syndrome. What happens is the mind locks on a team and the number put up on the team. It becomes devastating, because you become convinced there is absolutely no way the team can't get the money. You become unable to clearly see the whole picture. The bias within your own mind blinds you from looking objectively. The mind amplifies the positive while diminishing the negative. These teams do lose and they lose quite often. I've rarely, if ever, had a poker hand I felt that way about. Thirdly, poker has a structure within the game that enforces a form of discipline on behavior. In other words, you can only play stupidly so long before the ego is humiliated to the point that it takes over and forces you to tighten up. In sports betting, you are the only player. No one but yourself will ever know of the amount of stupid bets you make. Justification is easier in sports betting. Opinions are more dangerous and costly in sports betting. It easier and more costly to play God when you are not exposing the self to public scrutiny. Another reason and the best, is sports betting is a contest that hinges on physical skills. All players at all levels are relative in their skills to each other. (If they're not, the line makes up the difference).

Poker is a mental contest, an emotional leverage game. Mental and emotional capacities are easier to exploit than physical traits. All football players are muscle-bound. A muscle-bound poker player has no advantage over a 132-pound woman. Physical skills are constant. Most football players get tired at the same rate. Emotional and mental skills shift unequally. It's a constant state of flux. Almost one half of sports betting contests are decided by pure luck. In poker, luck is a factor, but skill is the long-term dictator on where the money goes. Physical errors happen less frequently then mental mistakes. If this was not so, then you would fall down the stairs more often than you would forget to do some task.

Poker is the perfect game because it involves imperfect players. It is a game that lends itself to the constant expanding capacity of the human mind. The more you're willing to put into it, the more dividends it returns. The more skillful you become at understanding people increases the hands you can or can't play. When we say "person" what we're really saying is not the person, but rather the person's personality. The part that makes them tick. When you can use and understand the personality part of the individual, you will become an above-average player, both in poker and in life. The worst trap you can find yourself in when playing poker is to have to depend solely on the cards you're dealt. You will get ground down, or at best be mediocre. In poker your opponent should become your helper. If you still view them as the enemy, it means one thing, they are winning, you're not. The purpose of this book is to give you added insight into your opponents and how to realize that in reality they are your great helper. When you sit down at the poker table you are naked, exposed and alone. It's not quite so lonely when you are able to use the help that others so subtly offer you in dozens of little ways that add up to small, ever-increasing edges over a period of time. The only requirement on your part is the ability to recognize, then use them to your advantage.

As a group, poker players are tough. I've yet to meet one who I think is easy. If I were involved in a life and death struggle and could make only one bet, I would choose 500 poker players over 500 stockbrokers, lawyers, engineers, etc. The reason is simple, they are better at surviving. They understand the jungle better. Most poker players live a life that is always close to the edge. I don't view this as good; however, it speaks volumes about resolve and basic survival instincts. My hope is that this book will help you, not only to survive, but also to prosper.

For illustrative purposes, the game of Texas Hold'em is used unless otherwise stated. The principles that are set out in this book are useful in whatever game you frequent. The structure of the games will be different, the personalities that play the game, not the game itself, are the constant.

IN THE BEGINNING

SIT DOWN AT ANY POKER GAME and you'll soon get the nagging suspicion that this game is not as easy as it appears. In fact, you might even suspect that it's inherently unfair. After all, there are ten players and only four Aces. One day you look down at your hand and find two Aces and an instant love affair, then you look at the board and find three Kings and heartburn. If you play long enough, you may even get to the point where you start hoping you can look at your hand and not find anything that plays. Poker is a difficult game. The survival rate is akin to dribbling a live grenade every day and not having it explode. Poker is a game of intense highs and lonely despair. Win three pots in a row and your memory of bad beats will disappear faster than the morning dew in the Mojave Desert. Get three bad beats in a row and you're in danger of circumcising Fee-Fee, the family pet.

Poker has no peers in terms of complexity, challenge, exhilaration, frustration and income potential. Poker is a legally-sanctioned narcotic. Play in one good game and you'll probably choose to avoid the bowling alley the remainder of your life. Play enough poker and you may wind up rich. Play enough poker and you may wind up poor. The choice is yours. From a statistical and historical viewpoint, it can be proven that the game can be consistently beaten. Conversely, the same viewpoint can be used to prove that other games of pure chance (craps, roulette) cannot be beaten. All dice are created equal. All poker players are unequal.

Some are better, by their choice. Some are not so good, also by choice.

In the insurance actuarial business, there is a God. This God is "The law of large numbers." In layman terms, what this law means is, "Spread the risk and all co-dependent factors among enough people and we, the insurance company, will get rich." This same law applies to poker players. The worst poker player in the world can beat the worlds best poker player in one game, two games or ten games. However, if they play a large enough amount of games, all the money will wind up in the possession of and in direct proportion to, the skill of said players. In poker, luck is a short-term aberration. Acquired skill is a God. Skill is the separating factor of all players at all levels. In this respect, poker is no different than any other profitably-run business. Skill wins. When was the last time you heard an executive of a large insurance company say, "Gee, if we get lucky maybe no one's house will burn today?" The fact is, they don't care if your house burns or not. They have become so skillful in the application of the law of large numbers, that what happens to your house simply doesn't matter. It wasn't always this way. 100 years ago, insurance companies were gamblers. They lost a lot of money, many of them went broke. Today they own a large portion of the world. What caused the change? They became skillful. How did they do it?

A. Hard work.

B. The ability to discover, understand and use information to their advantage.

Is it any different in any endeavor, poker included? I don't think so. We get back from life exactly what we put into it. It requires a lot of hard work to become skillful. The main reason it's such hard work is because skill can best be defined as an accumulation of small edges over your opponent. It may be unfortunate, but accumulative skill does not come to us in large chunks. It comes in painfully small, often slow, bits and pieces. This is a book about acquiring skill. This is not a book about how to play poker, per se. This is a book about people, or more precisely, a book about human personality traits.

Poker Chips And Personality Traits
(They all have differing values)

All poker players have equal opportunity at cards, position, maneuvers, strategy, etc. If you check raise me, I likewise, have the same opportunity. If you get a pair of Aces it's ok. I eventually will also get a pair. Position at a poker table changes with regularity. None of the above can be considered long-term advantages. Therefore, I can state that in the overall scheme of things that cards, check raising, position, etc., are of secondary importance in a poker game. So, what is important? Well, let's say I'm getting ready to check raise you. Is that important? Maybe. But what happens if you have information that says I know you're going to check raise. Don't you, through information (skill), really have the advantage? Let's use another example that's easily understood. You and I are both going to walk down the same dark street on the same night, only at different times. You know that halfway down the street a vicious dog lies waiting, I do not know there is a vicious dog waiting. Which one of us has the advantage? Information is a God, on dark streets and at poker tables.

A few years back, there was a popular theory in pop psychology that said you could determine a person's psychological makeup by the type of automobile they drove. As an example, Volkswagen was thrifty, a sports car was fun-loving, a Cadillac was success-oriented, etc. I think they had it backward. We say, "Don't worry about what the man drives." It's not important, what is important is to try to understand what drives the man. If I know that your personality characteristics and makeup are of a nature that makes it likely you're the type that check raises, I, through this information, have gained a small edge. (Information that leads to acquiring skill). A few years ago Kenny Rogers had a popular song called The Gambler. In this song, there is a line that says, "He spent a lifetime reading peoples faces." Again, we think someone got it backward.

If you're going to spend a lifetime reading anything, spend it in the quest to learn an individual's dominant personality trait. Your reward will be greater and far more profitable than wasting your time trying to read a professional poker player's face. All poker players have poker faces. Even bad players have good poker faces. Often, they have more than one face to fit what they perceive the situation at hand is calling for.

I once had a long conversation with a professional poker player. I had previously played in many games with him where he was always stoic, dispassionate and seldom made critical mistakes. During the course of the conversation, he revealed that he had lost the championship of a tournament to a player he considered clearly inferior and who consistently played bad cards and got away with it. As we talked, his bitterness and resentment came pouring out. He made two statements that stood out in my mind. He said "I was right he was wrong. You gotta lay down bad cards. I know in the long run I'll be proven right." Later he said "You know why I respect your game, you're not one of these bastards that's always trying to turn nothing into something."

He was wrong! From this one conversation, I was able to begin to understand his driving, dominant personality trait. (A Worker Moralist). I also learned that if I could show him a few good cards, I could run him off a few pots with bad or marginal cards. He once showed me down and caught me with nothing. I quickly told him I was stuck and playing bad. In a typical Worker Moralist vein, he leaned over and whispered that I needed to take a break. Again: Information that leads to acquiring small edges at the poker table results in a tremendous advantage when you apply the law of large numbers. (Small edges over many players over the course of many games).

What Really Matters

Let's talk about survival. In gambling, it can be said that survival is a form of winning. If you play ten days, survive seven and win three have you not, in reality, won all ten days? Survival is a form of winning until you can really win. If you and I are in a life and death struggle, what do I need to know in order to survive? Is it most important to know that you're armed with a .38 and your intentions are serious? It helps to know this! (However, you're sitting across the table from me with a big pile of chips, so I already know you're armed, I just don't know how dangerous you are). However, this is not the most important information I could have. Be it a .38 or a .22, what difference will it make? For my basic survival, it's more important that I know your habits, traits, your decision-making process, how you act, react, do you come straight at me or do you set elaborate traps. You're good with a .38, but how good are you with a sling shot. (A great poker player will make more money with a pair of nines than an average player can ever make with a pair of Aces). The very best way for me, you, anyone to know of the things that really matter is to understand that we're all personality-driven and that surviving and winning is a lot easier when we start to fathom the "whys" and "how comes" that lurk behind the masks we publicly wear.

Who Are We, Who Are They?

This is not an easy question to answer. The human race is a complex, difficult, species to understand and deal with. We are stubborn, temperamental, paranoid. We are generous, gifted, adventurous. Perhaps more important than who, is why we are as we are and why we do what we do.

Genetic Engineering

The genes we have determine many things as it relates to an individual. Skin color, height, eye color, hair texture, etc. It also determines many things beyond physical traits and characteristics. Genetics determine the traits of human personality. To what extent this is predetermined no one can say for sure. There is a huge body of evidence that clearly shows we are what we are, personality wise, primarily because of the genes that form us. There are other factors besides genes that help shape personality. Experience, environment and relationships also shape the way we act and react to the world we share.

No Excuses

This biological determination that forms us is not to be construed as a license for unaccountability. We also have free will in making decisions on how we use this personality that defines us. We can choose to use it positively (love, accomplishment) or negatively (abuse, destructive behavior). If we become the CEO of AT&T it's because we have the free will to choose that course. If we become a convicted criminal, rotting away in a prison, we also had the free will to choose that course. The personality we have simply dictates the style by which we accomplish the end result.

Human Behavior And Personality Traits

As we were yesterday, so we are today and will be tomorrow. Think back to when you were in grade school and to the individuals who were your classmates. If you were to visit with them 25 years after grade school, you would find they are basically the same today as they were back then. The class bullies are still dominated by the aggressive traits of their personality. The one who exhibited eccentricity is still odd by your standards. The one who was theatrical and spontaneous is still driven by their emotions. These dominant traits in their personality may have been tempered by age, experience, and circumstances, but nevertheless, it is still the dominant part of their being. It is the part by which we identify them (Rachel was always a loner). There is a lot of truth to sayings like, "You can't change a leopards spots. . .You can't make a silk purse out of a sow's ear."

Personality Is Neither Good/Bad, Right/Wrong

Most of the trouble in the world is not caused because a particular personality trait is right or wrong, good or bad. Trouble arises because it's different (clashes) from the traits that we have or the ones we enjoy being around. What we deem as objectionable may be quite acceptable in the eyes of another. The term "personality clash" was coined to express this view. Ultimately, we are not concerned with the good, bad, right, wrong aspects of personality traits. We are concerned with the different aspects/facets of personality so that we recognize and use them to our benefit. By identifying and being cognizant of the different personality traits, we are able to understand the resultant behavior (the what, why and how of the person). When you can successfully identify the part of a person's personality that is dominant, you then have additional skill, knowledge, information and insight that can be taken to the poker table. While it is not an exact science, I will state that mastery of it will give you a significant edge and a better understanding of the players against you.

Personality Is One Dominant Trunk With 12 Subordinate Branches

Picture in your mind a great tree that stands in the forest. This magnificent tree is dominated by its trunk. The trunk is the tree's main line of support. Going out from the tree are 12 branches of varying length and size. Some of the branches are long and powerful. Others are small and insignificant. This tree is you. The trunk symbolizes the dominant trait of your personality. The 12 branches symbolize the remaining facets of your personality. The 13 facets of personality dovetail, one to the other, to for the total you. You've probably heard the expression "A well rounded personality," no doubt it was coined to express the many facets of personality.

Facets Of Personality Are Discovered Through Deviation From Normal Behavior

I didn't discover the traits that comprise personality. Most of this discovery was done in the field of psychiatric medicine. By identifying behavior that went beyond normalcy, they were able to pinpoint the different facets and traits. In the *Diagnostic and Statistical Manual of Mental Disorders, Third Edition Revised* (published and copyrighted by the American Psychiatric Association), the 13 traits are listed along with their accompanying mental disorders. They are identified by their clinical name; paranoid, schizoid, schizotypal, etc. We are not concerned with the abnormal traits that comprise serious mental disorders; therefore, we will not use terminology like schizoid or schizotypal, but instead we will use a descriptive word that will encompass and define the trait in layman terms (Loner, Aggressive, etc.). It was from this brilliant work that I began to understand that sometimes you can best understand sanity by first looking at insanity.

Using Their Personality Traits To Accomplish Your Objectives

When you start to understand the total spectrum of personality, you will have within your means a better way of understanding exactly what you're up against as you deal with individuals who often seem a contradiction, even to themselves. An individual's dominant personality trait reveals why and in what manner they will act and react. Personality controls the person. The person doesn't control the personality. In many ways, it is a preset program that controls us. We can't say that it happens "in spite of us." We can say that it happens because "it is us." Personality determines:

♠ How we process information

♠ The values we have

♠ Our decision-making process

♠ The way we act and react to another individual

♠ What motivates us

♠ What causes fear within ourselves

♠ How we view risk-taking

♠ The risk we're willing to take

If you, as a poker player, can determine any of the above in your opponents, you have gained a significant edge. From these small edges should come superior strategy on your part to exploit the weaknesses and to proceed with caution against an individual's strength.

Our Dominant Personality Trait Is A Tyrant

We can't change what we are. The genetic engineering that formed us is not something that we can alter, nor is it something that we had a hand in choosing. When we were conceived, the dice were rolled, so to speak, and whatever came up became us, the individual "I." By fully developing other aspects of our personality, we can broaden the individual "I," but we will never change the primary trait that holds dominion over us. As mentioned previously, we all possess, in varying degrees, all 13 facets of personality. If we possessed only one or two of these facets, we would be a robot instead of a human being. (Or we would be in a mental institution). If the dominant trait of our personality is out of proportion to the other 12 facets of our personality, we become unbalanced. When this happens, we become too much of a Loner, or too Vigilant, or Co-Dependent.

It is our dominant trait of personality that rules us. It is this trait that dictates how we deal with ourselves and with the other individuals of this world. Inevitably, in almost all situations, we use this trait to negotiate for ourselves, to negotiate with others, we use it in our personal relationships, in our reasoning capacity, in our internal language and in our decision making. Furthermore, we are the way we are because we receive immense pleasure from it. Let me use an example, myself.

I was once playing in a 10/20 Hold'em game and raised before the flop from an early position. After it was all said and done, I won a very small pot. Now there's a young guy sitting to my left and he says to me, "You raised before the flop with bad position and a hand that only ranks 27th, as a starting hand. Do you always play that way? That was a bad play on your part. You must not know the rank and value of starting hands." To answer his first question (Do I always play that way?), The answer is yes and no. It depends on the severity of the punishment. As for his second statement/question (You must not know the rank and value of starting hands), the answer is no, I do not. A better set of questions is should I, and if I should, why don't I? Let's take the first question (If I'm going to play poker should I know the rank and value of starting hands?) The answer is an unequivocal YES! With no room for argument. If the answer to the first questions is yes, then why don't I? The answer is really quite simple. I receive no pleasure from it. Therefore, I don't do it. It doesn't feel good. It bores me. The reason it doesn't feel good and I find it boring is because it's not in my dominant personality trait or in my two major subordinate traits. I once memorized the 15 best starting hands. As I write this, I can only remember the first 14. Am I going to change my ways tomorrow and memorize starting hands? The answer is no. I, like everyone else, am too much of a slave to my dominant personality trait and its demand that we do that which gives us the most pleasure.

If my dominant personality trait was that of a Worker Moralist or Loner, you can be assured that I would know the rank and value of all starting hands. The reason I would is because of the immense pleasure I would receive from it. The Aggressive dominant personality is aggressive because it feels good to commit acts of aggression. The Loner is alone because they find little pleasure in other people. Remember this: The fastest, easiest way to throw an individual off balance is by denying them an avenue to express their dominant personality trait. We call this "creating psychological tilt." If I had to memorize 10 zillion starting hands, it would be the equivalent of committing self-induced psychological tilt. So what is the end result of the above-related story? Who was right, who was wrong? As in many situations involving poker and poker players, there is simply no right/wrong. The young gentleman was technically right; however, I was instinctively correct. I suspect that being technically correct will get you more of the pots you choose to enter, while being instinctively correct will get you more money.

When The Pressure Is On, When The Situation Is Critical, The Result Is The Tyranny Of Our Dominant Personality Trait.

If you want to discover an individual's dominant personality trait (and you do), all you have to do is put them under pressure, or observe their reaction under pressure. Just like the cavalry coming to the rescue, the dominant personality trait comes charging forward to deal with the situation. It literally takes over and dictates the way the person deals with the situation and all others involved in it. This is a real key in predicting the most likely course of action another player is going to take. By knowing and using the dominant trait of their personality, you will know in advance some or all of the following:

♠ The style of poker they will respond to

♠ The silent objection that your style creates in their mind

♠ The agenda has to be fulfilled in order for them to play effectively

♠ How they view you

♠ How to counter attack, to get the results that you want.

The dominant personality trait is both an asset and liability.

This dominant trait is what makes us unique, functional, creative and responsive. It is the main asset that we carry through life. The dominant personality trait is also our Achilles's heel. It makes us predictable, easy to read, easy to manipulate, and susceptible to the whims and desires of the tyrant that rules us. In layman terms, it makes poker players easy prey for the seductive power of other poker players.

How To Use The Information Herein

A. Things will change. The first thing to understand is using this information is what I call the rule of 10-90. This rule simply states that at any given time the behavior of 90 percent is working to create an advantage for 10 percent. The vast majority of poker players who buy this book will reject the material out of hand. To them the value will never exceed the effort needed to understand and use it. Others will use it only to confirm what they already know and discard the remnants of what they don't agree with. It is this behavior of the 90 percent that creates the advantage for you, the 10 percent. I said earlier that information at the poker table is a God. If you have information that your opponent doesn't have, you have the advantage. Additionally, information tends to become exponential in nature (information begets information). The next thing to consider is the game itself. In the next ten years, the game will explode in both popularity and societal acceptance. For any endeavor to experience radical growth it must have, in this country, social acceptability or government-backed sanctioning. Poker is on the doorstep of both. Once the wave is set in motion, history teaches that the next step is an explosion of information. As an example, computers have been around for decades, but it wasn't until the explosion of information on "How To" that they really became a mainstay of this society. The next wave in this cycle is new, better and more dangerous players. These will be players educated with technology and armed with information. If you don't believe this will happen, then look at Wall Street. The stodgy, establishment-run brokerage firms of the 1960s and 1970s were hijacked, torn asunder and taken over by a new, different, bolder type of player that changed the economic face of this country in the 1980s. The same thing will happen in the world of poker. When there is sufficient money on the table, you can be assured that a better informed wolf will show up at your door. The reason it hasn't happened yet is because there is not enough money available just yet.

B. Preconceived notions equal bad beats. An Ace is always an Ace. It looks like an Ace, plays like an Ace, has the shape of an Ace, gets attention like an Ace. Poker players are different. What you think is not always what you get. First impressions are often worthless at a poker table. When you start looking for an individual's dominant personality trait, assume nothing. It's superficially easy to say John's a Loner or Barbara is an Aggressive. Demand of yourself. Hearsay is not admissible in a court of law, yet at many poker tables it's counted as gospel. You need hard, convincing and conclusive evidence when you're dealing with something as explosive as human nature. If you don't demand of yourself, what you're doing is dealing yourself a potential series of bad beats.

Let's illustrate this further. I have a friend who's been playing poker for 20 years. One day we were talking and I asked him his opinion on who he thought the best poker player in the world was. After much deliberation he said Doyle Brunson. I said "Why do you think that?" He said, "Well he's got the most money and he's so damn aggressive." Okay, that sounds sorta logical. I then asked three other poker players to give me one word they would use to describe Doyle Brunson. All three said aggressive. One said aggressive but nice. I've never met Doyle Brunson, never played with him, know nothing about him. If I were to go on the hearsay evidence of four poker players, I would have to say that Doyle Brunson's dominant personality trait is that of an Aggressive. However, I don't go on hearsay and neither should you. It's quite possible that Brunson's dominant personality trait is Aggressive. However, it's just as likely that it's I-Dominant with strong subordinate traits of Vigilant and Adventurer. While these two traits have similarities there are also major differences, knowing the difference could determine whether you survive in poker. The point I'm trying to make is if you make a mistake mowing the grass, it's no big deal. If you make a mistake in judgement with another man/woman in a poker game it can cost you a lot more.

C. To know of thyself...the road to wisdom. Want to know the most dangerous opponent I've ever faced? (No, it wasn't you.) It was and is myself. Likewise, I suspect the above is true of all of us. Poker is an explosive game. It's centerpiece is MEE, Money, Ego and Emotions. It's not enough to know, have information and insight regarding your opponent. You must know of yourself. If not, you will soon find yourself being passed around the table as a sacrificial carving. If I were to give a 200-question psychological test to 100 people to determine their dominant personality trait, (we have) a strange occurrence happens in a pretest interview. I briefly explain all 13 personality traits and ask the participant to choose the one they feel most aptly describes their dominant personality trait. Guess what? Almost 50 percent will choose a personality trait that is incorrect. Almost ten percent will choose a trait that is at the opposite end of the personality spectrum. What this means is what we see ourselves as not what we really are. We see ourselves in the role that gives the most pleasure to our ego. . .dashing, daring, adventurous, but never a grinder. Stop and ask yourself, "How do my opponents view me?" Your game will immediately go up one level if you can start to view yourself through their eyes.

When you can remove the mask, set aside the ego and become unemotional about a very emotional subject. . .yourself, you will have taken a giant first step toward an insurmountable edge at the poker table. That edge is to take from your opponents the biggest advantage they have over you; their ability to know you better than you know yourself. The real problem that this altered view of our-selves creates is that we can never correctly discipline ourselves. It's like trying to discipline the wind. We discipline what doesn't need disciplining. We constantly say to ourselves, "Glad I'm not like that player," when in reality we may be exactly like that player, but we can't see it (or we refuse to believe it). When you can't correctly discipline yourself (play, temperament, ego) you are, in effect, engaging in a form of behavior that the mind will soon label as punishment. Once the mind becomes confused about punishment and discipline, we start rejecting both as bad and begin a long downward spiral.

The first step to knowing yourself is to determine exactly what pleasure, and to what degree, you receive when you engage in any activity. I was once asked why I played 8-7 so often? I answered quite honestly by saying that these two cards could create a lot of pleasure for me and misery for you if I got the right flop. If I didn't get the right flop it was easy for me to get rid of 8-7. If I flopped a pair of 8s, 7s, two pair, straight or flush draws, I could snap off a lot of A-Ks, etc. I know that certain dominant personality traits receive immense pleasure when they find A-K in their hand. So much so that they are willing to absorb a lot of punishment just to receive the pleasure of holding these two cards, many times to the bitter end, even after being check raised twice. Remember: We are motivated by pleasure. The desire for pleasure influenced past behavior, and will influence present and future behavior.

I was once playing in the 20-40 game at the Horseshoe when a player who had been sitting at the other end of the table caught up with me on the way to dinner. He said, "God, I love building big pots. I can't help it. It excites me. If I can turn two a night, it's worth it." After that conversation, it became a lot easier to put him on a hand. After all, I knew exactly what gave him pleasure. I don't mow the grass. The reason is simple. I receive no pleasure from it. I play poker in a certain style because I receive pleasure from that style of play. I will alter that style, or mask it, if I can see the possibility of realizing more pleasure because of that course of action. Ultimately, the style will revert back to its original form, in most instances. Any long-term change will come only if the pleasure turns to punishment. The second thing that's extremely important in understanding yourself is to observe your behavior as an independent spectator. This may seem like a contradiction, but it's really quite easy to accomplish. Just let the windows of your mind float above the table where you're sitting. Go high enough to where you can observe all the players, including yourself, still sitting there. Now just watch, observe, take mental notes. If you will be honest with yourself, you will start to see yourself as others see you. If you do this mental exercise often enough, you will receive all the answers you need to master yourself. There is one last step. Even though you have given yourself the answers you need, you have to be willing to come floating back down and ask yourself the right questions. You see, dear friends, most of us already know the right answers. It's ego and fear that doesn't allow us to ask the questions of ourselves. Think about it.

D. Concentration. The very worst time to learn anything about yourself or your opponent is when you're involved in a hand. The information is skewered, prejudicial. Too often you will see only what you want to see or what you don't want to see. If you're involved, the information you receive and store will always be emotionally tainted. Additionally, your brain will always reference back to it first as a pain/pleasure index, not as a barometer of usable reality. I'm not saying that information you receive, or lessons you learn while playing a hand should be ignored. After all, how did you learn not to put your hand on a hot stove? What I am saying is that on a long-term basis, information that is gathered without any emotional coloring is more valuable, more reliable and more often correct; and therefore, more reliable. If you want to become immediately superior in the game of poker, start concentrating when you're not involved in a hand.

The very nature of the game dictates that you will have a disproportionate amount of time in which you're not actively involved in the game. I've never played in a poker game in which I didn't find at least five or ten bits of information per hour that directly related to the "Why" and "How Come" of different players' behavior. This information is free. It's available to anyone sitting at the table. All that's required on your part is observation and the willingness to concentrate. In terms of value, it should be considered the same as winning one extra pot per session without any monetary investment on your part. What you're looking for is what I call unmasking of emotions. It happens with every player in every game. The end result of this emotional unmasking is that it will sooner or later become a factor in how hands are played and strategies formulated in future pots, in which you may be involved in.

An Absolute Rule:

> *In poker games, true emotional barometers are revealed later, after the fact. Emotions revealed in or immediately after the hand are usually residue of the battle and not indicative of how the player will respond later.*

I'll expand on this most-important concept by using a few examples. First, I'll use myself. Let's say I've been involved in a big hand and just lost a big pot. How do I immediately react? I don't, per se. I don't throw cards, I don't get into arguments, I don't moan and groan, I don't tell the other player how he should have played the hand to have gotten more money. I just accept the fact that I got beat. To the untrained eye it appears that I have silently shrugged my shoulders and said "So what." But folks, I've spent a lot of time with my mind floating above poker tables trying to figure out just who, what and why as it relates to me. What you're seeing when I lose a pot is not what I'm actually feeling, so therefore, it's not a reliable barometer to what my future behavior is going to be. This current behavior will only tell you how I'm going to react the next time I lose a big pot (I won't throw cards at you). Here is what really happens a couple of minutes after the fact.

First, I'm both highly introspective, (to look inside) and retrospective, (to look back). As human beings, we all have an inner voice that we have a dialogue with. The make up of our dominant personality traits will determine the breadth and scope of this inner dialogue that we engage in. As an example, a highly aggressive dominant personality trait who loses a big pot will literally have an inner dialogue with themselves that will consist of something to the effect of "Okay you son-of-a-bitch, just try to run over me again." End of conversation.

45

Other individuals with dominant personality traits such as Vigilant, Reflective, Emotional, etc., have, and engage in much deeper, more complex dialogues, since I have a subordinate personality trait that is highly introspective, I'm always involved in a debate that sometimes borders on chaos, if emotions are involved. If you are my opponent in a poker game, it's to your advantage to know this. It will help you to formulate a superior strategy. Here's why. When I win a pot, I'm twice as good as I normally am. When I lose a pot, I'm one half as good as I normally am. The reason for this is I'm still preoccupied with what happened when I lost the last pot. You're firing chips at me from all directions and I've got a voice in my head that's taunting me by saying, "Regarding the last pot, I told you she had a flush but you wouldn't listen to me." But it gets worse. Now the retrospective trait kicks into high gear and says, "Remember that time two months ago when you had the same hand, you raised, he folded?" So what do I do? I'll probably raise. I can't begin to tell you the number of times or the amount of critical mistakes I've made by playing in a pot immediately after losing a big hand. I now try not to get involved in the next hand if I'm emotionally distracted. Now, here is the critical point. I know all of this about myself, but if you want to become better "YOU" have to know it. Your chances of winning my money are much greater if you know not only how to attack me, but also when to attack.

An even more crucial point is, I, and everyone else, reveal this and other types of information constantly through the course of a poker game. If you're not concentrating, if you're not making a conscious effort to detect it, then the best you can hope for is that the cards you're dealt are superior to any your opponent holds. If you depend only on cards, you will ultimately lose. Time, discipline, tokes, vices, vig, impatience and bad luck will eventually eat your bankroll at a faster rate than good cards coming to your hand.

Again, the choice is yours. Concentration is a simple word, but a difficult subject to master. Here's just another example. I'm playing in the 20-40 game at the Horseshoe, I start playing about six in the evening and at about two in the morning a player who's been there the whole time leans over and whispers to me, "You and I are the big winners tonight." He keeps glancing at my stack and his stack then he says, "But I think I'm a couple of hundred ahead of you." I said nothing, but I thought his comments were indicative of what transpires in the course of a poker game when you don't concentrate. At the time of his comment I was stuck $2300 in a 20-40 game on a Tuesday night with only four players left, and the best I could hope for was to sit there and trade dollars and steal blinds. Even more ironic is the player who make the comment is probably the most intuitively great player I've ever played with.

Remember the absolute rule spoken about earlier? (True emotions revealed later, not sooner.) Let's continue on that road, using myself as an example. First, you can be assured that I went to poker school. I also know you went to poker school 'cause I saw you there. Now the very first class at poker school is poker face. What this means simply is, if it hurts, don't show it. Sometimes it also means, if it hurts show it only as a demonstration to allow others to know you have had advanced poker face class. There is nothing wrong with poker faces, per se. In fact, my favorite one is when player A looks at player B sighs, then says, "Well, I know you got me beat, but here!" He then throws another handful of chips in the direction of player B (if player A happens to lose the pot, raise him at the first good opportunity. If player A wins the pot, check raise him at the first good opportunity, trust me. Even if you lose, you will still win. It's an axiomatic truth "As a man thinketh, he is" . . .both you and Player A.) Human beings are not robots. We think, feel, hear, see, laugh, cry, plot, devise, scheme, give, take and so forth, till the day we die.

Our neurological system is first and foremost a response mechanism. It interprets what we're experiencing and translates it into a physical and emotional message, both for ourselves and for others. Put your hand on a hot stove and what happens? You jerk it back and scream,"OUCH!" Get a bad beat in poker and what do you do? Likewise, you scream "OUCH!" The difference is, you do it more discretely. You contain the pain until it's not so obvious to others. You may not say, "ouch" until two minutes later, ten minutes later, or an hour later, or you may say it in a language, strategy or maneuver that sounds more like joy than pain, but eventually we exhibit telltale clues to what we're experiencing. If you didn't have this emotional valve, you would explode. Furthermore, your neurological system will automatically override any silly pretenses or masks you choose to use to alter this life-giving spirit within us. It's as if when we were created, God looked down at us and said, "There are some things so important to your well being that they are out of your control." I'll give you two silly examples. Tell your heart to stop beating. Guess what?. . .It keeps right on ticking. Your command is automatically ignored through superior genetic and biological engineering. If the heart is too extreme of an example, let's choose an easier one.

Just tell yourself that for the next five minutes you're not going to blink your eyes, starting NOW! By the time you have gotten to the end of the sentence you are now reading, you have blinked. Why? It's a neurological prerequisite that to comprehend information your eyes operate as switches to give pathway signals to your brain. To do this, your eyes must move. When your eyes move, you blink. One more example. Pretend to mentally blow up a balloon. Notice what happens as air comes from your lungs to fill the balloon. The balloon expands in an even and predictable manner. Now, pretend you're going to blow up the balloon again, only this time restrict the natural flow of air into the balloon by wrapping your thumb and forefinger in a circle around the balloon half way up it. Now, as air fills the balloon, it expands in a distorted manner, uneven, unnatural. The very same thing happens to your neurological system when an attempt is made to mask or distort what you're experiencing. It's relatively easy to see this distortion in individuals. The difficult part is how to interpret the distortion and to have the commitment to put forth the concentration needed to both notice and understand it. After all, it's not nearly as much fun as playing poker hands, watching the ball game, ragging the waitress, counting your chips or any of the hundred other activities we engage in while pretending to play poker.

I've already told you of two things that happened to me when I entered this neurological warp, (became engaged both introspectively and retrospectively), but other things are also happening a couple of minutes after the fact. First, I have to shift my weight from the shoulders up. Why? It's the way I release any physical anger or frustration I'm feeling. The second thing I have to do is snap my chin (face) above the opponent who beat me. It's a way of saying emotionally, and verified through internal dialogue, "It's OK, here's my chin (ego)." The third thing that happens is I have to physically touch myself, sometimes the face, sometimes the arms or hands, sometimes the tongue flicking across the lips. Individuals who have a high dominant trait that is emotional, will continually touch themselves in some manner. Emotionally Dominant people have to continually bond to themselves to access how they are feeling at any given time. The fourth thing that happens is I have to move my lips. I literally have to come into contact with my lips. It is through this movement that I regain emotional balance. Our lips are extremely sensory-rich conduits that help us deal with what we're experiencing. Even unemotionally detached personality types will use their lips as a way of centering and balancing their inner being. The fifth and final thing that I do is look away. Almost always up, over, away. For one to two seconds, I'm literally out to lunch. For a split second, the eyes are blank. If you were to ask me a question, I couldn't hear you at this moment. It's here, at this split second, that I'm marshalling all my forces to make a return.

All individuals are different, we all act and react in a manner that is unique to what we're experiencing emotionally. Concentration and interpretation are the keys. Let's look at a couple of other examples. Day in and day out the toughest 20-40 Hold'em game in the country is at the Horseshoe. One of the better players in this game is a lady who plays almost every day. Her emotional recovery time between losing a hand and being fully competent to play the next hand is almost instantaneous. She reveals her intensity by coming forward and through a particular set of lip movements. This is one player I've always found to be more dangerous after losing a hand. I used to think she was a bluff because she could come back so often with a hand immediately after losing a tough hand. Experience is a good teacher. This particular lady gets my undivided attention and respect when she's in back-to-back hands.

Another player, also very good, in this same game reveals his emotional state of mind in an entirely opposite manner. This particular player has to have an extremely long period of time to become emotionally balanced when the cards don't come. Invariably, when he's emotionally upset he will stoically stare at a spot about six inches in front of his stack. Shortly thereafter, his right hand (fingers) will gently and protectively snake around his chips. When his fingers move from this semi-protective stance, he's prepared to resume play. So, often I've heard others remark that _____ never goes on tilt. They were wrong, he regularly went on emotional tilt. They simply weren't aware of it. While he was in this state of mind, he lacked aggressiveness, he would never raise the blinds and if he raised off the boards, you could be almost certain he had nuts and more.

Listed below are a couple of things to look for, be aware of and concentrate on. The list is far from complete and you should be able to expand the list as your expertise grows. When you start, just concentrate on one or two players at a time. Pick out one player you feel is inferior and one who you feel is superior. Soon you can pick both their pockets.

1. Are they negative or positive? All human beings will at one time or another express how they are feeling through what we call position modes. The only two we're concerned with are whether it's negative or positive. Don't expect to discover anything if the player is involved in a hand. The information would be inaccurate at best and guarded at worst. Almost all information that's useful comes after the battle. Positive is forward. Negative is back. Positive is open. Negative is closed. When human beings are experiencing something that feels, looks or sounds pleasurable, the human carriage opens up. The lips become fuller, often parting slightly. The hands and arms tend to move away from the body. The eyes become engaged in a more focused manner. The entire body carriage tends to project itself forward toward the action.

Exactly the opposite happens when we are experiencing pain, discomfort, stress, etc. Under these conditions, a human being has a neurological need to draw within themselves. The lips are tighter, the arms and hands closer to the body. The projection of the entire body tends to be back away from the action. If you make a habit of constantly monitoring an individual's position mode, you will start to pick up bits and pieces of precise information that will prove to be valuable to you in later battles. You will have a quick, reliable index to their emotional state at any given time. Remember: It's much easier to attack an individual when they are in a negative position mode. An individual in a negative position mode is more susceptible to mental errors and their level of aggression tends to become muted or ill-timed. Certain individuals, because of their dominant personality traits, are ineffective in their actions when in a negative position mode. Other individuals with different dominant personality traits are just the opposite. They actually become better under extreme pressure or stress. Concentration is essential as the difference between a positive or negative position mode is often slight, almost imperceptible.

2. Deviation from the norm. As human beings, we all tend to do the same things over and over in the same manner. The reason for this is two-fold, habit and comfort. Most men who shave daily start at the same spot on their face each time. Women put make up on in the same manner. We get into the habit of doing something, become comfortable with it, and soon we adopt it as part of our procedure. Poker players are the same way. They generally play in a style that is recognizable to someone who has played often with them. They become known as aggressive, tight, stupid, etc. Even someone who seemingly has no identifiable style is really a player with a highly identifiable style of play. Certain players will, with regularity, check, raise, bluff, limp, draw, etc., in a highly identifiable pattern. They perceive this style of play to be most effective. What they are doing is conforming to their personality trait. Once you can establish a player pattern, such as plays nut hands only, raises before the flop, check raises, slow plays, you can start punishing this player with precise regularity at two different times. When he's in his comfort rut and when he decided to start deviating from the norm. If you normally write with your right hand, try switching to your left hand. Obviously, this is awkward and uncomfortable. It's the same with all that we do, poker playing included. When you have identified a player's normal pattern, you can, with time, become accurate in predicting the what, why and how of their behavior. By identifying the style, you can then start matching it to the correct personality trait and add a much deeper understanding and insight into probable future behavior. In doing this, you should be able to formulate a superior strategy in dealing with each personality trait. As an example, a Worker Moralist Dominant trait needs complete information to feel comfortable making a decision; therefore, if a Worker Moralist Dominant Personality is betting or raising on the river, you should be fairly certain they have the nuts or close to it.

Remember: In poker, an inch is as good as a mile, provided the inch is on your side and not on your opponent's side. The second time you can punish an opponent is when they start deviating from the norm. In poker terminology, this is often referred to as shifting gears. Once you have established a players normal style, any deviation will stick out like a sore thumb. It's not easy for a human being to switch gears. It's psychologically uncomfortable. All deviations from the norm are best understood when compared with the individual's dominant personality trait. They may switch gears. That's not the issue. It's the effectiveness that follows the gear jamming that's debatable. An Aggressive Dominant Personality who becomes passive is crippled. It's not a natural state. To their inner self, it's an unpleasurable experience. To be passive is confusing to the mind. It creates questions, not answers, that stalls the process of dealing with the world as they best understand it.

A good example of this is the late Woody Hayes. Woody was a successful football coach at Ohio State for many years. He was an Aggressive Dominant Personality. Woody best understood the game of football by sending the fullback up the middle and off tackle. This satisfied his aggressive nature. When that didn't work, and he had to go to a passing game, he was uncomfortable and unhappy. Having to resort to a passing game was the equivalent of being in a passive state. Neither he, nor his team, was effective when they had to turn to the passing game. Superior opponents often recognized the fact that he was susceptible when he had to switch gears and adjusted their game plan accordingly.

There are some personality types who regularly and successfully switch gears. To the I-Dominant Personality it's a natural part of their personality make-up. The real key in strategy is determining if the gear shifting by the individual was because they wanted to or because they had to. If it evolves down to "had to" then the individual is going to be easy prey. When players shift gears, they fall into one of two playing modes. They start playing tighter or they try to become overly aggressive. When you can recognize this deviation from their normal style of play, you will have acquired an advantage.

The single biggest advantage a player has when they switch gears is the confusion it causes. If you easily detect the deviations in playing style, you have eliminated the element of confusion.

Your ultimate goal should be to become their shadow. Shadows create psychological fear. Soon their mind is invaded by the belief that they have no secrets to which you are not privy. When this happens, their resultant behavior is one of confusion and timidity. Both of these traits are eventually destructive at poker tables. If they suddenly start playing tight, your most effective weapon is aggression. If you look far enough and deep enough into the psychology of tight play, you will eventually find the element of fear, or more accurately, the fear of losing something they deem valuable (money, prestige, ego, exposure). When you find fear in an opponent, you have acquired a license to regularly snap the individual like a rubber band on a Michigan bankroll. If the said player suddenly becomes aggressive, your best course of retaliation is to try and match the aggression.

One of the biggest mistakes that occurs at a poker table is the perception that aggression is directly related to the cards the player is holding. This is most often not correct. True aggression is an attitude that is independent of time, circumstances, opponents, cards, etc. When a player has deviated from a normal playing style, to become aggressive it's just as likely that the hand is of minimal value, (J-8) as it is likely to be one of real value (K-K). Yet, the perceptual mistake often made is if it's suddenly aggressive, then there must be a valid reason for it; when in reality, it's image aggression as opposed to advantage aggression or personality aggression. While it's true that matching aggression to aggression will sometimes trap you, this is a price you must be willing to pay for long-term success in poker. From a psychological standpoint, it's imperative that you try and dominate the table you play at. This is not always possible, as some days the cards don't fall your way.

The second way to dominate an individual is through shadowing their play, creating the real fear in their mind that at any given time you're perfectly capable of pouncing from the shadows to take advantage of whatever maneuver they attempt. If you have superior skills in human nature, you will be feared as a player even when you're not involved in a lot of hands. If you have superior skills in human nature, it will allow you to selectively play certain hands against certain players that you otherwise wouldn't be able to play. Additionally, these opponents will start to sense this superiority in you, which in effect, starts to limit their style.

Poker: A Magnet For Extremes

If one was to give psychological tests to determine dominant personality traits in different industries, I doubt that you would find many that have the extremes that predominate in the world of poker. With the possible exception of the entertainment industry, I can think of no business that attracts as many divergent and pronounced personalities as poker. If you were to test 500 doctors or lawyers or factory workers, you would find the vast majority fall into a mid-range psychological mode. As an example, on a scale of 1 to 10, the majority would score 4-5-6. Using the same scale with poker players would result in an extreme amount of 1-2 and 9-10 scores. If you are a poker player, this is good news. It's these very extremes that make the players interesting, volatile and ripe for plucking.

When you start dealing with a profession where everything has the appearance of being the same, of melting together, it's not as easy to jerk chains. It would be like everyone wearing red everyday and you being asked to determine the difference. When you start looking at the personality extremes who play poker, it becomes obvious that the individuals are more Aggressive, more Reflective, more I-Dominant, more Vigilant than any normal segment of the population. The rigors and demands of the game itself seems to dictate that this be necessary for survival. This is also a double-edged sword because the more extreme the personality traits are, the more susceptible one is for both riches and/or ruin.

As an example, having a high trait of vigilance is good if you want to be successful in poker. There is, however, a thin line between being vigilant and crossing the line to become a Paranoid Dominant Personality. When an individual becomes too vigilant (paranoid), they can't play effective poker. At this point, the personality trait ceases to be an asset and becomes a severe liability. Suddenly, this individual will be snapped off with startling regularity by someone more skillful in human nature. As you become acquainted with the 13 different personality traits, you should start to formulate a strategy for playing with each type. This should be incorporated into the overall style of poker you play.

As an example, if you're up against an Aggressive Dominant Personality trait you should never raise the pot thinking the raise will cause this type of individual to fold. This type of personality may fold the hand; however, it won't be because the raise intimidated him. Conversely, if you're wanting to build the pot, this is an excellent individual to attack as they are just as likely to re-raise your raise. The remainder of this book will be devoted to the 13 personality traits and their individual style. We will highlight both the positive and negative and look at the strength and weakness of each trait. We will tend to look more at the negative as the game of poker creates advantages within the emotional cracks of the personality, which can then be exploited. To be most effective, look for insight concerning how you can play your strengths against their weakness. Remember: Half the battle in poker is knowing which fray to enter and against whom. . .Ego has destroyed more bankrolls than bad beats and superior opponents combined.

The 13 Dominant Personality Traits.
(The Distinguishing Facets Of Personality)

♠ The Adventurer .... First in war, never in peace

♠ The Aggressive .... The wolf who ate grandmother

♠ The Co-Dependent ..... A nation without identity

♠ The Eccentric .... Square pegs and round holes

♠ The Emotional .... Color me red (blue)

♠ The I-Dominant .... And on the 8th day, God created you

♠ The Loner .... Barbed wire souls

♠ The Masochist .... A painful truism

♠ The Reflective .... Life's difficult journey

♠ The Theatrical .... All that applause

♠ The Underachiever ...... Willows twisting in the wind

♠ The Vigilant .... Clint Eastwood on a pale horse

♠ The Worker Moralist .. Perfection in an imperfect game

JACOB CALLED HIS SONS AND SAID, "GATHER TOGETHER THAT I MAY DECLARE TO YOU WHAT LIES BEFORE YOU IN TIME TO COME."

RUBEN you are my first born...Foremost in pride, foremost in strength. Uncontrolled as a flood.

SIMEON and LEVI are brothers...They carry out their malicious plans...Accursed be their rage...

JUDAH is a lion cub...The scepter shall not pass from Judah.

ZEBULUN lives by the shore of the sea. He is a sailor.

ISSACHAR is a strong ass...He saw how good it was to take his ease...He became a slave to forced labor.

DAN is judge of his people...May Dan be a serpent on the road, a viper on the path, who bites the horse on it's Hock and it's rider falls back.

GAD, robbers rob him, And he, he robs and pursues them.

ASHER, his bread is rich...

NAPHTALI is a swift hind, dropping beautiful fawns.

JOSEPH is a fruitful creeper near the spring...

BENJAMIN is a ravenous wolf, in the morning he devours his prey, in the evening he is still dividing the spoil.

Genesis 49: 1 through 27 (The twelve tribes of Israel)

THE ADVENTURER

CLINICAL NAME:
ANTISOCIAL PERSONALITY DISORDER

Positive:

Independent

Positive-Oriented

Risk Taker

Challenging

Daredevilish

Spontaneous

Carefree

Generous

Sexual

Impulsive

Courageous

Yes or No Decisions

Fighters

Live and Let Live

Forgiving

Negative:

Undependable

Lackadaisical

Cruel

Liar

Disrespectful

Violent

Rude

Socially Inept

Pushy

Arrogant

Self-Centered

Insensitive

Boorish

Ill-Mannered

A Positive Overview

The Adventurer Dominant Personality can best be described as kin to the wind. They are high-adventure, free-spirited individuals who are not bound by conventional behavior. They live for the challenge of the moment. Working nine to five is not for them. The higher the risk, the greater the challenge to participate. As a group, they are dynamic, carefree, daredevils who need thrills. The Adventurer is not acquainted with fear, nor are they bound by the need to play it safe. Often they are spontaneous and generous, filled with never-ending wanderlust and a spur of the moment "let's do it" attitude. They are not given to a lot of mental introspection as to where they are going or why they are doing it, but rather, their energy is spent on just doing it.

Of all the 13 personality traits, it is the Adventurer who is the most physical (both men and women) in their presence and being. They often have the gift of conversation in a light, easy manner. They laugh heartily and kid easily. They often attract other personality types that are not blessed with the attributes of the Adventurer. They are often gifted in many areas as they are quick to learn, often through the willingness to experiment first-hand. These bold Adventurers are not afraid of hard work, nor are they prone to walk away from a good fight without first making an impact. They are yes or no individuals. They make decisions easily and effortlessly. There is little, if any, area of gray in their lives as their course is primarily black or white. They truly have the courage of their convictions and live their lives accordingly.

The Negative Side

The Adventurer Dominant Personality is often an individual without restraint, either toward themselves or with others. Their "this is all there is, life in the now" attitude is often confrontational. They will often have contempt for society and the rules that govern people. It is the "I want it now, never mind the consequences" that often leads the Adventurer Dominant Personality down the road of no return. When they are refused permission to have it their way, the end result can be, and often is, violence. They can be undependable in many areas:

- ♠ They may or may not show up for work
- ♠ They may or may not be financially responsible
- ♠ They may or may not be telling the truth
- ♠ They may or may not give 100 percent effort

The list could go on. Antisocial behavior is unlimited, proof positive is the bulging prison population. An Adventurer Dominant Personality who is unmotivated will often be pushy, lackadaisical, and self-centered. If they cannot be free to do that which thrills them, they can be boorish, self-centered, and totally insensitive to others' needs. If this normal trait of personality is so dominant that the personality is skewered, the result can be cruelty to others and to themselves. The next step up would be total disregard for law and order.

Identifying And Playing With The Adventurer Dominant Personality

These individuals are fairly easy to recognize. While most people process and make decisions on a combination of emotion, logic, and reason, the Adventurer processes almost entirely on their physical self. While we could say that this is a form of emotion, it is also much more. The Adventurer Dominant Personality must have physical satisfaction. There is a part of their being that can only derive pleasure from the physical act of doing. They certainly have an air of distinction that sets them apart from other individuals. This air of distinction takes many forms:

- ♠ A sense of restlessness
- ♠ A challenging demeanor
- ♠ A daredevilish grin
- ♠ A dare you to win attitude

Of the 13 personality types, it is the Adventurer who is the most charismatic. They are highly sexual beings. In many circles, their sexual prowess is legendary. They often have a physical beauty that attracts others. This physical attractiveness is sometimes an air or aura more than it is actual physical beauty; however, it is a powerful magnet that tends to suck others into the vortex of the Adventurer Dominant Personality.

The Adventurer is primarily male; however, there are quite a few women who are also of this mode. They were probably referred to as tomboys when they were children and they still possess the dare-do sense of challenge and wanderlust. Most of the Adventurer Dominant Personality types have a sense of eagerness about them and when they are excited about a subject, this eagerness shows through in their speech and mannerisms. When engaged in a conversation with these individuals, you will easily detect how interested they are in the subject. When you are on a subject they find interesting, they have animation. When they are disinterested, they shift their weight restlessly, nod their heads in absent agreement or at a time not relevant to the conversation. They will often appear to have a dream-like stare that is out of sync with the ongoing reality. If you continually bore this personality style, they can become sarcastic, dry, belittling to your viewpoint; ("Gee Billy Boy, I'm going to have to start hanging out at the car wash. You make it sound so exciting").

The Adventurer Dominant Personality will often have a thousand acquaintances and maybe only one true friend. They often have more friends of the opposite sex, as their smoldering sensuality makes members of their own sex paranoid, suspicious and protective of their self interests. The one thing this personality trait values above all else is their freedom. When forced into regimentation they suffocate. Like an animal caged, they strike back in any way possible to gain the freedom to do, go, be, as the whim strikes.

Another trait of this personality is the unique way they process information. The only time frame that really matters is the present. They are concerned about the past and future only if it relates to something they are itching to do now. They will use past experiences as benchmarks to possibly enhance or intensify their present reality. Don't expect to find this personality type in any 9-5 endeavor. They equate this to the equivalent of a slow torturous death. They often speak despairingly of those they perceive as trapped in this type of lifestyle.

The Adventurer Dominant Personality Is A Most Dangerous Poker Player

You will find many, many players who have this dominant trait. Equally important, is that this personality trait is highly susceptible in the game of poker. With all 13 personality traits the degree and intensity of the dominant trait must be taken into account when formulating a playing strategy.

As we stated earlier, the nature and demands of playing poker tends to create and attract personality extremes. This is especially true of the Adventurer Dominant Personality trait. Obviously, the superior playing strategy should always be to match strength against weakness first, then as a viable alternative, to match strength against strength. You lose substantial money in poker when you become trapped into putting your weakness against an opponent's strength. The best way to guard against this is to have a working knowledge of an individual's personality trait weaknesses and strengths.

To understand the Adventurer Dominant Personality, you must first understand how they view time. This is their mortal enemy. This personality trait truly has a lust and zeal for living life that is unparalleled. Adrenaline is the God they bow to. It is this very lust for life that so often creates a conflict within this individual. Deep within this psyche there is always a subtle fear that on a near or distant horizon time will cease, death will prevail, life will end. It is this subtle, unspoken fear that drives and creates conflict in the person. It is this unrecognized fear at the unconscious level that prompts the destructive behavior that is often attendant to this personality. To overcome this shadow on their being, they simply verify life by being unable to process fear as an emotion. Fear is something they don't feel. Because time is the enemy and adrenaline the God, life is always in the fast lane. It is this constant need for excitement, the need for the rush of adrenaline, that drives the Adventurer Dominant Personality.

Among the numerous assets that this personality type brings to the table is their ability to play poker fearless of the consequences. This personality type can, and does, use money as an effective a tool as any cards they hold. They are perfectly willing to shove in any amount of chips necessary to control or dictate the flow of the game. Furthermore, they are willing to do it as often as necessary. They process risk, not as a price you pay, but rather, as the greater the risk, the greater the pleasure reward. Anytime you're against an opponent who is willing to lay it all on the fateful turn of a card, you have a dangerous opponent. Their lack of fear creates fear in more mortal beings, causing many of their opponents to play a more guarded, cautious style, which plays straight into a second asset the Adventurer Dominant Personality possesses, namely a keen insight into human nature.

There is a lot to be said for individuals who possess the savvy often referred to as street smarts. The best thing I can say about them is: be careful, they often get the money. Many of the individuals of this personality trait left home at an early age to see what was over the next hill and have never returned. They have spent a lifetime living on the edge, surviving by intuitiveness and instinctual correctness. This personality type moves in and out of lives with disarming ease. They attract people with the ease of a pair of comfortable shoes or well-worn jeans. It is this seductive ease of attraction that traps other players. These people feel good to be around. They are fun, they make life appear easy, just reach out and grab it. Once you're lured into their web, you soon will be unconsciously playing their style of poker, loose, fast, it's only money after all. This is exactly what this personality type courted you for. Because they are highly instinctive and intuitive, they are skilled at using another person's emotions as a yo-yo. The manipulation will continue as long as it serves a purpose. Do not be deceived. The Adventurer Dominant Personality trait carries few, if any, emotional bonds through their life. They come and go as they please and have little sense of responsibility. They use and manipulate people to get their need for physical satisfaction fulfilled. They easily detect fear and apprehension in other people and use it as a weapon to attack lesser-equipped individuals. The Adventurer Dominant Personality is hot, impulsive, driven by the need for action. It is this need which leads to the downfall of this personality type.

They lack discipline. They have a low level of tolerance toward the ordinary, the mundane. Individuals who lack discipline take risks that are not appropriate to the potential rewards. The Adventurer Dominant Personality is the gunslinger, the warrior, the soldier of fortune at the poker table. The Adventurer instinctively moves towards risk. Their underlying desire is for involvement. The moment must be seized, not wasted. They dare to do, willingly and naturally, what other personality types can do only after a debating, weighing and calculating of the risks involved. The Adventurer Dominant Personality cannot accurately access the risk because what they do is not processed as being risky, per se. They can, and do, play hands of lesser value than other personality types. They can feel as strongly about a pair of sevens as another personality type would _feel_ with a pair of Queens. The key word is feel. Their outward actions are the result of what they feel and process inwardly. This personality type doesn't have to ponder the image they project. The most overpowering projections they have is they know that they have the warrior capacity. This projection is from the inner self that constantly feeds the feeling of bravery.   An example of this inner projection that the Adventurer Dominant Personality has toward the self would be in an endeavor such as skydiving. They don't question whether they can do it, they instantly feel that they can and the next thing you know, they are jumping from the plane. Many of the other personality types would either shy away completely from such an activity or have to first prepare carefully. The best way of playing an individual of this trait is by frustrating them. Don't get trapped into their fast and furious style of play. Play strong hands.

When you have a playable hand, let the chips fly. Always be aware of their sense of restlessness. When they can't get the action (fix) they need, they tend to try and force action. When you catch this individual in a state of restlessness, of forcing too much action, you can then selectively play hands of lesser value. Too many times, the Adventurer personality will play in a style that's more conducive to a head up situation than being cognizant that they are in a ring game with many players. Often, these individuals are easier to attack later in the game as opposed to earlier, especially if they are frustrated or stuck. Seldom will this type of individual try and play a deceptive style of poker (slow playing). They prefer a straightforward, two-handed approach. The issue with these individuals is not whether they win or lose. Ego doesn't play. Winning and losing is secondary to the excitement they derive from being involved in action. Because ego is not a factor in their play, it's important that your ego be controlled. If you start leading with emotions, you become susceptible to their superior instinctive skills.

The crucial factor in this personality type is the degree of discipline they've developed. Some individuals of this personality trait have, through age and experience, been able to temper their style to such a degree that they are world-class players. The great majority have not. Because of their lack of respect for money, you may find them walking down the street one week with a million dollars in their pocket and yet a week later they are totally broke. They loan money easily and borrow even more frequently. They are better suited and more dangerous in no limit than in limit games. However, many of these individuals trap themselves by playing in limit games where their style is ultimately ineffective because of the structure of the game. They seldom show much negative emotion at the table. Bad beats don't affect them. They are often complimentary of your skills. Many of these individuals are soft-spoken with a dry sense of humor. They tend to stretch their muscles often, much like a jungle cat. Their tongue flicks across their lips with regularity as they constantly access how and what they are feeling. If they throw away a hand that would have won the pot had they played it, then they will often make a soft comment to that effect. The most telltale word they use is feel (I feel, I felt, I had the feeling. . .).

At the extreme end of this personality spectrum you will find total disregard for laws and/or rights of others. At this point these individuals are full-fledged conmen, hustlers and crooks who often wind up behind bars, or in their need and drive for action and physical stimuli, they wind up dead. Almost all truly great poker players will have a high degree of this facet of personality in their overall makeup. If they didn't have it, they would not have the necessary "gamble" needed to engage in such activity. If this trait is accompanied by subordinate traits that provide balance and a degree of discipline, then these individuals will be as tough an opponent as you'll want to face. If they don't have the necessary subordinate traits, they are still dangerous, but even more so to themselves. Their lives will be a constant conflict of war, struggle, incredible highs and devastating lows. Ultimately, superior discipline grinds this individual down.

Above all else, you (as their opponent), must be patient. Eventually, their craving for action will trap them or allow you to trap them. It will often appear that this personality type is streak-prone, pulling in one pot after another as they catch fire. If they are streaking, it's because they are playing hands (and catching cards) that other individuals would not consider playing. Remember, to win five in a row requires that you play five in a row. Always be aware of how easily individuals of this personality trait let go of cards. If they have enough discipline not to buck long odds, give their play more respect. If they tend to ignore over cards or draw long to straights and flushes you can start to move in on them with regularity. Further erosion in this personality can often be observed by their attraction to other vices. The love to bet sports (often high-priced favorites with parlays), horses (long shots) and many times they are well-acquainted with drugs or alcohol.

Many times when they are flush with cash they become involved in outlandish business deals, often as the victim to someone else of this personality trait. However, it must also be said that many of these individuals are hard-core survivors. One thing you can always count on with the Adventurer is they are always willing to put the "gamble" in gambling.

The Adventurer Dominant Personality as a Buyer

You can't go anywhere unless you know where it is you want to go. That statement is a simple truth, which you're probably aware of. Yet, to be a successful selling agent you must be constantly aware that many individuals with certain dominant personality traits have no idea of where they are going. Their style is to simply exist. Their experience is that life happens, a constant series of events in which they find themselves as participants, either willingly or unwillingly. As the event happens, they act or react. Their action or reaction is usually based on their experience of the moment itself.

The Adventurer Dominant Personality types fall into the category just described. What all this means is that these type individuals are not always easy to deal with in the context of buying/selling. This doesn't mean they can't be sold. They can be great buyers. Their interest level depends a great deal on the product or service you're selling.

You, (the selling agent) are a unique individual. You have a dominant personality trait that drives you. Within this dominant personality trait you have values and beliefs that gives your life form, content and motivation. Yet with all your uniqueness, with all your talent, all of your training, you still must do one very important thing to realize your ultimate potential. This one thing is the most fundamental rule of understanding and overcoming human behavior. You must set aside your ego for a moment and realize that your values and beliefs are not always the values and beliefs of your client; and therefore, they are only important to you, not to your client.

Do you think life insurance is important? How about a college education for your children, or a savings account for emergencies? If you're like a lot of individuals you consider these things important. They may be so important to you that they form a set of values and beliefs for running your life. However, to an individual with a different dominant personality trait, the above-mentioned items may have no value at all. Their values may be having a boat at the lake, a race car in the garage and enough money to get drunk on Saturday night.

Have you ever heard someone say he/she is such a great selling agent that they can sell anyone anything? What a bunch of crap! You, me or anyone else is not that great, nor will we ever be. The reason we're not is because we constantly forget whose values and beliefs are important to who.

The No. 1 reason why we fail to make a sale is because of personality clash. Personality clash is caused by devaluing someone else's values and beliefs. We inadvertently devalue an individual by not understanding the dominant personality trait that controls them.

The Adventurer Dominant Personality trait is one which constantly looks to satisfy the physical self. Of all the 13 personality types, it is the Adventurer who most needs a product or service that matches their personality. The reasons for this are they are not great buyers beyond the area of necessity and those items that satisfy their physical cravings or enhance their particular lifestyle.

They will buy a raft to shoot the rapids with, while probably postponing indefinitely the purchase of life insurance. They will buy a new racing engine while being totally unconcerned about a roof that needs repairing. Responsibility is not a word that carries motivational weight with this type.

If you are involved in large commercial or corporate business selling you won't confront many individuals with this personality as they are ill-suited for this type of working environment. Their fierce independent nature tends to propel them toward entrepreneurial enterprises. Many of this type own their own business or they find work in an unstructured type of business.

As a selling agent, you need to quickly identify these personality types and adjust your presentation to their style. The presentation needs to be short, fast, colorful and have a heavy emphasis on what the product or service can offer as it relates to immediate satisfaction. Often they will listen to a sales presentation for a couple of minutes and if they can't find a point of reference that excites them, they'll simply cut the presentation off with a curt, "I'm not interested," or they will just walk away.

The Adventurer Dominant Personality types do not need a warm-up before the actual presentation. They have no fear; therefore, they don't experience the mental process of, "Do I trust or distrust this person?" Instead, they will decide in their moment-to-moment reality whether they like or dislike you. The fastest way to turn these individuals off is by boring them with endless, mundane details and dry facts and figures. They don't care about or need engineering details, per se. They tend to ask about the information that's important to their mental process. As an example, they may ask questions pertaining to performance (how fast, how big, how much, etc.). Your answers should always be in the same context. If they want to know how fast it goes, tell them it roars down the road at 180 mph but don't tell them it does so because of superior workmanship.

Don't try and sell these individuals by establishing emotional bonds with them. It's fine if they decide they like you, that you're an okay type person. However, the reality is they really don't care whether you like them or not. Being accepted is not a high priority with these type individuals. Being free to do their own thing is more important to them than any kind of social acceptance.

Never show fear with the Adventurer Dominant Personality. They live on adrenaline, and the fear shown by others is fuel for this need of adrenaline. They have a certain intuitiveness in their personality that allows them to use the emotions of others to achieve whatever results they are wanting at the moment. They can be manipulative in their dealings if it furthers their cause. The more sinister part of this is that they seldom feel remorse if they use someone. Their line of thinking is that there are users and abusers and it is better to be the one who uses. The best way to sell these individuals is with a straightforward man-to-man (man-to-woman) approach. Give it to them with both barrels. If they have an interest, they will come forward rapidly. Since they have a low tolerance for detail and financing, you need to keep the presentation interesting, yet simple. They become frustrated easily and will blame you if there are glitches in their getting immediate satisfaction. You will make more money if you are adapt at creative financing. Many of these personality types are financial disasters. They are seldom concerned with money. If they have it, they spend it. If they don't, then you will have to find a way to finance them. Don't try to play games with this personality. If you do, you may well find that it's a losing proposition, as many of them are shrewd and conniving. Don't be afraid to walk with the deal. They will often respond to the challenge of losing something more so than any type of reason or logic.

This personality type is often interested in you to a certain point. They will often inquire to see how you match their own unique style. As an example, if you are selling airplanes they will inquire if you have flown the particular plane in question: "How did you like it?" "How did it feel?" "What did you think?" etc. What they are searching for is the on-the-spot verification that if you are like them then they can duplicate your experience through ownership. Once there is a spark of interest, quickly fan the flames into a fire. The Adventurer Dominate Personality buys to fan their lust for life, and if you can address this slant to their personality, you will be able to sell them successfully.

When the Adventurer Dominant Personality wants something they are hot, impulsive and instantaneous. They move in a straight line toward the object. Since they are yes or no individuals, they do not procrastinate. They seldom argue or barter the price, as want and desire takes precedent over cost. Once you've established a basis for working with them, you don't have to worry that they will shop the deal with others, their mental process at this point is to get whatever it is that they are desiring as quickly as possible. As a selling agent, it will benefit you to move as quickly as possible.

The Adventurer Dominant Personality type's primary response mechanism is feel, either how they feel now or how they could or would feel. As a selling agent, you want to use a presentation that will evoke or enhance their feelings. The mind of the Adventurer is always associated, never disassociated. When the mind is associated, it sees pictures where it's actively involved in the scene. When the mind is disassociated it's like looking at yourself in a snapshot, you're there, but you're not really involved in the moment. Because they are always associated, it's important that every facet of your sales presentation be associated. If you fail to do this, you won't be able to trigger the response mechanism in the Adventurer's mind. They won't be able to get the feeling, nor will they be able to see themselves in the picture.

An old lion is not as ferocious as a young lion. Likewise, age will sometimes temper the Adventurer's free-wheeling spirit. When this happens, they can sometimes be called upon to buy through logic and reason. If and when they reach this stage of their life you will find them somewhat more responsive to responsibilities.

A big factor in the life of the Adventurer Dominant Personality is their spouse. Oftentimes you will make a sale to the spouse because he/she is of a different personality trait. It's the spouse who is the anchor. It's the spouse who has the practical side in the relationship and is the one who takes care of the business that the Adventurer cannot relate to or be interested in.

In dealing with the different personality types, I've always found it useful to have a mental picture of each type and what would satisfy the emotional and mental needs of each type. The mental picture I carried of the Adventurer was of a tiger in a cage that stalked restlessly. How did I handle it? I threw it a piece of raw meat with a big rope tied to it. The more I jerked the rope resulted in the tiger moving in the direction I desired.

THE AGGRESSIVE

CLINICAL NAME:
SADISTIC PERSONALITY DISORDER

Positive:	*Negative:*
Power	Rude
Focused	Ruthless
Daring	Violent
Bold	Sadistic
Disciplined	Unemotional
Tough	Demanding
Straightforward	Temper
Competitive	Harsh
Yes or No	Cruel
Black or White	Exaggerates the Truth
Courage	Boastful
Principled	Selfish
Goal-Oriented	Intimidation
Leader	Sarcastic
Fighter	Belittles Others

A Positive Overview

The Aggressive Dominant Personality is driven. They need to be No. 1. They are often brilliant and gifted leaders who can, and do, provide inspiration to those who follow them (General Patton as an example). These individuals are often creative, impulsive, and to the point. They are personally courageous and live to do battle. They are often dashing, dare-you-to-win types who have great self-confidence. They love the challenges that life holds and will often challenge others to join in. They are positive in their outlook and love a good party. They often have amazing stamina and their feats and accomplishments have been well-documented. They like people, like to intermingle with people, and can be quite charming and disarming in conversation. They believe in, and demand, discipline. They are often highly disciplined people who have a code of honor that they live by. Beneath the tough exterior, there is often a compassionate, caring individual who makes a wonderful parent, spouse, or friend. They value their opinion but will listen to advice if it is given in a non-threatening manner. The Aggressive Dominant Personality has a very strong sense of their own personal self. Many times they feel, and believe, that they are endowed, created, or chosen to do something special, a divine task.

The Negative Side

The Aggressive Dominant Personality is as the name applies. Their being is through force. Their style is to take, demand, and enforce. Seldom are they overly concerned with the consequences. They can be bullies toward others. They often possess a sharp, caustic tongue and will verbally berate any and all whom they perceive as being the enemy. These individuals are highly cognizant of order, territory, rank and power. Their world is mostly black and white, yes or no, right or wrong. All too often it becomes a case of "I'm the boss" (right), and "you're the underling" (wrong). When the aggressiveness is severe, these individuals are prone to settling matters in the way they best comprehend the world, violence. Their aggressive personality is not well-suited to tact, diplomacy, or negotiations. They tend to have the urge to want satisfaction immediately. Even in non-threatening situations, they sometimes are rude, indifferent, and vulgar. If you are perceived as an intrusion, you will likely be treated as an unwelcome intruder. They are often boastful individuals who play loose with the truth if they can see where it's to their advantage. Their ruthless nature often severely affects those to whom they are the closest. They simply derive a great deal of satisfaction from belittling or demeaning others.

Identifying And Playing With The Aggressive Dominant Personality

You come into their presence and you might be greeted by a harsh "What do you want?" "What are you wasting my time for?" The most identifiable characteristic of the Aggressive Dominant Personality is their straightforward, demanding demeanor. They seldom ask, rather they give orders. ("Bring that here;" "Get me that.") Aggressive Dominant Personalities seldom waste their words. They are to the point. Their main drive is to the objective they are wanting to accomplish. The manner in which they achieve the results is secondary. This personality tends to use the shortest sentences in the universe.

- ♠ "So"

- ♠ "How come?"

- ♠ "Why not?"

- ♠ "All right"

Another identifying trait is the style in which they move (brisk, directed, and abrupt). Most human beings have an element of fear within their psyche that lays just beneath the surface. The Aggressive Dominant Personality has no fear of either people or things. Because of this lack of fear, they tend to get to the subject matter quickly. Many of the other 12 personality types need a period of time to warm up, to accept that which is occurring in front of them. The Aggressive Personality doesn't. They simply wade right in. If you try to do a warm up, they will often cut you off in mid-sentence and tell you to get to the point. With most personality types in social situations, there is a common position mode that both individuals assume, which is where both are sitting back until their acceptance of each other is completed. The Aggressive Personality is different. They immediately lean forward, feet firmly planted on the floor, and elbows on the table. In playing with the Aggressive Personality it is important to remember that there are no rules, per se. These fiercely competitive individuals go for the jugular. They are excellent at accessing the situation and taking advantage of any weakness.

It is of importance to always remember that the Aggressive Dominant Personality is compelled and driven to do one thing, win. It's impossible for them to even contemplate finishing second. They are goal-directed, purposeful and often have a battle plan and a contingent plan to back it up with. Many aggressive personalities are fascinated by strategy, planning and discovering weaknesses. It is part of their goal and discipline mechanism. Ego is a powerful and dominating force within their being. Winning is the one sure way they can verify their self-esteem. While they love action, love the battle, as does the Adventurer Dominant Personality, there is a big difference between the two personalities. The Adventurer craves and needs action to satisfy their physical being. Winning or losing is not as important as just being involved with the action. The Aggressive is totally different. They want action, battles, to prove they are superior. Winning is supreme. Winning, being first, establishes rank and order, both important aspects of life to the Aggressive Dominant Personality.

The Adventurer Dominant Personality is fairly easy to recognize because of their physical and sensual being. The Aggressive is a different type animal. While they may have a physically imposing nature, they are just as likely to be scrawny, rawboned, nondescript, sloppy, bald headed, wear glasses, etc. Aggression is a mental and psychological trait that often spills over into physical acts. These individuals are easier to identify by their temperament and course of action than by any physical description. Immediately after their need, compulsion and drive to win comes their insatiable need for power and control. In many instances this need for power and control borders on dictatorial obsession. It is this personality type, along with the Underachiever, Theatrical and Worker Moralist who is most likely to tell dealers, floor personnel and other players how the conduct and play should be at the poker table. The Aggressive Dominant Personality does this because they just naturally assume they are in charge.

The Underachiever does it because they have a compulsion to find fault and assign blame. The Theatrical Dominant Personality does it to draw attention to themselves. The Worker Moralist does it out of a compulsion for details and the need for precision in everything they are involved with. The Aggressive Dominant Personality is straightforward. There is no indecision about where they are going or how they are going to get there. They process the world they live in as primarily black and white. They have powerful beliefs and convictions about themselves and about others. Being indecisive, wishy-washy or allowing their world to be colored with areas of gray, would be the equivalent of weakness, and therefore, unacceptable.

Many individuals of this personality trait are CEOs, presidents or otherwise powerful individuals who have clawed and fought to get to the top. Often their road to the top included the wrecking of other individuals who stood in the way. Many of these individuals were excellent military people. Even if they were not in the military, they have and enjoy a militarist hierarchy in their lives where power and position is clearly defined.

In poker, aggression is one of the key forces that drive both the players and creates the very nature of the game. Aggression is the single biggest factor in money being won at poker. It is also the single biggest factor in money being lost at the table. In the hands of those who have a natural ability to use it, it's a powerful and intimidating weapon. When it's use is ill-timed or inappropriate, it's a costly and foolish maneuver.

It's important to realize there are three types of aggression that are revealed and used in poker games:

A. Image Aggression. This type is most often used by those personality traits that are not aggressive by nature. Often it seems like a light goes on in their heads that says, "You gotta be aggressive, you've gotta get some respect." Often this type of aggression is ill-timed, inappropriate and backfires on those who perpetuate it.

B. Advantage Aggression. Almost all poker players have this type of aggression. It usually means the individuals believe and sense that they have superior cards, draws, outs, position, etc. Whatever the reason, it usually translates into a reward greater than the risk category. When this type of aggression is used by certain personality types such as the Underachiever, Co-Dependent, Eccentric, Theatrical, etc, I'm more prone to lay down the hand. You always need to be aware that when non-aggressive personality types become aggressive during the course of a hand, it's usually because there is little, if any, risk involved to themselves.

C. Personality Aggression. This type of aggression is inherent to the person themselves. It is their Dominant Personality trait at all times. The world is a jungle, it's dog-eat-dog and they are always ravenous. It is this aggression that we're dealing with in this section.

One of the identifying traits of an Aggressive Dominant Individual is that they are always coming at you in some way. They continually test the water (opponents) so to speak. They are always looking for a chink in the opponent's armor. They are highly intuitive of a weaker or bloodied opponent. Of all the personality types, it is the Aggressive Dominant Personality that is the most skilled at finishing an opponent. When they have firmly seized control of the situation, it is often their nature to become caustic and belligerent toward the opponent with an overemphasis on their perceived skills.

In playing with the Aggressive Dominant Personality, it is important that you control the flow and tempo of the game. Aggressive Dominant individuals respect and understand aggression, they secretly admire aggression in others, grudgingly so. A highly aggressive individual must be kept off balance. When Muhammad Ali fought Sonny Liston, an individual with an aggressive fighting style, he succeeded by putting a lightning quick jab in Liston's face, continually frustrating him. He continually stopped the forward thrust of aggression by counterattacking and creating an unbalancing effect on the opponent. It's the same way with poker. When the Aggressive personality has you going backward, retreating, they are both dangerous and deadly. When you're standing up, putting the jab in their face, they are not nearly as effective. The Aggressive Dominant Personality is territorial, meaning they want your territory, chips, position, rank, reputation, as their own. The fastest, easiest way to stop this is by being willing to counterattack, forcing them to spend time and money defending their own territory.

Most Aggressive Dominant Personalities are supremely disciplined. They equate it to strength of character. It is this discipline that is a major asset to this personality in the game of poker. However, when the discipline becomes too rigid, it often becomes a liability. They have rigid rules they adhere to. They also have rigid rules on what constitutes good poker playing vs. what they consider foolish, undisciplined play. It is between this right/wrong spectrum that the Aggressive personality tries to enforce their particular brand of dominance at the table. They are quick to attack any and all things they perceive to be a weakness in your style (their standards). It is this rigidness that often traps this individual in poker.

Poker is a game of many subtle hues and tones that can change drastically with the turn of a card. Aggression can change people, aggression can make opponents weak, timid, unsure; but, aggression cannot change cards. A pair of deuces will always beat A-K if no help comes. Highly aggressive individuals often have trouble with big hands, especially big starting hands. They look at their cards and see a big pair, or big suited cards and it becomes the equivalent to a baseball bat in a dark alley. Much like the proverbial red flag in front of the charging bull, the Aggressive Dominant Personality is unable to alter their course. As an example, K-K is virtually useless if the flop comes J-J-6 and there is bets before or raises after the Kings position. Yet, time after time, the Aggressive Personality's most probable course of action is to re-raise. Don't be impressed by how easily a player gets involved with a poker hand. Do be impressed by how easily they can let go of a hand. There are a lot of world-class players who will take a pair of Kings, get an Ace on the flop, and instead of laying the hand down, they drown in oblivion all the way to the river.

Another downfall of this individual is they often let personality clashes cloud their judgement. It is their need and drive to force their exacting standards on the world that causes this. In terms of belief and lifestyle, the Eccentric Dominant Personality is at the opposite end of the spectrum from the Aggressive. The Aggressive Dominant Personality has a compulsion, not only to beat, but also to punish those who are radically different, or indifferent, such as the Eccentric. This compulsion often leads the Aggressive to attack those who are different at times that are not appropriate or with ill-advised strategy. Besides the Eccentric Personality the Aggressive Personality often has a strong dislike for the Reflective, Co-Dependent, Emotional, Theatrical, Underachiever and Masochist personalities.

Position is an important factor in all poker strategy. Is a most important consideration when playing with the Aggressive Dominant Personality. It's always preferable when they have to act first, as it tends to make their aggression less effective as the possibility of a counterattack will keep them off balance. Be aware that a highly aggressive personality will often check a big hand early in the hope that they can lure you in.

Another consideration is it's to your advantage to play the Aggressive individual head up if possible. They tend to overreact to man-to-man, hand-to-hand combat. It becomes a personal indignity to lose while the whole table watches. When it's head up ego tends to sometimes become as much of a factor as the cards.

Another liability of this personality trait is they are not the most cognizant and perceptive of individuals. Because they process the world through force of will, they can, and do, fall victim to intellectual superiority. Because they tend to play, and react in a rigid, programmed manner, it's difficult to switch courses easily or to adjust to changing situations quickly as the game of poker so often dictates. Instead of being willing to admit there are other courses of action that might work better, they say to themselves, "This is the way that worked last week, last month, last year so it's what I'm going to do today."

Aggressive Dominant Personalities go on tilt frequently. However, because of their supremely-disciplined being, their recovery time is fast. When they recover they will tend to screw it down a notch as a form of self-discipline. Of all the personality types, it is this individual who has the most stamina. Once they set the course for their life, they seldom deviate in their quest to be No. 1. Even though they can suffer severe setbacks in the game of poker they have the ability to recover, and in time, they usually manage to extract punishment against all who stand in their way.

Some individuals who are highly aggressive have a habit of rubbing the top of their head in a brisk manner when they are feeling stress. When angry or upset, their lips become tight, straight lines and they often involuntarily flex the tendons in the neck. When they are upset or angry, their speech becomes shorter with a staccato rapidness to it. Another quirk of Aggressive individuals is they have a tendency to steal quick looks at an opponent's stack of chips. All human beings tend to look or glance often at that which they are most fond of. Many of the other 12 personality types will glance more often at their own stack of chips than they will at their opponent's stack. Another telltale clue to an Aggressive Personality is how they handle money. The count their money in an open manner, often holding it out in front of them for all to see. They also count it frequently, as they believe in keeping score. Other personality types are different. Some never count their money, some must constantly rearrange their stack or re-buy because they can't play effectively unless they have a mountain of chips in front of them. The Aggressive can play effectively without having to have a large pile. Some individuals are so vigilant (paranoid) of the table that they will push their chair back and count their money in their lap beneath the table.

Aggressive Dominant Personalities do not like disorder or confusion. They are not introspective by nature. They do not want to debate with themselves the road to take or the right/wrong possibilities of that road. To insure that disorder, chaos or confusion is limited, the Aggressive does one thing consistently. They take direct action. For the Aggressive, the easiest road to travel is the one that yields the desired results the quickest. While it's true that the Aggressive locks on to a course of action then drives hard toward that goal, it doesn't mean they are blind to the obstacles. The Aggressive is shrewd. They can protect their asses if the danger becomes too great. This doesn't mean they abandon the goal or give up the objective. It simply means they are willing to wait until a more opportune time presents itself. The Aggressive is a hard-nosed negotiator. They will go to great lengths to both prove a point and make a point. Their nature is to lead then protect the lead by fighting in whatever manner necessary.

When the aggressiveness is severe in this personality, the result is often violence toward others as their quest for power and control spirals out of hand. Many of these individuals become involved in a tyrannical dominant relationship where abuse of a spouse or children predominates their actions. From this weakened state, they can only control or exert power through violence. This state is often caused by the inner realization that they are actually powerless; hence, the violent reaction.

For this personality trait to enjoy world-class success at the poker table, it is absolutely necessary that they have a strong subordinate trait to balance the Aggressive trait. If they don't have a trait that tempers the aggression, they become prone to predictability, as much so as the individual who only calls bets in poker. If it's tempered by I-Dominance, Vigilant, Worker Moralist, etc., then their chance for success is greatly enhanced. If the only trait they can bring to the table is aggression, then they are committing a form of suicide as the more intuitive, diversified players will use their aggression to their detriment and eventual down-fall. You will find many highly Aggressive Personalities in low-limit games. They periodically will move to a higher-limit game only to find themselves being kicked back down by those players who keenly understand aggression.

When the aggression can be controlled and used as just another tool or skill as opposed to the only means, then the chance for success is much greater. They then become tough, cut-throat competitors who are dangerous and deserving of respect. It's important to remember that a large part of an Aggressive Dominant Personality's success is because many of the other 12 types simply do not have the stomach to do what it takes to combat the Aggressive. Therein, you must look inside to decide what course you prefer.

The Aggressive Dominant Personality as a Buyer

The Aggressive Dominant Personality is one of the best buyers in the world. This is true because they seek and attain positions of authority and leadership. When one attains a position of authority or leadership, they are forced to make decisions. A great majority of decisions in this world pertain to buying and selling. The Aggressive Dominant Personality is also one of the toughest buyers in the world. You don't get to the top of any profession by making wishy-washy decisions, by getting run over by fast-talking sales agents, or by getting the short end of the buy/sell transactions.

You need to make a distinction in your mind as it pertains to aggression. This distinction is between controlled and uncontrolled aggression. If you want to see uncontrolled aggression visit your local jail, that's where individuals with uncontrolled aggression wind up. Individuals with controlled aggression use it as a form of drive, determination and discipline to accomplish their desired results.

The Aggressive Dominant Personality has a game plan. Unlike the Adventurer Personality who deals with situations as they happen to occur, the Aggressive has a strategy to deal with each situation. The driving force within the Aggressive Personality is to win, to be No. 1. Their mental process is "if you want to win," if you're going to get to the top, then you must be willing to pay the price. The price they pay is self discipline. This form of self discipline manifests itself in many different ways. To put it into a manageable form that can be understood we can say, "The Aggressive Personality is willing to do what others aren't willing to do in order to win."

The next logical question is are you, the selling agent, willing to do whatever is necessary to sell the Aggressive Personality? Most selling agents fail miserably when they try to sell an Aggressive Personality. The reason is, they are not as mentally tough as the Aggressive. Here is a hard, fast rule if you want to successfully sell to the Aggressive personality on a long-term basis. "You must develop unemotional aggression within yourself."

Most sales agents fail to sell the Aggressive Personality because when they are confronted with the aggressive nature of the individual they counterattack by allowing themselves to become emotionally aggressive. When this happens, you're severely disadvantaged because you've taken your ego, put it on the platter and placed it directly in the hands of the Aggressive. From that point on, the Aggressive will toy with you and your ego like a cat plays with a mouse. When it's tossed you around enough to bemuse its own ego, it will then devour you. The Aggressive Dominant Personality is driven and consumed by the need to acquire and exert power. They destroy egos that are exposed emotionally. In contrast, unemotional aggression is result-and goal-directed. It earns the respect of the Aggressive Personality. The Aggressive has disdain for those whom they perceive as weak and undisciplined. In their mind, if the individual is weak and lacking mental toughness, then the product or service you're offering is likewise tainted. Therefore, you deserve to be run over in a roughshod manner to the point where they can outright steal your product or service. Either way, you, the selling agent, will lose.

The Aggressive Dominant Personality has an enormous ego. You can divide it into different categories. One is the need for power. One is the need for control. One is the need for success. The most powerful category is the need of results that verify and feed the above-mentioned ones. In the business world, almost all results come from how successful you can buy or sell, be it ideas or tangible products and services. For the Aggressive to reach their personal or their company goals, they, like everyone else, are in the buying/selling business. Not only does the Aggressive buy. . .they have to buy! Therefore, it all just means one thing. They can be sold!

When you remove the ego, you force the Aggressive to deal with and think in terms of results that can be accomplished. Tough, hard, matter-of-fact selling is what the mind of the Aggressive respects, understands and needs. When the Aggressive is first confronted, their personality slant is to attack you in some way that puts you in reverse and on the defensive. When an individual is in a constant attack mode, they develop a closed mind and a limited view of reality. When you sell the Aggressive, you need to counterattack in such a manner that you are not the issue, while at the same time making the Aggressive mind concentrate on and enhance the necessity and value of your product/service. The fastest and most efficient way of doing this is to have the Aggressive's mind think that you are exactly like them. The Aggressive is not emotional about their aggression. Pushing, shoving and being abrasive feels natural. It's the way you accomplish results. It's the way the world works.

If you make a sales call on an Aggressive Buyer and you're thrown out of the office with an abrupt, "I'm not interested," don't react emotionally with insults, the desire for revenge or tucking your tail between your legs as you mentally tell yourself that they're just too tough to sell. Please realize they buy so much that it's worth your effort to sell them. Instead of becoming emotional about the individual, become hard-nosed about how your product or service will benefit the individual. If they throw you out of the office, show up the next day and matter-of-factly make another proposal. If you get thrown out again then make a written proposal. Most agents won't do this because they fear offending the Aggressive again. Yet, ask yourself what the Aggressive would do if they were in your shoes. Do you think an Aggressive Dominant Personality who's fought and clawed his way up the ladder is going to quit? When you quit, you lose.

The Aggressive Dominant Personality is not a good first-call buyer. They want the best end of the deal. You will often have to make several calls and engage in some tough negotiations to get to the closing stage. Be prepared to have to give up something in the bargaining process. In their desire to win, to always exert power, the Aggressive's mind needs some concessions from you in order to buy. Their ego demands it.

Another key to successfully selling these individuals is to find out the specifics of their game plan. If these individuals are successful they probably have their business planned out several years in advance. You must be able to show how your product or service will directly enhance their success strategy. The Aggressive is not an impulse buyer. They are cold hearted in their mental toughness. They won't buy anything unless they can clearly see how it will directly enhance their goals and plans.

The Aggressive has a rigid mind. Their view of reality is often limited. If you want to sell them a copy machine and they haven't previously considered buying one, they will automatically reject the idea. Since they haven't previously thought of it their minds are closed. It's the ability to deal with this particular mind set that often determines success or failure in selling many different personality types. A most important concept in understanding and controlling human behavior is to realize and use the following:

The first step in breaking anyone's resistance is not getting them to do or buy something against their will, but simply get them to consider and entertain the idea in their mind as a possibility.

What you've been told and trained to accept as gospel about first-call closing is not the reality of how the world works or how the human mind processes information to make a decision. If I want to sell you something, my first objective is to sell you nothing except the planting of one simple seed in your mind. If I can get your mind to entertain my idea, it becomes your possession. In a poker game, it's not necessary that I raise or re-raise every bet that you challenge me with. However, it is necessary that I make you entertain the idea that if you bet against me, I'm going to punish you by forcing you to risk even more of your money. If I want to sell you a copy machine, I need one thing from you as a first-step process to breaking your resistance. I have to get you to consider the idea that it might be to your benefit to own the copy machine.

As an example, suppose I wanted to get you to tell a lie. If I come right out and ask you to lie, you probably won't. However, if I can plant one tiny seed in your mind about lying I will eventually succeed. If you don't automatically and immediately reject lying as morally repulsive, you will lie. If I plant the seed and get you to give the idea consideration, the mind will automatically start growing the seed. The mind doesn't ask itself if it's good, bad, right or wrong; it simply takes what we give it and starts directing us toward its fulfillment. After consideration comes justification. Soon we're telling ourselves, "No one will get hurt," "It's only a white lie," "I'm only going to do it once," "No one will know," etc. Now you're going to get your chain jerked. If I can get you to consider doing one little tiny thing knowing full well that you'll supply the justification to soothe your own conscience, how long do you think it will be before I can get you to consider other bigger, more sinister possibilities? If I want to sell you, I first want to get you to talk to me. Then I want to get you to meet me. Next I want to get you to consider possibilities to the point that you'll want to start eliminating my competition for me. The next and final step is I've got you isolated with me. At this point I own you because you've created enough justification in your mind that that's the way it should be. I don't have to sell you anything now, all I have to do is sit back and watch you buy. Not once do I have to tell you that my real objective is to sell you a copy machine. Consideration and justification are the great seducers of the mind. Why should I tell you I want to sell you a copy machine? It's much more effective if I allow you to seduce your own mind, because once you've committed the act (bought the copy machine) your mind will make you bear the responsibility. . .Not Me!

When you first start dealing with Aggressive Dominant Personalities you'll find they often reject your product or service automatically. Their rigid mind set is controlling their behavior. It's saying, "I've never thought of buying a widget; therefore, I don't need a widget. Furthermore, since I haven't thought of buying a widget, I must not like widget selling agents; so therefore, I'm going to throw you out of my office." With the Aggressive Dominant Personality you must plant the idea then build it around the results that are important for their continued success.

In the business world, the Aggressive Dominant Personality is more of a force to be reckoned with than in the world of poker. Without discipline, aggression is of little value in a poker game. I've yet to meet on Aggressive Dominant poker player who impressed me, the reason being that this type individual could bring nothing to the table to complement their aggression. In the business world, the Aggressive is often a blend of traits that make them superior, accomplished people. If the Aggressive is willing to surround himself with individuals who complement his talent, then you are probably going to be dealing with an individual who is success-oriented, and has the results to prove it.

If an individual allows aggression to override intellect, then the reality has to be that you're dealing with nothing more than a chump. The more successful Aggressive Personalities have control of their aggression. They have learned the value of having some intellectual capabilities, where listening and reasoning are components of success.

Don't directly challenge the Aggressive in a selling situation. When you do, the issue becomes you and not your product or service. Ask for help. It's the Aggressive's nature to tell you what's wrong and exactly what it will take to make it right. The Aggressive is straight-forward. A black and white individual. When you remove yourself as an object of confrontation and increase possibilities in their minds the sales process moves into high gear. The decisions are quick and final. Start closing as soon as they indicate interest plus willingness. Expect to negotiate even as you're closing. Once you've sold an Aggressive, work hard to keep their business. It's valuable business. If you will ask, they will provide excellent referral business to you. The reasons being they have no fear that they might be steering a friend or business associate into a bum deal. Their mind set is that they have total confidence in their decisions, therefore, there is no risk to their friends or acquaintances. Never promise something to an Aggressive that you can't deliver. If you can't deliver what you've promised, you will never get their business again. In your presentation, stick to facts and figures that conclude with hard results. Conceptual selling is not effective. Be brave, have heart, have courage. You'll make lots of money if you get this type of individual.

In life, business and in poker games, there is no substitute for heart and courage. The technical boys who play poker and write books on theory can't win in proportion to their skills, because they don't have the heart and courage to gamble. Don't get me wrong, there is nothing wrong with the technical, theoretical, probability side of life, business and poker games. However, it's only one part of a many-faceted, complex equation called life. Heart, courage and the 4-7 of spades will win as much money as a pair of Aces in the hand of those who have no gamble. Life takes heart and courage. It also requires a willingness to gamble. You're guaranteeing yourself mediocrity if you think you can ride the fence all your life while avoiding chance and risk. There is not enough Preparation H to heal the wounds you'll inflict upon yourself if you choose this course. The Aggressive Personality often has an abundance of heart and courage. Plus it's a trait that they admire in others.

THE CO-DEPENDENT

CLINICAL NAME:
DEPENDENT PERSONALITY DISORDER

Positive:	*Negative:*
Caring	Vacillates
Loyal	Gray Areas
Trustworthy	Passive
Loving	Lack of Identity
Dependable	Inconfident
Helpful	Can't Make Decisions
Team-Oriented	Lacking Initiative
Cooperative	Distorted Reality
Thoughtful	Non-Competitive
Reliable	Helpless
Dedicated	Submissive
Honest	Depression
Moral	Anxiety
Sincere	Hypochondriac
Devoted	

A Positive Overview

A good wife. The dependable husband. The loyal secretary. The faithful son. The good and reliable neighbor. The Co-Dependent Personality comes in many forms and shapes. It can be stated unequivocally that the world is a better, nicer place to live because of these individuals and the contributions they have made. They are warm, generous human beings who care and have genuine concern for others. They are people-oriented and seldom, if ever, have ulterior or underhanded motives tied to their actions. In many ways they are the supporting fabric of society. If it were not for the love they feel and their generous nature, many, myself included, would have missed some of the better parts of life. They are team-oriented individuals who will, and often do, sacrifice the personal "I" for the betterment of a goal. They are harmonious in their outlook and friendly in their demeanor. Their reliability and trustworthiness is beyond reproach. Through thick and thin their dedication is unwavering. Many of these individuals have endured great personal hardships to ensure a better life for their spouses, children, and those who employ them.

The Negative Side

The individual with the Co-Dependent Dominant Personality is, as the name implies, co-dependent. This is a judgement call and a very difficult subject. We are all, because we are human beings, somewhat co-dependent on other individuals. The old cliche that says "No man is an island" has an abundance of truth in it. We are all co-dependent on others for love, companionship, friendship, and success that we enjoy in the work place.

Like all traits of personality, the Co-Dependent must be viewed in the context of "how much." If the co-dependency is taken to the outer limits, it becomes a form of vicious manipulation against another and can only be viewed as destructive behavior. The Co-Dependent Dominant Personality is essentially one who is unable to find their own identity. They are in need of another to function.

They vacillate when asked to take a stand and their lives are marked by an extreme amount of gray areas. The lack of a yes or no mentality often leads to their existence being a burden upon someone else. Since they do not have the confidence in their own decision-making capacity, they often appear passive, disinterested, and helpless. Their non-competitive nature is often a liability in the work place as they are prone to accept many things at face value. Their overwhelming need to find their identity through another can and does make them victims of manipulators. They often, when removed from the source of their dependency, suffer bouts of depression and anxiety.

Playing With The Co-Dependent Dominant Personality

The Co-Dependent Personality is not a major force in poker, either in number of players or in playing skill. The primary reason for this is their personality make up doesn't include the traits necessary to withstand the rigors of the game. We will include some work on this personality type in order that you can have a working knowledge of all the personality traits.

In identifying this type personality, it is important to look for telltale signs that indicate a reliance on others. Depending on how co-dependent the personality is, the individual may only need an approving look from another person to the extreme, which would be never making a decision. The Co-Dependent seldom, if ever, functions as an individual entity. Their decision-making process is tied directly to how the other person will react and feel. The telltale signs to look for cover many areas:

Their reaction to you. The Co-Dependent Dominant Personality wants to please you. They are concerned with your comfort. "Can I get you a glass of water?" "Would you like a magazine to read?" Take this comfortable chair." They are genuinely happy to see you. They show more than just a social interest in you. They will inquire about you on a personal level. "Are you married?" "Do you have any children?" "How do you enjoy your work?"

The language they use. Many times the language they speak reveals their personality. "We are going..."; "What concerns us..."; "John and I..."; "Our family is..." The Co-Dependent will speak in terms that include others. Seldom will you find one that uses "I, me, myself" as a form of identity. The second way they use language is to defer to the other party. "Whatever makes John happy." "If it is what Mary wants, then it's fine with me." "What do you think, honey?"

An air of apprehension. The Co-Dependent is often unsure in their movement. They just don't come charging into the room. They move with tentative ill ease, they avoid being the center of attraction. If they see you standing, they will willingly vacate their chair. If they are with a spouse/companion they are apt to be behind a step or two. They are constantly involved in a game of mental deferment such as, "I'm not smart enough to do that," or "I could never do it as well as you do." Furthermore, because this is the way this personality actually thinks and believes, they make such statements sincerely, without guile.

When the Co-Dependent Personality plays poker, it is usually in one of three formats.

1. Low-limit social games. The vast majority of these individuals are female, older and are either temporarily or permanently without a mate, most probably due to the death of a spouse. Often they come to these games with a friend. Their intent is not to win money. They are there to have companionship. Often the friend they are with has become the surrogate partner in the Co-Dependent relationship hierarchy. If the Co-Dependent shows any initiative, boldness or aggression in poker, it's most likely to occur in these type situations and games.

2. Playing in a lower-limit game while dominant companion/spouse is in higher-limit game. In many respects, this is the proverbial dog and pony show. The majority of the time the Co-Dependent personality companion is an Aggressive Dominant Personality. The Co-Dependent is simply part of the entourage. If the Aggressive Dominant partner grows tired of the

Co-Dependent being close by or becomes irritated, he will often order the Co-Dependent personality to go play in a low-limit game. I was once playing in a pot-limit Omaha game with a very Aggressive personality who had a highly Co-Dependent companion sitting behind him. This individual wasn't running particularly good to start with, then he made a wrong move that cost him a considerable amount of money. A couple of minutes later, his companion meekly asked him a question about the previous hand. He exploded in rage, literally pushing her chair away from him. He then angrily peeled off some bills, gave them to her and ordered her to go to the other side of the room and play poker. An hour or so later she returned with less than she had started with. For the next 20 minutes, her Aggressive companion berated her publicly. In great detail he told her why she couldn't play poker, why she shouldn't play poker, why he could and she couldn't. While the above example is extreme, it happens in a less-dramatic form, quite often with the Co-Dependent personality.

3. Co-Dependent personality playing with dominant spouse/companion in the same game. While the scenario doesn't happen frequently, it's usually the most telling and interesting of the three situations. Invariably, they will try to sit side by side. The normal procedure is the Co-Dependent glances nervously toward the Aggressive Personality while trying to make the correct decision. The Aggressive Personality spends most of his time shaking his head in disgust or ridiculing the play of his companion. This same scenario is repeated much more frequently at the 21 table than at poker. At the 21 table, the Co-Dependent Personality will ask the dominant personality about every decision, (hit, stand, split, etc), particularly revealing in this situation is the Aggressive Dominant Personality will often angrily insist that the Co-Dependent individual make the decision when the call is tough to make, such as the dealer showing 10 and the player having 15 or 16. What is important to realize is these situations have more to do with relationships than they do with gambling. They really reveal how different individuals realize and receive pleasure.

The Co-Dependent Personality seldom, if ever, leads. They seem to have an inherent need to follow. This is a deadly trap to fall into, especially in poker. The most striking characteristic of this personality is their inability to have the initiative of purposeful decision-making. Because of this short circuit, they become easy victims at the poker table. If, and when they play poker, their style of play is noticeably absent of risk-taking, boldness, bluffing or even the most limited of strategies. In the truest sense, these individuals tend to play hands in the manner that they perceive as the least likely to offend anyone. This personality type tends to become regimental in their style. Their most likely course of action is to check (defer to another), or in lieu of being able to check, they will simply call (follow another) every bet.

In the few times I've played with Co-Dependent Personalities, especially in home games, I've witnessed, on occasion, a simple call at the end of the hand even though they had the absolute nuts and could have raised with no possibility of penalty. Even more striking is that if you try to explain the advantages of aggression to them after the hand, you realize they were perfectly content to simply call. Often their explanation is "Oh, I would never do something like that."

A common mistake that other more dominant personality types make when playing with the Co-Dependent individual is, (A) trying to execute sophisticated maneuvers and (B) being too aggressive. It's important to understand that an individual without a clearly defined will or sense of individual purpose is likely to surrender or quit when confronted with unusual or difficult circumstances. When you try to trap these individuals or intimidate them, you will often lose an extra one or two bets that would have otherwise been forthcoming if the threat was not so alarming.

The Co-Dependent Personality will win some pots on the sheer force of cards that play. Another mistake that is easy to make when playing with these individuals is to assume that their hand is weak based on the way they are acting. Even on the simplest of decisions, they often appear tentative, lacking confidence and vacillating between courses of action. This should not be construed as probably being a weak hand; but rather, it should be viewed as a trait of this personality. They quite possibly could have a monster hand and still be unsure of what to do.

The Co-Dependent Personality is relationship oriented. They need people. As a rule, they are stable, straightforward and not vindictive. Because of their need for others, it's almost impossible for them to view you (other players) as either an opponent or enemy; thereby, they lack the killer instinct so necessary in poker.

Another trait of personality is they will be highly apologetic to an opponent if they win a pot, even more so if they give an opponent a quote "bad beat." Other personality types will also manifest this trait. The Aggressive, I-Dominant and the Theatrical will often exhibit a bedside manner when beating up the opponent. The difference is that a personality type like the I-Dominant does so in the hope that the opponent won't get pissed off and leave the game while they still have money. The Co-Dependent acts in this manner because they are truly frightened of offending someone.

The best way of playing with this personality type is through a straightforward, somewhat laid-back approach. Because they are security-oriented they will never have a high degree of gamble within them. They are much more likely to be at the poker table for the social or relationship values as opposed to any serious intentions of winning money. If you want to keep them in the game, it's best accomplished by chipping away little chunks at a time, even to the point of checking more often than usual. If you want to drive them from the pot, then a style of hard aggression works best. They are also highly susceptible to being mentally beat up through verbal intimidation and psychological warfare.

Many Co-Dependent individuals are lonely with lives that border on desperation. Many times their self-identity is so skewered that they have no idea of what their needs are or what they want. They can tell you everything that their partner or spouse wants and needs; yet, if you ask them what their favorite color is or where they would like to vacation, they cannot find an answer as it pertains to their personal self. The Co-Dependent Dominant Personality is ill-equipped to play poker. While poker is a complex game, it also has an elementary simplicity to it. This simplicity evolves around one thing, making decisions. If you are a poker player and someone asked you what you do for a living you can truthfully reply. "I'm a decision maker." When you play poker, that is all you ever do. The not-so-simple part is the complexity involved in making some of the decisions. The Co-Dependent is ill-equipped to play poker because they have surrendered their will, thus, their ability to make decisions.

If you want to become a better poker player you can: (A) make superior decisions or (B) take advantage of the personality types who exhibits weakness or vacillation when they have to make decisions. There are many telltale clues that you can zero in on, e.g., checking, calling, etc. (C) Lastly, you can complicate the ability of others to make the correct decision. The best way to do this is through constant and unrelenting pressure.

Many personality types can play poker, but only a handful can play effectively when under constant pressure. Remember: creating a little bit of fear in a poker game will get you a lot of money in two different ways. (A) You can outright steal it, or (B) You'll win it by forcing an opponent to make the wrong decision by creating pressure that cripples their decision-making process. The fastest way to cripple an opponent is to put fear into his heart. Once the fear is there it takes a long time for the individual to recover. Of all the emotions that human beings experience, it is fear that does the most long-term psychological damage.

The Co-Dependent Personality as a Buyer

The Co-Dependent Personality is not a buyer. At their best, they will buy as part of a partnership. This type individual does not have the power of their own mind. An individual who gives control of their mind to someone else will never make decisions. It's sad, because many of this type are very loyal, trustworthy individuals who have big hearts and a generous nature.

Most often the Co-Dependent Personality is matched with a dominating partner who makes the decisions. The Co-Dependent shies away from the spotlight. They find their strength and meaning through the life of someone else.

In a selling situation, it's futile to try and get a decision from these personality types. They become nervous, upset and vacillate over the slightest exertion of pressure. It's very easy to get them to say "yes" to anything. The problem is that the "yes" has no value. "Yes" is nothing more than a way to escape the pressure at the moment. As soon as the selling agent has left, the sale will be canceled.

It's very easy to identify the Co-Dependent Personality in a selling situation. Simply ask for the decision. If you hear "I'll have to ask my husband," or "I'll have to call my son," etc., you're wasting your time. If this becomes the case, you need to make the presentation directly to the party that has the decision-making capacity. It's a waste of time to do anything else.

If you're fortunate enough to make a sales presentation with both the Co-Dependent and the dominating partner present, concentrate solely on the individual who has the decision-making capacity. There is a sinister little power game going on between the two parties. You do not want to be caught in the middle, aligned with the wrong individual. I've seen a lot of sales agents lose sales because they didn't understand what was going on.

Many times the aggressive partner will, in the middle of the presentation, ask the Co-Dependent Personality what they think or what they want to do. The Co-Dependent Personality looks weak, bewildered, scared. Now the selling agent starts to smell blood and begins to zero in on the Co-Dependent. The real truth of this situation is that you don't want a decision from the Co-Dependent.

If they say, "Yes," the aggressive partner is going to berate them because they've already been told a thousand times the reason they're not allowed to make decisions is because they don't have the capacity to make right decisions. If they say, "No," you've lost your power by giving the aggressive partner an easy escape route. As soon as the dominating partner hands the ball to the Co-Dependent, you need to take it away from them and hand it back to the decision maker. There are dozens of ways you can do this, such as:

♠ Let me give you some more information. (Look and speak at the dominating partner).

♠ Ask the Co-Dependent if they would be comfortable with whatever decision their partner made, (you will always get a "yes" and probably a sale).

Another facet of this personality is they are most willing and eager to buy for anyone but themselves. They will often encourage their husband to buy a new boat while they sacrifice something they need. I used to feel pity for Co-Dependent individuals. I no longer feel this way. I finally realized that they actually feel safe, secure and probably relatively happy in their Co-Dependent role. It's easy to think of a Co-Dependent as a victim, yet the dominating partner is just as much a victim. It's a heavy responsibility to have to carry 130 or 140 pounds of dead weight with you at all times. It's more like a caretaker role than any kind of relationship role.

If you're not involved with in-home sales or sales that involve selling to a family unit, you probably won't deal with any Co-Dependent Personalities. They almost never have any position of authority in the business world. They simply shy away from any position that requires decision-making.

The Co-Dependent Personality is largely female, although there are a surprising number of men who are co-dependent to their wives or mothers. Since that would be a large book by itself, I won't even get into that.

Most Co-Dependent individuals are financially responsible. They tend to be thrifty individuals with solid values. They place a high value on the comforts and security of their home and their mate. They shy away from the extravagant and tend to think in very basic terms.

When selling the different personality types, it's useful to ask yourself what each type needs most to fulfill their inner self. The Adventurer needs adrenaline, action, challenges. The Aggressive needs power, ego enhancement and results that supply concrete proof of their success. The Co-Dependent needs someone else to secure their inner being. They want a world that acts and reacts in a manner that never threatens their existence with the unknown. Decisions equates change. Change equates the unknown. You will have more success dealing with the Co-Dependent if you can maneuver within their world in such a fashion that you never rock their boat.

THE ECCENTRIC

CLINICAL NAME:
SCHIZOTYPAL PERSONALITY DISORDER

Positive:

Independent

Creative

Observant

Analytical

Intelligent

Self-Motivated

Self-Sustaining

Passionate

Doers

Visionaries

Energetic

Driven

Idealistic

Intuitive

Negative:

Magical Thinking

Suspicious

Iconoclastic

Compulsive

Anti-Establishment

Arrogant

Rude

Manipulative

Condescending

Odd

Aloof

Paranoid

Eccentric Behavior

Preoccupance with Self

Vindictive

A Positive Overview

The Eccentric Dominant Personality is perhaps the most misunderstood of all the 13 personality types. They are different. They, through their strikingly different personality quirks, are often recognized by labels that have been assigned by society. When I mention these labels, see what mental image forms in your imagination.

♠ The Mad Scientist

♠ The Nutty Professor

♠ The Beatnik

♠ The Hippie

♠ The Flower Children

♠ The Left Bank

♠ The Revolutionaries

♠ The Odd Genius

Beyond the labels we have words that also identify the individual with the personality.

♠ Drop Out

♠ U.F.O.s

♠ Ghosts

♠ Cosmic Forces

♠ Crystals

♠   Channeling

♠   Spaced

To some degree, a few or all of the listings listed above apply to this personality. The extent is dependent on the amount of eccentric behavior in the personality. Aside from the conventional labels assigned by society, these individuals are highly creative, talented people. They are fiercely independent. They are passionate in their causes and persuasive in their beliefs. They have bright analytical minds that go beyond commonly accepted standards to search for new and better ways to accomplish tasks. They have the ability to be highly observant of all that transpires in the world. They are often vocal political activists. They demand responsive actions to any and all perceived wrongs. They are highly self-sufficient individuals. They are internally motivated to do what they want, when they want to do it, and as often as they want to do it. They process from emotion. This emotion is intensified by their own unique form of logic and reason.

The Negative Side

It is important to stress that each and every one of us has the trait of Eccentric in our personality. We all have little quirks that if others knew about would cause them to think of us as a little odd. The difference between us and the Eccentric Dominated Personality is the degree. When it is the dominant, driving part of the personality, these individuals can be many objectional things. They have a high degree of suspicion. This suspicion will be directed toward your motives. They will often feel you are secretly making fun of or silently disapproving of what and how they are. They are often compulsive in their behavior, driven to be unconventional if for no other reason than not to appear conventional. If they form a bad opinion of you, they will become rude, arrogant, and highly uncooperative in any and all endeavors. Because they often perceive that they are endowed with special gifts and powers that you couldn't possibly possess, they will have a condescending attitude toward you, your values and your beliefs. This form of arrogance will make it difficult for them to fit into conventional social situations. They will often become more odd, more eccentric and more aloof as they become preoccupied with the slightest perceived injustice toward them.

Identifying And Playing With The Eccentric Personality

Do you know the trouble with many poker games? They are boring. The reason they are boring is they don't have the right mixture of personalities. This is especially true of the Eccentric Dominant Personality. The fun thing about being an author is you can write what ever you want, just as long as you put it in the middle of the book and don't offer refunds.

Therefore, I think I'll create my own poker game. In seat one, I'll put Shirley "Crystals" McLain. In seat two, I'll put Jerry "Moonbeam" Brown. We'll let old Al Einstein and his pipe have the three seat. We'll put Professor Irwin Corey in four. We'll have Timothy Leary and his pipe in number five. We'll seat Howard Hughes in the six seat (it's been sprayed with Lysol). In the seven seat, we'll put the guy with funny hair that writes for poker magazine. In the eighth seat, I'll put Buddha. Then just to be Christian we'll put Reverend Jimmy Swaggert in number nine. Then just to be unchristian to the Christians, we'll put the happy hooker in the ten seat. Wait a minute. . .just to make it interesting, we'll make it an eleven-handed game and put General Patton (an avid squirrel hunter) in seat eleven, and since I thought of the game, I get to deal, and since I get to deal I get to make up the rules. First rule is, whoever has the biggest pile of money gets only one card before the flop. . .(before the game starts it's a toss up between Swaggert and Hughes). The second rule is the guy in seven with the funny hair has to play his cards face up. Third rule is dealer gets tithed 10 percent. Fourth rule, no praying or chanting. Wait a minute. . .I just decided to make it a 12-handed game, I get to put Mizz Dolly J. Parton in the twelve seat. Dolly gets five cards before the flop.

To insure that none of our esteemed players get their feelings hurt, Dolly will not be allowed to sing her hit song "Why'd You Come In Here Looking Like That." Now, as they say in Missouri (and elsewhere), shut up and deal or, in this case, shut up and write something important.

The Eccentric Dominant Personality is easy to identify in one of three ways:

1. Appearance. To the keen observer they are easy to spot. They are different, different in the sense that upon meeting them we can sense that we are normal and they are slightly abnormal, (of course, this normal/abnormal standard is by our judgement only, not theirs). If we were them, this judgement would be reversed because they perceive "us" as the part of the world that's out of sync, therefore the problem. When confronted with the Eccentric Dominant Personality, you will notice they often give the appearance of being slightly disheveled, like each morning they had to rush to get put together. Even when they take meticulous care to put themselves together, it doesn't quite work. They appear to have plastered it together to get it to stay in one piece. The necktie is crooked, a shoelace is undone, earrings don't match, a $1500 suit and a $10 tie, etc.

2. Mannerisms. When the Eccentric Dominant Personality is out of their natural habitat, out of their social comfort zone, they lose the sense of naturalness. They give the impression of being slightly stiff, slightly awkward, tentative and unsure of both people and of the situation. The eyes will dart, they scan the horizon more often, they will either shuffle along or speed up to where their movement is out of sync to the flow around them.

3. Speech. Their speech is different. Sometimes to explain the simplest thing, they ramble on and on making less sense as they continue. Other times it's vague, abstract, more of a riddle than an answer. Often their answers lack synchronization because they are internally asking themselves 100 questions about the question you asked or because they distrust you for asking a simple question.

POKER, SEX & DYING

To understand the Eccentric Dominant Personality you must deal with them as an individual as opposed to dealing with them as a class of personality. As an example, an Eccentric Dominant Personality who lives in Santa Barbara and strings love beads together to sell on the street corner is one type. They may walk into the poker room and sit down. If fact, they may do so by the dozens.

On the other hand, there is an Eccentric Dominant Personality type who may walk in and sit down at the table who doesn't string beads for a living. This individual may be the most brilliant poker theorist alive. Their theoretical mind is sometimes several levels beyond the average player's ability to comprehend. Every field of endeavor attracts a small, or large, percentage of individuals, who are brilliant in theory, perfect in their strategic understanding, conceptual in their moment to moment ongoing reality. Poker is no different. It has its brilliant minds. On one occasion, while playing at the Mirage in a Hold'em game, I sat next to a couple of these individuals. I was both amazed and delighted, because after an hour or so of listening, I became convinced of one absolute thought that refused to leave my mind, which was: They cannot win. They are too brilliant. They are too far above the game. They can win only when the masses become educated to the point that there is only one level, instead of five, separating their play. They can't use what they know because it goes over the head of the average player. It's like being in a gunfight where they are armed with a cannon, but to me, their opponent, it looks like a water pistol; so therefore, my actions are formulated accordingly. The cannon is not effective because it takes too long to load and cannot be fired rapidly enough. This doesn't mean that they don't win or can't win, it simply means they don't win in a ratio to their knowledge or skill. They are esoterically superior, but are trapped by a parasitic table, (players).

Another way of understanding this is to say the seducer is prey to the non-seducer, because the seducer eventually wants to seduce no one but himself. Many individuals (mostly men) view themselves as gifted seducers, both sexually and professionally. In reality they are not. They are simply endowed with stamina, force of will, persistence and a parasitic nature. They are not skillful, per se. Many are rude in their actions, clumsy in approach, vile in their reproach and vindictive (rape) in the final analysis if the possibility of punishment were slight or the circumstances can be justified? (e.g. date rape). As Brooks so aptly puts it, tongue in cheek, "You couldn't get laid if you were the warden in a woman's penitentiary and you had a handful of pardons."

It is not seduction if you ask 100 and find one who says yes. However, because they have perseverance, determination and the refusal to quit, they succeed. These are skills that the seducer views as secondary to intellectual skills. Meanwhile the one who has the true seduction skills. . .smooth in approach, perfect in theory, becomes so enamored with the endless possibilities of seduction, that they forget about the object being seduced. The eventuality is at some point they seduce their own mind. At this point the circle becomes complete because in doing so they give seduction skills to the non seducer. The parasitic nature of the non-seducer will devour the seducer because in poker the essence of the game is parasitic in nature. The mind that seduces it's own mind has no natural defenses. It can't comprehend success earned by being a parasite. It's too ugly. It doesn't fit into any esoteric formulas of theory. They can't comprehend that poker is more closely akin to survival in the jungle than to ivory tower perfectionism.

Part of the inscription on the Statue of Liberty reads. . .Give me your tired, your poor, your huddled masses, yearning to breathe free, the wretched refuse of your teeming shore. Send these, the homeless, tempest tost to me. These words are symbolic of the American spirit of freedom for one and all. However, these words, I think, also symbolize the spirit of the poker table. If you want to play poker, it doesn't matter if you're different. There are no quotas, barriers, prejudices, or class distinctions set up to prevent your participation. All are welcome equally. If you're aggressive and overbearing, it's okay, sit down, if you're an adventurous hell raiser, it's okay, sit down. If you're a vigilant, superstitious individual, it's okay, sit down. If you're an eccentric, odd individual you also can sit down. Just because you believe you have clairvoyant powers and act accordingly will not get you thrown out of the poker room. You can show up with your lucky frog, lucky chip or any other trinket that soothes your mind. You can dress in whatever manner you feel best describes you and it's still okay Poker is the only profession where the individual is more valuable than the product, service or image of the organization itself. If you don't believe this, go to work for IBM and tell the management your work style is based on the belief of hunches or intimidation or slow playing the opponent down the street. They will kick you out on your ass and send the one who hired you to a psychiatrist.

It is this open-minded acceptance of all personality types that gives hope to the Eccentric Dominant Personality. In the real world, they have difficulty not only in fitting in but also in being given the opportunity. They are often referred to as squirrels, odd-balls and sometimes in more unflattering terms. In some respects, it's only natural that this personality type would find refuge at the poker table. They are socially accepted and they can find all the freedom of expression they'll ever need to try out their unique belief as it pertains to the cold, hard facts of odds and probability. The only requirements is—bring money.

As we said, there are two types of this personality, your average Eccentric and the ones who seem to possess the many qualities of true genius. Since the genius types are few and far between, we'll concentrate on the more prevalent Eccentric type personality. Needless to say, however, is the fact that the Eccentric Personality who possesses a high degree of specialized information/knowledge is a dangerous foe and should be treated accordingly. I'd rather be bitten by an aggressive dog than a rabid squirrel. The pain is less severe and the antibiotic is more clearly defined. The highly specialized Eccentric Personality will often possess many of the qualities of the personality trait discussed in the next section (Loner), so it's advisable to combine the two personality types when formulating a playing strategy. The genius Eccentric tends to have less emotional coloring to their thought process, while the average Eccentric Personality is often emotionally tainted inwardly.

The Eccentric Dominant Personality believes they possess special powers that are unique to them or their type. Because of this belief, there is always a me vs. them mentality at work. This constant and unnecessary creation of adversaries results in a weakening of an individual's state of mind. They eventually can't perceive real opponents from imagined opponents. It's these supposedly "special powers" that create the lifestyle and also is the source of much of the conflict within and with their difficulty in dealing with other personality types who tend to believe in a different type of reality. This belief in the possession of special powers is exposed under the category of:

Magical Thinking... and is manifested in various ways:

A. Hunches

B. Superstition

C. Psychic Enlightenment (Spiritual Guidance)

D. Cosmic Help

E. Predestination

F. Lucky Numbers

G. Clairvoyance (Fortune Telling)

A most logical question is, "Are there happenings that can't be explained through standard conscious knowledge?" The answer is Yes. The second question is, "Can you control it?" The answer is No. If I wanted to, I could make an overwhelming case, with evidence, that in the lives of many, things happen in a sequence of three, or that on special occasions, certain individuals have received knowledge not otherwise revealed. I'm not even willing to debate the fact that these things do happen. I am willing to debate the fact that I believe them to be useless, because you can't control their occurrence. My main form of gambling is sports betting.

A couple of years ago, I was having a very bad three-week run. After one particularly bad day, I laid down to sleep and the thought came to my mind that said, "Bet five particular teams." I clearly heard the names of the teams. I also heard my mind say parlay these teams. I don't like to parlay five teams and I live and die with statistical handicapping, so I didn't put much credence in what my mind was telling me; however, I wasn't willing to. . .couldn't ignore it either. So I parlayed five teams for ten bucks. All five teams covered. The next evening the same thing happens, only it is four teams. I'm still skeptical, but I parlay four at $100. All four win and cover. Next night the same things happens, I get five teams. Now, I'm not only skeptical, but angry at myself because I've had nine straight winners and won only $1200. I parlay five teams at $500. That evening I collected $10,000. I've now had 14 straight winners, won some money, but I'm even more skeptical, plus I'm perturbed because I'm not willing to believe it. Not only am I not willing to believe it, I can't believe it. My mind simply cannot accept it.

Later that evening, the same thing happens again, my mind says bet these four teams. I write the team names down and drift off to sleep. An hour later, I'm up walking the floor. Two of the names I've written down are Los Angeles and Baltimore. I've got a problem. The next day the Lakers, Clippers, Rams and Raiders are playing. There is no Baltimore in either pro football or basketball. I am beside myself. Maybe it meant the team that used to play in Baltimore and is now in Indianapolis. I'm racking my mind trying to figure out which Los Angeles team. I lay back down and wait for enlightenment. Nothing happens. I'm up all night. Finally at eight the next morning I say "screw it." I write down all the possible combinations on pieces of paper, close my eyes and tell myself which ever one I see first when I open my eyes will be the one. I decide to parlay $2500 and have to use two different joints to get it down. Three out of the four teams blow it. I kiss the $2500 goodbye. But guess what? I'm glad, even ecstatic. I can go back to my beloved statistics.

Looking back, 9 out of the 14 teams were teams that I would never have bet. The odds of picking 14 straight winners are prohibitive, but not impossible. What are the odds of picking 14 winners by hearing a team's name in your mind? I'm not sure about those type odds. It hasn't happened since. Another example: I used to play a lot of 21. I got to the point that I could, with amazing accuracy, call the Ace when the dealer had it under a ten count card showing. It got so bad that dealers cringed and pit bosses would eye me and the dealer suspiciously or inspect the Ace for markings. However, the real point of this was I couldn't predict the Ace far enough ahead to where I wouldn't bet or cut the bet back, but still play in order not to disturb the cards the dealer was to have received. So this ability (?) was useless. If you can't control it, you can't use it profitably. Just because I don't believe it or because there is no scientific proof to substantiate it, doesn't mean anything to those personality types who not only believe it, but also live by it.

I'll give you one more example of occurrences that happen to me personally. If I sit in a poker game 4 or 5 hours I will during that time experience an inner feeling that tells me to play a certain hand 2 or 3 times in 5 hours. These particular hands always prove to be the winning hands, yet I make Zilch, Zero money! The Reason is I don't ever play the hands. They are always shit hands such as 9-2, J-5, K-7. I can't play them because I've trained my mind to automatically reject them. The feeling that I experience is like an unidentifiable impulse that rockets through my mind for a split second. In this situation I'm a pitiful slave to my own mind. I suspect that this happens to others besides myself. The Logical question is from what source does this impulse originate. I can't even begin to answer the question as the analytical part of my being rejects the question as foolish. Perhaps also because I fear the ease with which I could find my ass parked in some shaman tent pitched in some distant jungle. These occurrences frustrate me. All my life I've lived and died in direct proportion to my Instinctive and intuitive skills. In my heart of hearts, I know I should follow these impulses. Because the only way I've ever made money in my life was through the willingness to find value in those things overlooked by others then gamble that I was correct and the masses were Incorrect. And just in case you're thinking I'm an Eccentric Dominant Personality, forget it. Eccentric is my 8th ranked Subordinate trait.

One of the first things to understand is that the Eccentric Dominant Personality will often play in a style that appears to lack synchronization. Initially, this style of play seems confusing as it often lacks common logic or reason. As a good general rule, it's best to downgrade the possibilities that they hold in their hand. They may have a playable hand, but in many cases it's just as likely to be a play based on superstition, a hunch, or a message from God. A second thing to understand is that the Eccentric Dominant Personality often misses the big picture, because they become hung up on a single issue and can't let go of it. This fixation on a single issue causes the self to become isolated to everything else that is happening. This single issue fixation can be something as simple as how come. Over and over their mind keeps asking how come, how come? As an example, if you raised their bet they can't just accept it as a part of something that happens in the game of poker. Instead, they must try to fix a greater or even sinister meaning to the action and your motives. If you watch closely, you'll notice that when in this state of mind, the Eccentric Dominant Personality constantly steals glances or stares incessantly at the one whose motives they can't understand or who they suddenly distrust. When in this state of mind, they can't play poker. They start to play a hand then abruptly abort it, sometimes three hands in a row. The single issue, whatever it might be, is still holding the mind prisoner.

Many times this personality type is highly perceptive with an observant and analytical mind. However, many times at the poker table these assets are voided because they stumble over the fundamentals. They often ignore or are oblivious to position, draws, overcards, etc. They fix on a course of play and can't adapt as the situation changes. At the more extreme end the style of play is marked by an attempt to lead, then at the first resistance they suddenly start following, even when they should still be leading. This quirk in playing style is often because of this personality type's great difficulty with authority figures. They fluctuate between grudgingly following, then wanting to strike back out of anger and spite because they did follow.

There is often distrust that is directed toward the more forceful personality types such as the Aggressive, I-Dominant and Adventurer. There is often a clash in beliefs and lifestyle between the Eccentric Dominant Personality and the more rigid Worker Moralist type. One is viewed as a deadbeat, while the other one is viewed as the ultimate square.

Many Eccentric Dominant Personalities have an identity problem. They often drift from one belief to another belief as they struggle to find or understand their purpose. Individuals who lack identity or have an ill-defined purpose for their lives are always susceptible to being pushed and shoved. Hard and constant aggression causes them to withdraw and the lack of purpose makes it difficult for anyone to be willing to engage in, or have a commitment to, bloody battles. This personality type is often guarded and protective of what they possess in the here and now (at the moment). This hold-on-to-it stinginess is not a good trait to bring to the poker table. They do not have the gamble necessary to succeed in gambling. Many times it's a constant test, test, testing of the water with the inability to take the full plunge because of the desire not to lose in contrast to a commitment to win.

Do not confuse superstition with eccentricity. Superstition is widespread in gambling and among gamblers. We would describe superstition as a one- or two-point issue while eccentricity is a full-blown lifestyle. As an example, an individual who can't play until their chips are arranged in a certain way and have to have on a particular hat is superstitious, but they are not Eccentric. Earlier in our make-believe poker game, we created an Eccentric dominated table. While each one of those individuals may have had a superstition, many of those personalities are far removed from the Eccentric category. They may even want you to think they are Eccentric, when in reality it's nothing more than an elaborate mind game. The Eccentric Dominant Personality is neither people-oriented (friends, companions), or thing-oriented (possessions, careers). They do have a tendency to be cause-oriented. Many of them will have a fierce commitment to a cause that they view as necessary. As an example, many of them are radical about the environment or they are passionate about animals and their rights. Sometimes, this passion is such that they value it as being of greater importance than human life.

When you get past the outward manifestations of the eccentricity, there is often an individual who has great difficulty with people. Their suspicions and constant questioning of others' motives often makes them dysfunctional in an endeavor such as poker. They become susceptible to personality types such as the shrewd and cunning Aggressive and the manipulative and trapping I-Dominant Personalities who feed well and often at the trough of others and their weaknesses. It's rather easy to create a state of emotional tilt in an individual when they view everything as a possible personal attack against the self. This type is highly susceptible to ridicule, personal jokes and innuendos.

If this personality type is extreme in its behavior, they are prone to try highly unconventional maneuvers. These playing tactics have nothing to do with trying to create confusion, stealing a pot, draws or probability. They simply believe they know something that will work and they play it accordingly. This abstract belief in sudden superiority is always reason enough to show down a hand. On the other side of the coin, they try to spring a trap only to find out no one is biting.

When the Eccentric Dominant Personality is stressed, angry or upset, they draw into themselves. Sometimes they stare angrily at nothing, or sometimes give the appearance of emotionally binding themselves too tightly, resulting in obvious constrictions to themselves.

This personality type will often develop very subtle tells. As an example, they sometimes create an enforced state of discipline when they have a big hand. They don't dare twitch a muscle until it's their time to bet. Almost invariably though, they have to keep trying to glance sideways to see what the player next to them has done or trying to see what the player might do.

I once observed one of the greatest players in the world in this position. He deliberately counted out his bet, chip by chip, twice; carefully set it back down and did nothing while giving the impression of having done something. After a couple of minutes, the dealer says, "Sir, it's up to you." The guy says, "Hell, I checked." The strange little guy sitting next to him looks like he's going to explode. His face burns red and veins bulge out in his neck. Then he screams angrily, "You didn't check, I was listening, you didn't do anything." The other guy stares at him disdainfully and says, " You're going to have to pay attention. I checked." He sits and stews for a moment, then says, "I check, too." Last card comes and the first guy grins and says, " Go ahead." The guy with the red face and popping veins is hunkered down in his chair chewing away on his lip. Suddenly he relaxes and says in a chipper voice, " I check, too." He then gloats as he turns over the unbeatable hand of Queens full and says, "You're beat." The other guy says nothing but looks terribly satisfied for someone who'd just got beat. I guess it just goes to show that some days you're the dog and some days you're the fire hydrant. However, some days you're the fire hydrant but the dog is enlightened.

The Eccentric Dominant Personality is better suited to low-limit games and games where clairvoyance and drawing possibilities can be easily confused (Omaha).

It's doubtful that an extremely Eccentric personality will ever enjoy long-term success in the poker world, if for no other reason than the fact that poker is people, and personality types who consistently cannot understand others (or themselves) are severely handicapped. In many ways, poker and big-time business mirror each other in how they deal the game to their opponents. In the business world, the Eccentric Dominant Personality has to find a special niche to succeed. However, most times the Eccentric is ground down by rules, regulations and rigid structural organizations. Ultimately, this is the best way to attack this opponent in poker, too. There are built-in restrictions to what you can and cannot do in poker, if you wish to succeed. Those who succeed most are those who constantly punish those who ignore these restrictions. Likewise, those who most often fail are those who, for whatever reason, believe they can play outside the restrictions with impunity.

The Eccentric Personality lacks consistency in playing style. Many times they give the appearance of trying to develop a style of play as the hand is unfolding. Their tendency is to try aggressive moves periodically and if the results are negative, they lapse into long periods of passivity. The Eccentric Personality is often the easiest of the 13 types to read. They are prone to reveal how they feel and what they are thinking through body movement and facial expressions. The disturbances of their inner state often are worn as an outer garment for all to see. They especially have trouble hiding anger that they are feeling. If you observe their style closely, over a period of time, you will notice they are constantly trying to fill straights and flushes as cheaply as possible. They take keen delight in giving bad beats to others by overcoming the long-shot possibility. Ultimately, this desire to inflict bad beats takes its toll on their bank roll, not yours.

The Eccentric Dominant Personality as a Buyer

Of all the 13 personality types, it's the Eccentric who is most likely to stall the buy/sell process because of a personality clash. This personality clash is a double-edged sword. The Eccentric is suspicious of the selling agent and their motives, and the selling agent naturally views the Eccentric as odd or different.

The Eccentric is not easy to sell because their style of buying or negotiating is often like the shifting sand. They have a tendency to use evasiveness as a counterattack when being pressured to make decisions or commitments. Another reason they are difficult to sell is because they like to speak and act with large generalizations. These generalizations take the form of, "I'm just looking," "I'm thinking," "someday," "maybe," etc.

To successfully sell this type of individuals, you must turn generalizations into specifics. To do this, you ask direct questions, (what color, how much, today or tomorrow). If you can't convert these individuals from generalizations to their specific needs and wants, go on to your next client. Your time is too valuable to waste.

Many of the Eccentric Dominant Personality types have a combative urge within their personality. This combativeness will often manifest itself in the form of mental games of one-upmanship or a condescending superiority on their part. In the buy/sell process they like to attack the values of a product or service. As an example, if you were showing them a house and mentioned that it's located in a good neighborhood, they will counterattack by saying, "In other words, all the people out here are boring." If you then react in a combative or defensive manner, they will continue to dig for so-called cracks in your psychological make-up. If you allow this to happen, you are in a never-ending game of personality clashes.

An important first step in selling an Eccentric Personality is to find out their goals, the purpose for their lives and what exactly is motivating their day-to-day existence. When you find out the above, it's much easier to formulate a selling strategy based on specifics. The Eccentric Personality often has 100 vague ideas that run through their mind, but until you can put concrete into these ideas they are too abstract to sell to.

The dominating feeling in the minds of many Eccentric Personalities is that often they really don't have a purpose for their lives. This will manifest itself by their moving from one cause to the next as they search for the meaning of life, and in particular, their life. If the Eccentric has developed a focused view of themselves, they are much easier to deal with. If they have reached this stage in their lives they tend to surround themselves with objects that reflect this; such as computers, art, research projects, etc.

In selling the Eccentric Personality, questions have far more value than statements. All the questions should be posed to discover a specific need, want or desire. These personality types also need a lot of reassurance in the buy/sell process. This is because they tend to object silently when questions or doubts pass through their minds. They may ridicule the stability and dependability of a product or service, yet they need to be assured of value for the dollar; because while they may be anti-establishment, they, like everyone else, are not anti-self. The Eccentric Dominant Personality is not a good negotiate when it comes to price. Their first line of defense is to walk away. As a selling agent, you can successfully deal with an individual who will make a counter offer, after all, it's what you expect. It's difficult when the individual protects the ego by getting up and leaving. When negotiating with the Eccentric, always give them multiple offers, as it will cause them to have to consider the possibilities and keep them stationary.

The sales process is smoother when the Eccentric Personality is forced to come forward into your territory, a somewhat negative type of selling presentation is useful. High-pressure tactics tend to put this personality type into reverse. Many times the sales process becomes difficult as the Eccentric personality tends to have a mind that drifts off the main subject and toward tangents that have little bearing on the matter at hand. You need to discipline the presentation by asking direct questions that assures participation.

Almost all Eccentric Personalities feel that they are different. This feeling feeds the belief that others have difficulty understanding their needs. If this is the case, then you, the selling agent, need to put yourself in their shoes. Most of us fail miserably when we try to put ourselves in someone else's shoes. Most times the fit is too tight. The reason it's too tight is because when we put ourselves in someone else's shoes, we invariably try to cram our ego in there also. It's hard to be objective when we involve our ego.

Overall the Eccentric Personality is a very small percentage of the buying public. Eccentric Personalities tend to either seek isolation or to cluster in groups. Many times when they are in a buying mode, they will seek out a selling agent whom they feel is similar to them in belief and style. They often have an uncanny sense that steers them in that direction.

Ultimately, the best way to sell the Eccentric Personality is to have a sincere desire to help them. If you can put aside the fact that they and you have different styles and personalities, you can more easily develop a common ground to stand on. Accepting the individual as they are is always a good starting point.

Procrastination is common with this personality type, especially when buying a product or service they are not comfortable with. When this happens, you must make this type individual understand that while you are sincere in wanting to help them, your time is valuable. Insist on a decision. Don't expect to get rich selling to this personality type. First, there is not enough of them, and second, their buying is often too far removed from mainstream products and services to seriously affect the buying market.

A key component in selling a product or service is often the ability of the selling agent to create a sense of urgency. It's difficult to do this with an Eccentric Dominant Personality, because most of them have no need or desire to compress time. We all live in a twenty-four-hour world. However, if you are an I-Dominant Personality, you may feel like it's a twelve-hour world because your personality speeds up or compresses time. The Eccentric lives in a 36-hour day; therefore, there is not the sense of urgency to do things immediately. Their mind and their world moves at a more leisurely pace than many other personality types. Given your choice as a selling agent, you'd rather have 10 I-Dominant Personalities as potential clients than to have 100 Eccentric Personalities. It's not prejudice, it's simple economics. You will sell more, more often, to those who compress time to create the sense that there is more time. The only way you can compress time is by the amount of action you create within any time frame.

An Eccentric personality will often become obstinate, stubborn and argumentative over something insignificant at the close of a sale. To handle this, you must realize that these types have difficulty seeing the big picture. They literally stumble over the flea while looking for the elephant. When this happens, you have to back up the presentation and give them the big picture again. It's often frustrating, but sometimes the only way you can change their focus is by creating a bigger picture that encompasses the stumbling block in their mind. Many of these individuals are in a constant disassociated state. Your presentation needs to be constructed in such a manner that the Eccentric becomes associated with the product. Selling through logic, reason and product/service function is more effective than emotional appeals. Just remember that many Eccentrics are also disassociated from their own emotions as well as emotions toward others.

THE EMOTIONAL

CLINICAL NAME: BORDERLINE PERSONALITY DISORDER

Positive:

Involvement

Intensity

Fiery

Spontaneous

Energetic

Sexual

Alluring

Daring

Passionate

Imaginative

Creative

Dramatic

Generous

Inspirational

Negative:

Unpredictable

Uncertainty

Volatile

Stubborn

Rude

Emotional Punishment

Self Hate

Self-Destructive

Low Self-Esteem

Arrogant

Lack of Direction

Lack of Purpose

Roller Coaster Behavior

A Positive Overview

The Emotionally Dominated person is driven by their need for involvement. They find meaning and purpose through and because of the other person. They are impulsive and often times compulsive. If it feels good, do it. If it feels good, buy it. Their emotional temperament is so powerful that we often use the phrase, "Wear their heart on their sleeve," when talking about this type. Other people with a different dominant personality trait can be motivated or demotivated by factors such as logic or reason with "The Emotional," logic, reason or caution have no value. Their fiery nature, their need to feel, their need to have emotional involvement in and with others, is the reason for their being.

In their world, there is no gray. Everything is black or white, or perhaps more appropriately, everything is red or black. Their style, be it work or play, is marked by intensity. Their motto is: "If you do it, do it with feeling; if you feel it, be passionate about it." There is very little room in this personality for the tepid, cautious way of life. Their level of intensity dictates that it be a 100 percent effort. If they can't feel the emotion that will allow them to give 100 percent, then they will totally lose interest or give a half-hearted, lackadaisical effort as they pout about having to do it in the first place.

The Emotional Dominant Personality is laced with frenzied energy. They go here, they go there. They can have the type of high-octane energy that would leave most individuals in a collapsed state. They are often bright, creative, spontaneously witty individuals. They have wonderful laughs and will often poke fun at their own follies and miscues.

The Negative Side

The Emotionally Dominated Personality is like the wind that blows in all directions. Their life is dominated by what they feel. If it doesn't feel right, if it doesn't feel good, then you will pay the consequences. They have violent tempers that are controlled by hairline triggers. They are jealous, revengeful, spiteful. If they perceive an injustice against themselves, they will always blame you. When they fail to get that which makes them feel good, they become moody, sulky, they pout, they become withdrawn. They use their emotions to manipulate. They can withhold emotions as a form of punishment, refusing to talk or interact because of the perceived injustices that they feel they are suffering.

They are emotionally demanding, even to the point of draining those around them. The clinical definition and its accuracy (borderline personality disorder) can best be seen by the fact that so many of these individuals are always on the edge of going over the line. Their impulsiveness to do, to be, often pushes them in directions that later create severe problems. These areas can be in money or business matters, love and sex relationships and alcohol, drug, or food abuse.

Identifying And Playing With The Emotional

The Emotionally dominated personality is easy to identify. They have personal style. They often move with the flow of their self-propelling emotions. They are extremely aware of the personal self. If they are feeling good, it shows. If they are having an extremely difficult day, then it will show even more. They are warm, bright, energetic personalities. They like people. You can often identify them by how they make you feel. You're not a stranger. They move close to you as their emotional outcharge overcomes any fear that they might have had about you or the situation. Their language is dominated by what they feel. Words like wonderful, great, I'm so excited, wow, brilliant, and super, lace their conversation. Their clothing is often alluring and sensuous. It is stylish and smart and very often accented with lavish ornamentation that may or may not match, but is a personal statement of some emotion that they felt, past or present. Watch the style and speed of their movement. They move poetically, they move energetically. Their movements are often calibrated to what they are feeling. An individual who has an I-Dominant Personality and any-one who has the Theatrical Dominant Personality will also move briskly and with force. The difference though is that the I-Dominant or Theatrical person calculates their moves to achieve a result or to make a statement. The Emotional Dominant Personality doesn't stop to think or reason about walking across the floor; therefore, it has a naturalness to it, based on what they are feeling and not what they think would make a good show.

The Emotional Dominant Personality is impulsive in their actions and in their lifestyle. This impulsiveness at the poker table can manifest itself in many different forms. This personality trait will play a hunch based on nothing more than a feeling they sud-denly develop. They will sometimes play a hand because of some ill-defined impulse from within that says "It's my turn to win." This impulse often overrides and disregards the actual circum-stances at the table. This personality trait often develops a love affair with certain hands. This love affair is often based on a previ-ous experience that caused them enormous emotional satisfaction. As an example, they may always play J-10 suited because they won a huge pot or experienced an intense high when they previously played this hand. The Emotional Dominant Personality tends to be highly retrospective. They will constantly refer back to favor-able experiences, both silently and verbally. In conversation they will often make comments such as:

♠ I remember when. . .

♠ That was an incredible game last week. . .

♠ I once won a pot. . .

Often their actions in the present time frame are being dictated by their need to try and duplicate some past experience. If this need to duplicate becomes extreme, this personality trait becomes highly vulnerable to other personality types who are attuned to the harsh reality of what the current circumstances are.

Another characteristic of the Emotional Dominant's Personality is they love to become involved in hands when certain other poker players are involved. This is a devastating trait to develop and it's a flaw of both good and bad players. As human beings, we all have certain people we identify more closely with. These are people we feel good around or who make us feel good. Because the Emotional Dominant Personality is the most people oriented of all the 13 types, they tend to let this need for involvement with the people they like (or don't like) separate them from a lot of their money at the poker table. If this flaw is severe in their playing style it will be such that it actually doesn't feel that bad if they lost to a particular person or persons.

So many times an Emotionally Dominant Personality will look across the table and see that someone they feel good about or someone they secretly admire is in the pot and they suddenly snap to attention. When this happens, they will, with amazing regularity, find something in their hands that plays.

If you're involved in this situation, you can, with restraint, play hands that you would otherwise throw away, knowing full well that your call or raise is going to lure the Emotional Dominant Personality into the pot. In this situation, it's to your advantage not to have position as you need to take the first action. Many times in this situation the Emotional Dominant Personality will, because of their spontaneous and energetic nature, become engaged in a game of one-upmanship. If you raise, they'll re-raise, regardless of the cards. Even if you're not the player that the Emotional personality wants to play with, you can, by paying close attention, often get involved as the third party and through aggressive play wind up head to head with the Emotional. By picking your spots carefully, you're odds-on favorite to have the best hand a majority of time. While the characteristic of wanting to get involved in hands with certain players is a trait of the Emotional personality, it is by no means limited to this personality type.

Through close observation in a poker game, you will notice other personality types who are itching to come flying out at another player. The reasons for this behavior are many. Among them are ego, revenge, spite, anger, reputation, etc. Again it's to your advantage to get into the middle of this scenario when possible. The player with the big itch will often have, at best, a marginal hand. Many times the player who was the target of the ego attack has no need to prove anything and can, and will, lay down a hand leaving you head up with a player on emotional tilt who first made a decision based on irrationality. Second, he's stymied in his emotional attack because his primary opponent backed out, not because of his illogical behavior, but because of the unknown strength you represent (or represented).

This personality type can suck in other personality types through their fiery nature and lust for living. Their daring, passionate nature can be a powerful magnet to those who let their guard down or their discipline become lax. When playing with the Emotional Dominant Personality, it is always wise to have a certain amount of indifference to their emotions. Not only does this serve as a protector to you, but also tends to unsettle and distract the Emotional personality, making them prone to mistakes based on their emotional, roller coaster nature.

To a highly Emotional Personality, indifference is the cruelest of any behavior that can be directed toward them. If you love or hate them, it's okay; they are equipped to deal with either emotion. However, stone-cold indifference throws a mental switch that often drives them to both distraction and the need to prove something (themselves). The results from the above are usually mistakes in judgment, strategy or ill-timed acts of aggression aimed at striking back at the hurt caused by the indifference.

Another characteristic of the Emotional Dominant Personality is they have a very low tolerance for details. Being patient or dealing with the mundane is against their nature. When they become frustrated, which is frequent, they lose both intensity and concentration. When this happens, they become susceptible to being ground down in a poker game. The personality types that are detail oriented, the plodders, the deliberate mentality types often win money from the Emotional Personality because of the distinct clash in styles and the Emotional's personality trait of feeling contempt and wanting to strike back at this type players. This emotional intolerance is often manifested by careless, sloppy play or by trying to run over or intimidate certain players or playing styles.

When playing with the Emotional Dominant Personality, it's extremely important to try and monitor their particular mindset at any given time. Of the 13 personality types, it is the Emotional who is most given to quick changes in temperament swings. When they are emotionally high, positively engaged, they are dangerous poker players. During these times they are keenly perceptive and highly cognizant and attuned to the ebb and flow of the game and to the emotional state of the other players. Because they live and die with emotion, they often seem to have an innate sense pertaining to others' emotions. When they are in this positive emotionally engaged state, they are highly skilled at detecting bluffs, weaknesses and strategic mistakes by others. It is in this state that this personality can dominate a table and do so with lightning quickness. They seemingly come out of nowhere and suddenly have a mountain of chips in front of them. When this happens, other players frequently grumble about the player being lucky. Don't believe it. More than luck is involved. A positive mindset is a formidable ally that has nothing to do with luck and everything to do with the most misunderstood power in the universe, which is the power of the mind.

It's just not poker players who misunderstand this power, but also, the vast majority of medical and science professionals. In the medical and science fields, it is called the "placebo effect" and because it's not what the researchers are looking for, it's stunning effects are ignored or swept under the rug. However, the fact remains that in controlled studies, the placebo effect on healing and controlling the body is oftentimes as statistically great or greater than the effect of the drug being tested. Both science and poker players would be better served if they quit looking for a magical pill and started realizing an undisputable universal truth, which is "as a man thinketh he is" or perhaps "as he will become."

At the other end of this personality spectrum is an opposite mindset. All human beings suffer low mental states from time to time. The Emotional just suffers it with greater intensity. It becomes personal, a statement about themselves, rather than a statement about circumstances. When they swing to this mindset, they become unpredictable, volatile, stubborn, self-destructive and will often engage in a form of emotional punishment toward themselves at the poker table. They become vindictive toward the self. They play unimaginable hands, they take risks that are not remotely in proportion to the possible gain. They show utter disdain for money, as they seemingly receive a perverse pleasure from the punishment of losing.

This self-punishment that the Emotional Dominant Personality experiences is often related to the message they deliver to themselves through internal conversation. Many highly emotional personalities have a life-long acquaintance with the seven bastard sons of despair: can't, don't, won't, shouldn't, couldn't, never, nobody. Internally the conversation is:

♠ "I can't do anything right."

♠ "I'm so stupid I shouldn't ever play poker."

♠ "I'll never get over this."

♠ "Nobody likes me."

Highly emotional people experience a lot of ruin in some areas of their lives, because they are susceptible to turning on themselves. However, there are also many, many times the most resilient of creatures can, in a short period, pull themselves back up through an amazing inner resolve to live and experience life to the fullest.

In a poker game, the best time to attack these individuals is when they are self-absorbed. Often they will come charging at you out of sheer spite. A common mistake is a misinterpretation of how an Emotional personality reacts when they are in a negative mode. They may push their chair back from the table in disgust, leave the table, throw the cards, berate your play, curse, look at the ceiling in disgust, or do 100 other things. However, these types of reactions are not the action of an Emotional Dominant Personality who is on emotional tilt, at least not in a negative, destructive manner. In fact, all of the above could be categorized as somewhat normal to this personality type.

When the Emotional Dominant Personality is severely stressed, upset, or beset by problems, they become dispassionately stoic. They withdraw into themselves. What moments earlier might have been a laughing, playful mass of energy, suddenly becomes quiet, withdrawn, totally oblivious to events and circumstances. It is in this state that they often have vicious internal conversations, directed both at themselves and at others who they perceive as the cause of the emotional storm. It's during this state of being that this emotional personality often attempts to strike out with disregard for consequences, sometimes in a short period of time. In this state, they are susceptible to innuendos, challenges, mental jousting and abnormal risk-taking.

Of all the 13 personality types, it is the Emotional who must constantly come into contact with their emotional feelings through physically touching themselves. Their hands often hold their heads, touch their cheeks or pull at their features. When they are in a negative mode, they appear to engage in a listless, unconscious form of touching. When they are positively engaged, they continue the bonding to themselves through touching. However, in this state the touching takes on a sensuous form, as they are highly conscious of the feelings that the touching is producing. A highly emotional woman will lean forward and stroke her leg from ankle to knee. She will use her hand to toss her hair to one side or constantly pull the hand through the hair. When they hear something pleasurable, the hand will lightly touch and stroke the throat. Highly emotional men will constantly lick their lips and often will use the tips of the fingers to lightly stroke the back of the hand or forearm. Another trait of this personality is to constantly look down to the left or right when they are trying to determine what action is appropriate. The longer the eyes remain in this position mode, is an indication of the difficulty they are having in reaching a decision.

Because the Emotional Dominant Personality demands of themselves to live life fully, the problem often becomes how much. There are only limited opportunities to ram and jam in a poker game. In between these opportunities there exist hours of the ordinary, hours of humdrum activity. The Emotional's success at the poker table is almost always determined by how they handle the times that require discipline and patience. Even though they have enormous creative talent, drive and determination, the end result is they often become victims because of others' ability to use their fiery nature against them.

The Emotional will always live and die by what they feel. If they exhibit aggressiveness, it's more apt to be based on emotions they are feeling than on advantages that have presented themselves at the table. The Emotional pays more attention to the players involved than to the game itself. The ability or inability to feel often is the determining factor on what course this personality will take. If the depth of emotion is extreme, then the risk involved is inconsequential. A frequent comment that the Emotional Dominant Personality makes to themselves and to others is, "I've got to stop this. I can't keep living like this." Yet this discipline is almost always artificial, as their emotional tides soon put them back on the roller coaster ride of ups and downs.

The Emotional Dominant Personality as a Buyer

The Emotional Dominant Personality is a terrific buyer. They are hot, passionate, impulsive, creative people. They live and die by their intense feelings. The Emotional Personality is a splurge buyer. What they buy is as varied as the imagination is vivid.

The Emotional Dominant Personality is the most people-oriented of the 13 personality types. They need and crave the emotional involvement of others. In the selling arena, the most important factor as to whether you make a sale or don't make a sale with this type is you, the selling agent.

The Emotional will feed off your involvement, excitement and zeal. Likewise, they will become moody, depressed and unresponsive if you present yourself or your product or service, in a gray, drab, ho-hum manner. The Emotional is a highly associated individual. They constantly check internal references as to how they feel about an object or about someone. They need excitement. They need to be actively involved in life. When forced to set on the sideline, they become prone to depression and anxiety.

The Emotional is a lover of both people and of objects. They have a distinct eye for beauty. They have a creative flair for design, decorating and art that far surpasses any of the other personality types. The Emotional is a great shopper. They have a unique ability to zero in on objects that others overlook, then transform these pieces into valuable decor.

The Emotional lives in a world of color. Their world is fast, bright, vivid and hectic. They have the type of energy that few can keep up with. They like instant results. Life is not some future event, nor is it something that is to be postponed until the time is right.

As a selling agent, the most important thing you can do is always be aware of how the Emotional Dominant Personality is feeling at any one moment. Because their feelings are so intense, they are often on a roller coaster ride between highs and lows. When they are in a low mental state they become self-absorbed. They draw within themselves, becoming moody and uncommunicative.

As a selling agent, you want and need the Emotional to verbalize their feelings. A constant barrage of questions directed at them produces the best results. Ask why, what, how come. . .tell me what you're thinking...tell me what you're feeling. You can get an Emotional to consider buying anything if you can get them involved. When they turn inward, they become like a kettle that seethes. When you get them to verbalize their feelings, they tend to blow off the low state of feelings and return to the highs that drive them.

There are two types of objections, those that are spoken and those that are spoken silently to the self. With the Emotional Dominant Personality, the silent objections have a tendency to populate into unrelated areas until you have something that's unmanageable, so much so that even the Emotional doesn't know what's bothering them. The result is a sales process that is stalled.

The Emotional responds best to a free-wheeling, unstructured presentation. The imagination of the Emotional is a great ally in selling to these individuals. Their imaginations will often provide the exact steps your presentation should take. Any and every time their body carriage position comes forward (leaning toward you) you should attempt to close the sale. If you can't close at that time, just back up and explore the objection then play the game of "what if" and "how would". . .What if you owned it and how would you feel...

Memories and past favorable experiences are powerful references for the Emotional Dominant Personality. The Emotional is highly sentimental. The Emotional spends a lot of money trying to duplicate an experience that created good memories from their past. If you can find out what these experiences were, than recreate them through your product or service. It becomes a powerful motivational magnet for the mind of the Emotional.

After getting attuned to the Emotional's state of mind, a next important step is to watch their hands. Emotional individuals speak volumes silently through their hands. This is true not only of the Emotional personality but of all the 13 personality types. In a poker game, you can detect accurate information by watching an individual's hands. In contrast, you learn almost nothing by studying a poker player's face. Human beings reveal an inordinate amount of unconscious information through their hands and fingers. This is information such as anxiety, tension, apprehension, eagerness, caution, fear, doubt, excitement, etc. We unconsciously move and place our hands and fingers to the silent emotions we're experiencing. If you master nothing except reading emotions revealed through an individuals hands and fingers, your sales will soar by at least 10 percent.

The Emotional has a fast thought process. Many personality types tend to have and deal with one thought at a time thoroughly. The Emotional tends to have dozens of short bursts of thoughts, thus the tendency to get lost or overwhelmed by the volume of what they are thinking. When this happens, their hand and finger movements increase. It's important to pick up the signs of frustration and impatience. At times like this you want to slow the individual down to where one issue at a time can be dealt with and overcome. If the Emotional becomes overwhelmed by their own thoughts, they tend to throw up their hands and quit out of frustration.

Many Emotional Dominant Personalities are highly successful in their chosen field. Yet many who are successful are financially strapped because they spend excessively. When the Emotional is hot they want it now. They are not overly price conscious, nor are they tough negotiators. If they can't get what they want, the blame will always fall on the selling agent's shoulders. At times like this, they can be vindictive and hot-tempered. Reason, caution, details, facts and figures are non-motivational weights with the Emotional, they're simply things that stall the gratification of ownership.

The Emotional will buy because of you. They like, need, even crave the approval of others. Your opinion carries a lot of weight in their decision making process. They will ask questions like, "Do you think it's really me?" "What do you think I should do?" "If you were me what would you do?" The Emotional responds to stroking and sincere assurances.

If you light the fire bright enough, this type seldom procrastinates, plus they tend to be honest and forthright in their dealings. Ultimately, the key to successfully sell this type individuals is to understand their feelings; and just as important, to help them understand their own feelings. Many "Emotional types" constantly stall themselves because they can't find, touch or understand the torrents of what they feel. Above all else, get involved with the emotional. Even if you don't make a sale, your life will be better off because of it. A rage and passionate desire for living is a good quality to have rub off.

THE I-DOMINANT

CLINICAL NAME:
NARCISSISTIC PERSONALITY DISORDER

Positive:	*Negative:*
I Am	I
I Can	I
I Will	I
Competitive	Me
Will to Win	Me
Ambitious	Me
Self-Belief	Cut-Throat
Purposeful	Manipulative
Leader	Narcissistic
Goal-Oriented	Hot-Tempered
Deal Maker	Unforgiving
Gambler	Carries Grudges
Dreamer	Unable to Take Criticism
Extroverted	Petty
High-Octane Energy	Not a Team Player
Generous	Scheming
Powerful	

A Positive Overview

The I-Dominant Personality is the material of legends. The Texas oil man who started with nothing. The automobile dealer who started by washing cars. The big time stock trader who wins or loses millions in one day. They are the gamblers, the dreamers, and deal makers who have become folk heroes in this country. The I-Dominant Personality is self-contained, purposeful and highly competitive. They are fueled by an intense inner fire that drives them day in, day out. They are often visionary, being able to see beyond current trends and needs to anticipate the future and that which is yet to come. They believe in the self. They have a list that is long and precise as it pertains to themselves and their goals and plans. They truly have the power of the "I." They process from the knowledge that "I am," "I can" and "I will." Their power is the confidence of their self. Self-doubt is overruled by self-belief. They are not led, because their purpose is to be leaders. They have the will, power, and stamina to produce results, "regardless." They are seldom deterred or distracted by emotional binges or sentimental musings of others.

The Negative Side

Because they are I-Dominant, they are often shackled by the very trait that gives them greatness. They can be so dependent on the I, I, I, me, me, me part of their personality that it becomes a liability instead of an asset. They are God and you are a mere disciple. They are cut-throat, they are vindictive, and they are manipulative. They view the world with a black/white me vs. them mentality. They are often ruled by a hot temper and a vicious tongue that knows no limits. You may have been a loyal confidant to them for 20 years and still feel their wrath over the slightest perceived act of disloyalty. They demand and take center stage. It is their belief that they have the inalienable right to be at the front. Many I-Dominant personalities will carry a grudge for years, all the time waiting for the opportune time to exact revenge. They are not a team player. Their mentality is that they have the God-given right to own the team. When the I-Dominant part of the personality becomes extreme, they cannot take any kind of criticism. They construe this as disloyalty, ungratefulness, and a personal attack of the severest nature.

Identifying And Playing With The I-Dominant Personality

There is a stereotypical Hollywood image of the I-Dominant Personality, which is primarily one of the swashbuckling, bold, dare-all individual. This image is both true and false. Many I-Dominant personalities have this persona. However, just as many have limited physical capabilities, as would any normal segment of the population. The I-Dominant Personality is not easily identified through physical characteristics, because I-dominance (the belief in and the power of the self) is a mental, emotional, psychological trait. There is an old proverb about a white tiger that stalks into a dark cave. This proverb would be a good example of the mental and psychological state of mind that propels the I-Dominant Personality. In many respects, this personality type is best equipped to conquer the game of poker for several reasons which we will highlight. However, it's wise to keep in mind that most proverbs have an addendum that is often ignored, forgotten or not stated as being pertinent to the proverb. In the case of being a white tiger that brazenly stalks into dark caves, we would hasten to add, especially as it pertains to poker, that one should be aware that if you walk into enough dark caves, there is the distinct possibility that you could wind up knee deep in bat shit, which has an adverse effect on both white fur and fragile egos.

If your purpose in life is to be a professional poker player, you are to be both admired and pitied. Admired because of your courageous undertaking; pitied because the deck is stacked against you in various ways. The most important way that this deck-stacking occurs is that the only support you have is yourself and the self-belief that you must have in order to sustain the self. I can state unequivocally, it's easier to be the president of General Motors than it is to be a successful professional poker player. The president of General Motors has a large and efficient (?) structural organization that supports and protects him. If he is wrong, so what? If he screws up, so what?

If you are a poker player, you have no structure supporting you. If you're the president of General Motors, you have a board of directors that, in theory, is supposed to be a position of oversight for the good of all concerned parties, when in reality, it is many times nothing more than a system of protection that covers the asses of those at the top. If you're the president of General Motors, you will receive a multi-million dollar salary, millions more in stock options and various other perks that have nothing to do with performance. If you perform poorly, the board of directors (your friends, associates) will normally give you a vote of confidence. On rare occasions, they might fire you; however, that's not a bad deal, because they'll send you off with a million-dollar retirement/pension fund. If you're the president of General Motors and you have a bad month, you can fire some vice-president, pretend to realign some divisions, blame your poor performance on unfair competition, blame it on the Japanese, blame it on lazy American workers or you can go to the government and get a billion dollar bailout.

If you're a poker player and you have a bad month, there are no vice-presidents you can blame it on or fire. As a poker player, you are always naked and exposed. Because there is no support organization surrounding you, you live and die based solely on one thing, your performance. To stand alone, naked and exposed requires an enormous amount of self-confidence, self-belief, self-reliance, therein the I-Dominant Personality is superbly equipped to challenge the game of poker, because this type of individual has all the previously mentioned qualities in abundance.

The I-Dominant individual is keenly aware. They are aware of where they are, where you are in relation to them and where they are going. Out of this awareness comes an individual who is highly positionally oriented in all areas of their lives. They understand and use position (leverage) as a weapon or advantage better than any of the other twelve personality types. Deep within the psyche of the I-Dominant Personality is the one abiding thought, which is the absolute necessity of the preservation of the precious self.

One of the ways they insure this preservation is through positioning themselves in a manner superior to their competition, be it at the poker table or at endeavors in the real world. Position is an important concept in both business and poker in which the value is often misunderstood. I once had a neighbor who was the largest builder of single-family dwelling units in the United States. One day I was talking with this highly I-Dominant individual and he mentioned that had purchased, over the years, $56 million worth of undeveloped real estate out in the middle of nowhere. I ask him why he wanted to buy land 40 miles from the city where no one lived. He said, "Because someday this city has got to have an airport and the only place they can build it is out where I own the land, and when they do I've got the advantage 'cause I'm already there." (Position). He was right, because eight years later they built K.C.I.

Poker is a game that dictates a constant process of decision making based on incomplete information. Position does two important things:

A. Exposes your opponents hand.

B. Creates an information advantage for you.

As an example, suppose that in a ten-handed Hold 'em game, all nine players just call the big blind before the flop. Now the flop comes and you're in the tenth (last to act) position. By the time you have to make a decision, nine other players have given you progressively more information on what your decision should be. You have a 9-1 ratio advantage from the first position, 8-1 from the second position, etc. Additionally, as each player has acted, they have in minute or gargantuan proportion exposed their hand through their actions (bet, check, raise, fold, etc.). How you interpret these actions in relationship to the cards you hold will determine your success. As another example, you can be a prolific card counter in the game of 21 and you are still going to get your head beat in, because you are always required to expose (act on) your hand before the dealer. This is such a serious disadvantage that I know of no one who consistently makes money at the 21 game.

Information at the poker table is a crucial advantage. Oftentimes the difference between winning and losing is the information that you are able to gather. If the situation were such that you had complete information, the result would be that you could make a perfect decision. In poker, the information is always incomplete; therefore, you make decisions based on what you know (fact) and what you don't know (supposition). It's here that the I-Dominant Personality is extremely dangerous.

These individuals have an ability to take a small amount of information and make the correct decision as it pertains to what the finished picture will look like. The I-Dominant Personality is oriented toward visual imagery more than the other personality types. They constantly visualize or fantasize in their mind the possibilities of how things, events, people, etc., will wind up as an end result.

As an example, tens of thousands of individuals may drive down the road and see a weed-infested cow pasture. The I-Dominant Personality drives down the same road, past the same pasture, and almost automatically does not see a cow pasture full of weeds. If you drive down the road a year later, you may be surprised to see a sparkling sky scraper setting in what was once a patch of weeds, and just as likely it's owned by an I-Dominant Personality who could see a bigger more complete picture than the other individuals who passed by.

It is this constant visualization or fantasy in the mind of the I-Dominant Personality that creates a huge advantage over other personality types. Because of this visual imagery, a different state of consciousness often emerges. Questions often predominate the mind. These are questions that tend to expand the realm of reality and therefore possibilities. These are questions like:

A. Why not?

B. What would happen if...

C. What could I do that...

D. How can I better...

Other personality types such as the Aggressive, Worker Moralist, Vigilant, etc., have a tendency to make statements, as opposed to asking questions, that limit or constantly replay the same day-to-day conscious reality. Statements like:

A. This is how it's done.

B. This is what works.

C. This is correct, that is incorrect.

As an example of how this process can enhance your life, the next time you're feeling down, defeated or depressed, ask yourself just a couple of simple questions:

A. Why not be happy?

B. What would happen if I just decide not to be unhappy?

And then make a conscious effort to stop making the same statements over and over to yourself. Statements such as:

A. I'm really down.

B. I feel bad, depressed.

C. It's tough to win.

Beyond your personal life, you can start using this simple (it works) concept to improve your perceptual, analytical and information-gathering skills at the poker table. It's a huge advantage to take an incomplete picture and see with clarity the different possibilities of the finished product (hand). The I-Dominant Personality is highly skilled at this, because they constantly look ahead as an exercise of consciousness.

Poker is a game of assumptions. The ability to make correct assumptions is directly related to how much of the money you get and how often you get it. The first assumption you have to make is, what hands your opponent would or would not play. Once you've made that assumption, the next assumption you have to make is, what the opponent would or would not do with the said hand. A third assumption, that's equally important is, what your opponent will do when you raise, re-raise, check, call, etc.

If you can be correct about the above three assumptions, more times than you are incorrect, you will be a winning poker player. If your assumptions are correct at the right time, you'll make even more money. Your assumptions have to be correct in direct relationship to the size of the pots you're involved in. It's a losing proposition to be correct on three $500 pots and then be incorrect on one $5000 pot.

Assumptions are more easily arrived at when you've played with an opponent on more than one occasion. If you can, after time, put an opponent on a hand regularly, it means one of two things: Either you are a superior player or the opponent is inferior. When it becomes easy to put an opponent on a hand, they are probably nothing more than a nut player. To put it more unkindly, they are flat-ass inferior. A pair of Aces vs. a pair of Kings is not much of a poker hand; yet, the majority of poker players think it's written in the Dead Sea scrolls. A pair of fours vs. a pair of fives is a more accurate gauge of poker skills.

If you have an opponent who you have difficulty putting on a hand, it will mean one of two things: That player is either a very inferior player or a vastly superior player. An inferior player will play any two cards that resemble a rag and a mop. Over time, this violation of the laws of probability will bust them. The best assumption you can make against this type of player, is that they will, the majority of time, have very little or nothing and play accordingly.

A superior player is difficult to put on hands, not because of the hands they choose to play, per se, but because of the hands they choose to play against an individual opponent. In reality, they make superior assumptions about opponents more so than about cards. Of the 13 personality types, it is the I-Dominant who is most capable of making correct assumptions. That, in itself, accounts for a large degree of their success. As an example, in a different context, suppose that IBM stock goes up 20 points today. When do you want to buy it? Yesterday or tomorrow? Be assured that successful I-Dominant individuals bought it yesterday.

A large majority of poker players have a built-in false assumption that they carry around with them at all times. It resembles a large anchor on their ass. This false assumption is the belief that the world is divided into two groups: Poker Players and the square world. This built-in superiority complex is nothing more than a cancerous growth of the ego. Too many poker players think that their profession is too elite, too complex, too macho for anyone from the square side of the world to master. Too many poker players labor under the false assumption that everyone in the world, aside from themselves and those of their genre, is a sucker in waiting (waiting to be separated from their money). The real truth is that there are a lot of big-time trial attorneys, stock traders, commodity players, business executives, etc., who could beat just about any world-class poker player if they really wanted to. On the other hand, I know of only a handful of poker players who could even start to run a major corporation.

Look closely at the assumptions you make and carry with you. They are closely related to winning and losing. When I was a kid, I spent a lot of time at the creek fishing. The biggest fish in the creek was called a sucker. They got their name because they were very adroit at sucking the bait off the hook. The real problem, however, was when you caught one, you couldn't eat it. It had too many small bones in it to make it worth the effort. Life is often like that. Be careful of assumptions you make.

The I-Dominant Personality is a charismatic individual. Other personality types such as the Adventurer often have a physical or sexual charisma born from their physical being. The I-Dominant personalities charisma is from a different source. Ask yourself a question. What is the greatest aphrodisiac in the world? Is it the legendary Spanish Fly? Is it the supposedly magical powder from the Rhinoceros Horn? Or how about the drug Papaverine? Thousands of men have spent millions of dollars from the beginning of time in search of the magical substance that would give them virility, stamina and unending potency. How foolish this quest. The single greatest aphrodisiac is self-confidence. If you think you can, you will. If you think you can't, you won't.

The charismatic persona of the I-Dominant Personality is born from self-confidence. It is the single greatest ally they have at the poker table. Out of this self-belief comes other assets that make the I-Dominant Personality a dangerous opponent. Self-confidence, self-belief, gives an individual deep roots. The deep roots of purpose and conviction make it difficult to throw an individual off course. Other personality types with shallow roots are easy prey, because when trouble comes or difficulty arises, they can't stay the course. They are ripped apart by the first ill wind or storm of self-doubt that blows through their minds. Individuals with deep roots have a rock-solid purpose for their life and goals set out to provide the proper direction. It's easy to set goals. Some personality types change goals as often as they change their clothing. The I-Dominant Personality sets the goal and it seldom changes. The goal is specific, to be No. 1. Fueling this goal is the willingness to gamble, to take chances.

The I-Dominant Personality is almost always entrepenurial in belief and lifestyle; therefore, they are not only comfortable with gambling, but have a personality desire to gamble. Winning without the element of chance, danger or risk, is not processed as satisfying by this personality type. The Adventurer or Emotional Dominant Personalities also have a personality need to gamble and often do so with contempt for the risk involved. However, the I-Dominant Personality is totally different in this regard for, or lack of, respect of risk.

The I-Dominant Personality is highly cognizant of risk and what is acceptable and what is not acceptable. It can't be any other way, because to blindly ignore the risks involved would possibly injure or destroy the precious personal self, and that is a risk that the I-Dominant Personality won't. . .can't take. The I-Dominant Personality may have a bankroll of a million dollars and will willingly throw fifty or a hundred thousand dollars on a highly speculative venture. They are perfectly willing to do it time and time again. However, they would never risk a large portion of their bankroll if it would endanger their self, their position or their prominence, even if the odds are more favorable than some speculative venture.

This is an asset, not a liability in gambling. You cannot be blind to risk even when the odds are prohibitively in your favor. In many respects, the casino owners are still the best gamblers, and in all their games they are the favorite. Still they are shrewd enough to impose a maximum betting limit on all their games. They have no need or intention of risking the whole house on one roll of the dice or turn of a card.

A central issue in playing with and understanding the I-Dominant Personality is ego, both as an issue with them and with you, their opponent. Having self-belief is a powerful component, going across the line to narcissistic behavior creates a reality that is out of touch with the human race, the real world and the harsh realities of winning and losing at the poker table. At face appearance, it often appears that I-Dominant personalities live charmed lives. Everything seems to come easy. They often appear to have more going for them than the average person. This superficial judgement often creates envy, jealousy and resentment against the I-Dominant Personality that results in back biting, pettiness and stupid play, born out of a desire, to quote, "cut him down to size."

Undoubtedly, some I-Dominant personalities have lived charmed lives; however, the great majority of these individuals have started with nothing or very little, and through belief, hard work and a willingness to do what others wouldn't do, have built a successful career. Many of these individuals have struggled for years and endured great hardships to get where they wanted to go. Often in these years of struggle and hardship, the only light that shined, the only encouragement they had, was their own belief in themselves. Sometimes their own worst enemy was themselves. Even when they desperately need help, they can't ask for or accept it. Their pride is such that any acknowledgement of such need would translate as a demeaning of the self. Instead, they stubbornly turn inward, depending even more on the self, and in the process wind up destroying their greatest asset, the self.

However, the I-Dominant is resilient, and sooner or later, even if it's years, they tend to rebound. When they do there is hell to pay. They, more than any other personality type, carry grudges and exact revenge that often borders on the destruction of other lives. Furthermore, they do it with a cold ruthlessness that is completely devoid of empathy or remorse. Not only do they exact revenge for themselves, they often take revenge against anyone who they feel mistreated their loyal allies during their years of struggle. The I-Dominant Personality is extremely loyal to those who are in their camp; however, their camps are sometimes lonely places as their intensity and fierce demands of loyalty often cause others to desert them.

Is the I-Dominant Personality egotistical? The answer is yes. Is this good or bad? The answer is, it depends.

Ego is the outward projection of an individual's inner reality of how they view themselves. A healthy ego serves as both an instrument for future accomplishment (drive, ambition) and as a protector against detrimental behavior (behavior that harms the self). When the ego is out of control, it gives an individual an altered view of reality that prevents it from functioning in the role of protector.

Of the 13 personalities, the I-Dominant Personality is the one who is most ego-driven. If the ego is within the boundary of actual reality, the I-Dominant Personality is dangerous. If the ego is outside the boundary of reality, then this personality can be viewed as one which willingly helps his opponents in beating him regularly. Any opponent who constantly leads with the ego, is an individual who fails to assign a correct and true value to the hand they play. Their reality is that a pair of tens in their hand is as good as a pair of Kings in an opponent's possession. They believe their supposed superiority in other areas can easily overcome this starting disadvantage (tens vs. Kings). This grandiose view of their personal ability leads them to try maneuvers that are inappropriate, such as check raising or bets sized out of proportion in an attempt to make a statement (create fear, the show of disdain for an opponent).

A subtle manifestation of egotism is stubbornness. They exhibit stubbornness in their refusal to acknowledge the possibility that their chosen course of action could have been improved. Another manifestation of egotism is justification. They easily and constantly find ways of justifying what they do or did as being correct. Many times, this stubbornness and justification is not easily detected, because it is internalized (told to and kept to the self). One of the keys to look for is an individual who displays stone-cold indifference to a situation such as losing and especially to other people. This mask of imperturbability is the I-Dominant Personality's way of protecting the ego (self) from exposure. Highly egotistical individuals go to great lengths to keep from ever having to expose fully any inadequacies for public scrutiny.

As another example, you may tell yourself you are the world's greatest Shakespearean actor. You might be. However, until you're willing to step from in front of the living room mirror to the actual stage of peer review, you're only deluding yourself. Behind the mask of imperturbability, the I-Dominant individual is engaged in an emotional storm when under stress or experiencing emotional difficulty. The most common emotions being experienced are rage, anger, revenge, hatred, envy and humiliation. The I-Dominant Personality reacts outwardly by first ignoring any opponent who beats them. They have the very real need to devalue any opponent who could possibly be superior. During this period of indifference, the I-Dominant Personality is creating justification and many times plotting revenge that is born out of stinging humiliation being experienced by the self. Almost invariably at some point, two or three minutes after the fact, the I-Dominant Personality will have the need to glance at any opponent who beats them. If you watch closely, you will often see hatred and a cold fury.

The purpose of this book is not how to create psychological or emotional tilt in opponents, but rather to differentiate the distinguishing facets of personality and to understand the motivations of the different personalities. However, the step that follows mastering motivation is the ability to manipulate, especially in poker. Personality is like a two-edged sword or the proverbial tightrope that one walks. There is always a balancing act going on. Are they Vigilant or paranoid? Are they I-Dominant or narcissistic? Are they Adventurer or are they really over the line and needing an adrenaline fix? Because of this fine line, it's wise to understand that manipulation is possible, either for you or against you. As an example, you can simply stare at an individual who is highly vigilant and create all kinds of problems in this individual's mind. You can intensify the effect if you beat the individual, then whisper something to the dealer or someone sitting next to you.

I was once dealt back to back Aces in a 20-40 Hold 'em game, and by mere coincidence, was head up with the same opponent both times. This individual, who was paranoid to the letter, spent more time watching others than he ever spent playing poker. After I won the second pot, I deliberately gave the dealer a large toke and grinned maliciously at the guy. He didn't win any money that night because he was too busy glaring alternately at the dealers and me. Another example is with the I-Dominant Personality when they are wearing their mask of imperturbability. By deliberately exposing them to public scrutiny or by amplifying a weakness you intensify their internal storm to the point that many of these individuals will sit and seethe for hours. If you beat them and they didn't show their hand, you simply ask them in front of the table what they had or you can insinuate loudly, "Bob, you're going to have to learn you can't play a pair of fours in this game," or if you wish to ignore all the rules of poker etiquette, you can state matter-of-factly, "Bob, your play is very amateurish." Beware! Before you decide to step up to manipulation, you had best decide first if you have the type of personality to engage in long-term psychological warfare. You will certainly be marked in the minds of many as a target worthy of extermination.

The two previous examples are of blatant behavior. Most manipulation in the game of poker is more subtle in nature. It's a kind of cover-your-ass manipulation to ensure you don't receive too much retribution in return. A good example of this is the name I chose to use in the above example. "Bob" is a generic name in the sense that there are hundreds of poker players named Bob. These players can't possibly take offense, because they can say, "I'm not that Bob." So in effect, I have covered my ass. If I had said, "Pug, your play is very amateurish," I would have created the possibility of retribution for myself. However, there is another possibility (it's the sinister part of manipulation), which is that maybe "Bob" is not generic but a real person whose play is very amateurish and will certainly recognize himself and feel rage when he reads this public whipping.

Because the possibilities of manipulation are endless, it's only fair to postulate that perhaps, in reality, "Bob" is a very fine poker player who regularly hung out the author and it's just sweet grapes on the author's part because he's I-Dominant and has been waiting for five years to pay back "Bob." Like we said, the possibilities are endless, because if the author is I-Dominant why use a characteristic of the Eccentric Dominant Personality such as saying sweet grapes instead of sour grapes? (A favorite tactic of the Eccentric is the use of odd language for the purpose of creating confusion. In reality, it's delusionary superiority.

So what is the real point of all the endless possibilities on manipulation? Two things you need to remember. First, the mind of a manipulator will always lovingly say to themselves, "There is a fine line between right and wrong." Don't believe it. The fine line between right and wrong is a chasm so wide you can fall into it and never climb out of it. Secondly, the I-Dominant Personality is the most manipulative of all the personality types. One of their favorite and most successful ways of manipulating is through the creation of endless possibilities in your mind.

If you'll remember, earlier we said the I-Dominant Personality is highly positional in their activities. So just what is position? I will, for this context, define it as "That which best serves to enhance the priorities of the self." Politicians are position-oriented. They tend to view themselves as someone worthy of special entitlement such as limousines, perks not accorded to others, favored treatment, etc. To ensure that they receive this favored status, they take positions that often have nothing to do with their actual beliefs, but are certain to perpetuate or sustain the position they desire. A good example of this is many politicians will take a position in favor of women's rights; however, many of these same politicians will confide to you secretly that they really can't stand women libbers.

It's the ability to work both sides of the street that the I-Dominant Personality is so adept at. They will solicit your viewpoint, not because they personally care about your feelings, but because they want to know your position in order to use it to protect or expand their own. Pay close attention to the language they use and how they use it. When this personality is positive in its balance (I-Dominant), they will use and say things such as:

A. John, give me your opinion.

B. John, how would you have played that?

C. John, what do you think would be best?

In conversation, the I-Dominant Personality is very adroit at using your first name as an inducement to win your confidence. When this personality is negative in its balance (narcissistic), they engage in extreme self-reference such as:

A. Yes, but. . . (yes followed by but is really no)

B. Well, what I would have done. . .

C. Here's what I think. . .

This personality often has a need to interrupt your conversation and interject a point that highlights their ability or calls attention to something that they accomplished. When you're engaged in conversation with them and they are secretly envious of you, they will often look over your head as you talk, or they will pick up the phone and make a call and only say "excuse me" after they have dialed or exhibited impatience with your viewpoint. The I-Dominant Personality is easiest to attack at two distinct times, when they are sitting on top of the world and when they hit rock bottom. When they are at the top, they are susceptible because they process themselves as being unbeatable. They start relying more on their perceived personal strengths than on what might be the actual reality of the situation.

A mistake that other players of a different personality trait often make is they sometimes exhibit a reluctance to attack a highly successful I-Dominant Personality who is sitting at the top. This is really an over valuation of reputation that not only happens in poker, but other areas also.

A good example is the line that is put up by the bookmaker on certain sports teams and the public buying of this betting line. Some teams such as the Chicago Bears, Los Angeles Raiders or Boston Celtics are consistently given a line greater than their current ability. These teams are receiving an inordinate amount of respect based on reputation more than any current playing ability. The Chicago Bears of 1991 are a mere shadow of the 1984 or 1985 Bears teams.

When playing with the I-Dominant Personality you need to look closely at what is and what isn't. You'll find many times that if you separate reputation from actual fact there are a lot of individuals skating on reputation rather than skill. Complicating the picture is that the I-Dominant Personality is often busily perpetuating the reputation. If you look closely at the success of I-Dominant personalities in the business world, you will notice that many of this type parlayed their success. They often started with one small victory and in rapid succession parlayed it again and again until they reached the top. It's at this ladder climbing stage that the I-Dominant is so dangerous. They have a razor-sharp edge. This edge is like being on the proverbial streak or roll. They are sharply analytic, highly intuitive, always three steps ahead of the competition in their positioning. This edge is like steel that sharpens steel. If you continue to look closely; however, you will observe that many times the I-Dominant reaches a certain level of success, and the narcissistic side of their personality begins to dictate more and more of their actions. In essence, what happens is they stop taking care of business and become involved with both actions and fantasies that are solely for the satisfaction of the ego.

They have ever-expanding fantasies of brilliance, importance, and often an insatiable need for power. It is when they are in this grandiose state of mind that they are more easily attacked. They become show-oriented instead of goal-oriented. The most serious flaw they develop is a prevailing belief that their own unique abilities are greater than any opponent or situation. They can never clearly see reality, nor can they see reality as others view it. It's at this point where if they continue to try and parlay, they meet disaster. They break the one rule that they value as most necessary, which is, "Never do anything that would totally endanger the precious self." It becomes a two-sided attack against themselves. First, they have become lackadaisical about taking care of what they already have. Secondly, they are blind to the values of risk-taking. When they are at the poker table in this narcissistic state, their style of play is to attempt to attack from the top down. They want any top dog sitting at the table.

In comparison, a personality type such as the hard-nosed Aggressive or the grinding Worker Moralist are content to attack from the bottom up until the situation is such that they can attack the strength at the top. So many times the I-Dominant gets blind-sided in this situation, because someone else moves in on them while they are trying to lure the object of their envy into the game. A favorite tactic of a narcissistic personality who's out of control is to win a pot with nothing, then attempt to embarrass the opponent by showing the hand, then rubbing it in. The I-Dominant Personality would be well-advised that most poker players have a memory that is longer than the New Jersey Turnpike and that a much larger toll fee will be due at some future date.

The other distinct time when the I-Dominant Personality is susceptible is when they hit rock bottom. A gambler who has lost his self-confidence will always make incorrect decisions and be in conflict with themselves. In gambling, a lack of self-confidence manifests itself in two glaring ways:

A. Too much action with disdain for ruin.

B. The inability to take action.

All human beings have within their neuro circuitry a stop-destruct switch. It's an impulse that comes to us that says stop! This is destructive to the self. It's there for our protection. It tells us we need to choose a less hurtful alternative. Because of free will, it's up to the individual whether they listen to the internal warning or not. Many personality types such as the Reflective, Theatrical, Worker Moralist, Vigilant, Loner, and in many cases the Aggressive, use this self-destruct switch as a form of discipline to preserve the self. On the other side, personalities such as the I-Dominant, Emotional, Underachiever and Adventurer override the switch and suffer the consequences. When the I-Dominant is at rock bottom, the switch is often ignored out of anger or the need to spite the self. The result is out-of-control playing (too much, too long). The style is being led by the ego. The mind becomes set and the money disappears. Self-doubt, self-blame and incriminating internal dialogue (you deserved it, you bastard) replace self-belief, yet the mask of imperturbability remains even as the internal voice is screaming, "Go ahead, lose it all so we can get out of here."

In gambling, the rush to ruin is marked by desperate maneuvers, play against impossible odds and resignation of spirit. On the other side of the coin, a gambler who has lost their self-confidence shows a marked inability to take action. They can't gamble. It's dying in slow motion while waiting for the nuts. The style is marked by vacillation, hesitancy and playing not to lose, which in effect, means you actually lose more because you miss betting opportunities. You keep calling and the phone bill keeps getting larger.

It's just not the I-Dominant Personality, but any personality that is susceptible when self-belief deserts them. However, it's more devastating to the I-Dominant Personality because they are then totally alone. None of the other 12 personality types can ever experience this total loneliness, because the loss of self is loss of spirit. At this time, opponents can, to a certain degree, play without regard to position, cards or money. It's easy to run over anyone who lacks self-belief. Be aggressive, even if you lose hands. That in itself will not, in the short term, restore the confidence of a losing gambler. As long as they are willing to sit there, you should be willing to fire back. After hitting rock bottom, the I-Dominant will usually begin the long climb back.

Some of the identifying traits of the I-Dominant Personalities and their style are:

A. Name. I-Dominant Personalities love to splash their names all over the place. As an example, Trump Plaza, Trump Shuttle, Trump Casino, Trump's Art of the Deal. Many I-Dominant personalities will have underlings regularly page them at public places regardless of whether they are there or not.

B. Traps. The I-Dominant Personality is most adroit at setting traps. Even when they are not playing, their head is filled with endless variations of possible scenarios and how they might unfold at the table. This personality type practices poker much like the football team practices daily, yet only plays once a week. The I-Dominant is skillful at inducing others to play at him because of his ego, haughtiness and condescending manner toward others. As you come toward him, the I-Dominant surrenders, surrenders then surrenders some more. He surrenders with easy disdain, often giving the illusion that he has beaten you by surrendering. In reality, it's just another trap being set, but first he wants to amuse himself and bedevil you.

An opponent who constantly attacks, but gets no booty, has his momentum stolen away. The I-Dominant creates superiority by causing others to come forward. He maintains position and superiority by causing others to exert effort in the expectation of an ample reward, only to find out they are being toyed with. Even though the I-Dominant sometimes loses blinds or initial bets by surrendering, he is, in reality, giving a little to get a lot more later. The I-Dominant Personality needs emotional adrenaline. The fix is realized through endless mind games with others. Ali, the greatest heavyweight of all time, was a masterful manipulator both in and out of the ring. His haughty, arrogant manner against opponents before he climbed into the ring with them caused them to play right into his hand once the fight began. Ali's fighting style was to surrender, surrender (territory), jab, appear to be there, but when the opponent came forward, Ali surrendered by backing up, dancing away, then taunting the opponent at their inability to get him to stand still and fight. When they were sufficiently frustrated, Ali would trap them as they came in, but only on his terms, not theirs. The I-Dominant wants you on emotional tilt against him and he knows how to induce it.

As an example, suppose I ordered you to go down the hall and check out a dark room, but be careful there's a maniac on the loose. You would do so very carefully. Likewise, you would be careful the second and third time if you were ordered to go there. However, by the eighth or ninth trip you have grown less careful, more susceptible, more brave, so much so that you're sure there is no maniac in the room. You're right! The maniac is outside the room and will come in behind you after you have entered the room the last time. Question? Who is the maniac? You or the one who set the trap?

When playing with the I-Dominant Personality don't readily assume that a check is weakness, regardless of where it occurs in the hand. The I-Dominant uses a check as a reference to see how you react or as a maneuver to change positions with you. If the I-Dominant Personality is in control (not narcissistic) they are not overly concerned that checking might cause them to lose a betting opportunity or win a pot that's shorter than it should have been. More important to the I-Dominant is the information they can accumulate and use over the long haul. Many I-Dominant personalities are ravenous in their need and ability to consume information and store it. Later they sort this information into bits that are useful when their head starts running the incomplete picture and they start formulating what will decide the ultimate outcome of future events.

The I-Dominant Personality is suited to play a variety of different games. Their restless nature and gambling nature makes them better suited for high or no limit games. Limit games require a grind it out mentality that is not always suited to this personality. Their ability to use incomplete information and their skill in understanding others weaknesses is perfect for no limit. These skills also make them excellent lowball players provided their restless nature doesn't find too many hands to caress.

Ultimately the question that has to be answered is how much? If the I-Dominant Personality is under control they are dangerous, forces to be reckoned with. They demand respect because their talents are enormous. If this personality has crossed the line to narcissistic behavior, they are not nearly as dangerous.

As an example, an I-Dominant Personality walks into a poker room and has no doubt he can do damage. Furthermore, he knows his opponents also know this. A narcissistic personality walks into the poker room and he believes every head turns as he walks in. If two people are having a conversation then naturally they are talking (admirably) about him.

At the extreme end of narcissist behavior this personality walks into a poker room and actually believes there is applause, that the games were being held up until he arrived. He believes that the game can't possibly start until he has arrived. In this last example he is probably right because undoubtedly the other poker players are waiting for him and they probably did reserve a chair for him. Beware of dark caves.

The I-Dominant Personality as a Buyer

One of the great stumbling blocks in the buy/sell process is the buyer's conscious or unconscious fear of the seller. This fear is caused by certain personality types' lack of confidence in their own decision-making process. The fear of making the wrong decision inhibits the ability to make any decision, correct or incorrect. Fear fuels suspicion, which creates an atmosphere that inhibits the free exchange of ideas between buyer and seller. The buyer's glass is always half empty, because their minds won't allow the seller to fill it up. It's infinitely easier to sell to individuals who have confidence in themselves and in their ability to control their own destiny. True, it's tougher to sell to these individuals because they demand the selling agent be better; yet, when the sales are made, you sell more, more often and at a substantial profit.

The I-Dominant Personality is a tremendous buyer. They have the power and confidence of their own decision making. The I-Dominant is a mover and shaker, a deal maker supreme. They love the world of transactions. It's the adrenaline and main purpose in many of these individuals' lives. The I-Dominant is a risk taker; they live and breathe with an entrepreneurial spirit. Of the 13 personality types, it is the I-Dominant who is most visionary. They are highly visual individuals who perceive things far different than most individuals.

To successfully sell any individual, it helps if you understand how they view both themselves and the world they live in. The No. 1 asset of the I-Dominant individual is that they can see and think ahead of the average person. Many talented I-Dominant people work and process events and transactions backwards. They see the completed project or the potential of the project first, then they work backward from that vantage point to supply the components necessary to make it a reality. This is a huge advantage when you contrast it to individuals who can only work with the piece of the puzzle immediately in front of them. An excellent example of this thought process is the game of chess. The best chess players are not concerned with the move at hand, per se. The reason being is because they can look at the chess board and see how the fifth or tenth move is going to impact the game. If I can only see one move ahead while you can see five moves ahead, who do you think has the advantage? The I-Dominant sees the big picture and everything in their lives is directed toward its fulfillment.

The I-Dominant is the most ego-driven of all the 13 personality types. Many of these individuals' entire existence is for nothing more than the need to build a successful career. Yet having a successful career is not enough. The career is simply the vehicle that spotlights the self. The I-Dominant needs and craves recognition for the self. The more they acquire serves as proof of the importance of the self.

As a selling agent you are valuable to the I-Dominant Personality. They keenly understand the world of buying/selling. One of the easiest appointments to get is with the I-Dominant Personality. They seldom say no. The reason being is that their mental process is to listen to every deal and to consider every offer. They listen to all deals and offers because they don't overlook or reject anything out-of-hand until they have enough information to make a decision. If you are in the entrepreneurial business, you know that you listen to a thousand proposals to find the next Hula Hoop gold mine. To the I-Dominant, the selling agent is the party who has the information that makes the world spin faster.

If the product or service you're offering interests the I-Dominant, you become a little bit more valuable. You now become a component they can use to enhance their self and their accession upwards. Please notice the emphasis on the word "use." The I-Dominant is a user of people. Furthermore, they have the ability to make you feel good while you are being used. The I-Dominant is shrewd, cunning, cut-throat, tenacious and manipulative. They are also polite, polished, charming and disarming in negotiating to get what they want.

One of the first tactics of the I-Dominant is to try and determine the exact strength of your position. They want to know the exact strengths and weaknesses you bring to the table. One of the ways they do this is by getting as much information as possible from you. These individuals are superb at conversational information gathering. Their next tactic is to give you short-term concessions in order to gain the long-term advantage. As a selling agent, you are severely disadvantaged if you take short-term concessions on the front end and lose the long-term advantage. If you do this, the I-Dominant will always win because they have tremendous willpower and staying power.

Once the I-Dominant has you counting your money and licking your chops over what you think is about to transpire, their next tactic is to string you out. They are masters at game-playing for the purpose of enhancing the power of their position. As a selling agent, you simply need to be able to understand and play the negotiating game as adroitly as the buyer.

When the ego listens, resistance melts. The Achilles' heel of almost all I-Dominant individuals is their ego. They need to buy, deal, acquire, build, etc., to fulfill their inner self and their inner image. An important first step in selling these individuals is to find out exactly what role they plan to eventually create for themselves. As an example, many I-Dominant personalities are politicians. They may only be at the level of city councilman; yet, their ultimate goal is to be governor. When they decided they wanted to be the governor, they started working backwards and decided that being a councilman was necessary to realize the ultimate goal. When you can see the big picture as the I-Dominant sees it, you only need to fit your product or service into it to succeed.

The I-Dominant values any and all individuals who will become loyal to them. Phrases that ring their bell and impact their minds are statements such as, "I'd like to help you," "I think I could work this to your advantage," "We might be able to pull this off," etc. What you really want to do is plant the idea of a partnership in the mind of the I-Dominant. Don't even worry whether you have the ability to pull it off. The I-Dominant has enough self-confidence for the two of you.

All presentations to I-Dominant types should be highly visual in content. This type constantly visualize and dream in vivid pictures with themselves at the center of the picture. Even more effective is to make it panoramic in its scope. The I-Dominant responds to big. They are also very responsive to challenges. Their ego and self-confidence is such that they will attempt, and often succeed at, what others fear or have failed at.

The I-Dominant is keenly aware of the position, power and status of their peers and/or competitors. They love nothing more than to do what others can't do or have failed to do. The desire to crush a competitor or to create an act of one-upmanship will motivate many I-Dominant individuals to take action. They are often jealous and envious of the success of competitors. These ill feelings supply a tremendous amount of drive and determination for the mind of the individual.

The I-Dominant is emotional. However, it's a very one-sided emotion. They are not emotional in an impulsive heart-felt manner such as caring, tenderness or compassion. Their emotions are for the self. It's an emotional rage to succeed, to be admired, to have a never-ending spotlight shining on themselves. Therein, they respond to emotions that enhance or build those feelings.

The I-Dominant's ego wants the best of every deal. As a selling agent, you should always be prepared to have competition, lots of it.

They will shop a deal mercilessly. If they can get you and the competition to cut each other up, it's even better. While getting the best end of the deal from a financial standpoint is important, it's usually not the deciding factor on who gets the sale. More important is the personalized service and attention they receive from you. Price is second to their ego satisfaction. Often the I-Dominant is a free-spending individual in that they will pay money to enhance their position, because to them it's nothing more than a type of future investment that will pay dividends in some future format. They mainly want to create competition because it enhances their ability to pull strings and creates a base of power for themselves.

The I-Dominant is very skillful at using the telephone. It's one of their most useful tools. Likewise, it should become an important part of your arsenal. You should touch base frequently with these individuals. Your purpose being to add, modify or restructure the proposal you're working on. The I-Dominant is not a rejector or a procrastinator. They tend to always leave the door open for you until the deal is finally fashioned in an acceptable manner.

The I-Dominant Personality is very good at joint-venture or partnership arrangements as they are highly skilled at taking parts of the puzzle and forming a complete, workable picture.

The I-Dominant is a creative, action-oriented doer. Their world is fast-paced. They respond to the people who are most like them. They like to deal with selling agents who are creative and imaginative. The I-Dominant individual is a gutsy individual. Don't bore this type and don't be afraid to dream as big as they do. They understand dreams and goals and respect others who are of the same fabric. They are excellent at giving referrals and will often provide valuable contacts that will further your career. Just remember, the I-Dominant is an ego looking for a spotlight. If you want to sell them, you only need to be the spotlight.

THE LONER

CLINICAL NAME:
SCHIZOID PERSONALITY DISORDERS

Positive:	*Negative:*
Intelligence	Unemotional
Self-Sufficient	Stoic
Reliant	Dispassionate
Quick Decision-Making	Indifference
Observant	Aloof
Creative	Empty
Confident	Cold
Imperturbable	Stern
Independent	Rude
Calm	Belittling
Great Thinking Capacity	Sarcastic
Disciplined	Condescending
Task-Oriented	

A Positive Overview

As a group, the Loner Personality may have a higher degree of intellect than any of the other 13 personalities. They are often brilliant, creative people; some having made enormous contributions to the world in fields such as medicine, physics, literature, etc. The Loner is self-sufficient. They function best by themselves and are reliant only upon themselves. Their creativity can, and does, extend in many directions and once interested, they have amazing stamina and will power in completing the task at hand. They are disciplined individuals who are unperturbed by the wants and demands of others. They are calm, detached, not easily swayed by the surge of public opinion. They are keen observers of all that happens in front of them, much like an individual sitting alone in a movie theater taking notes on what is transpiring. They are interesting conversationalists and can often cut through the emotional rhetoric of a situation to get to the crux of the problem. They are often highly conceptual and at the forefront of new and better ways to realize results.

The Negative Side

The Loner Personality is truly as the name implies. They are devoid of any and all emotional trappings. Emotion is excess baggage. It's not that they are against feelings, per se. They simply don't experience it. While most individuals need, want, enjoy, and even crave emotional involvement, the Loner Personality considers it a waste of energy, a hindrance to their core functioning. It is this inability to function from an emotional level that creates problems for the Loner. Because they are so devoid of emotional content, they have severe problems with other members of the human race. Their inability to interact with others on a personal level makes them appear to be cold, aloof, and dispassionate to the needs and feelings of others. This brusque manner creates conflicts with others and often leads to severe criticism and rejection on a personal level. They will seldom fit well into a social situation that demands interpersonal relationships. Many of these individuals never marry, have difficulty maintaining even the simplest of relationships, and often the only friend that they have is themselves. They are often lacking in fundamental social skills and appear to be rude and ill-mannered in many facets.

Identifying And Playing With The Loner

They are always by themselves. They are quick, abrupt, and to the point. ("What is that? What does it do? What's the issue?") As a group, this Personality type probably accounts for less than 2 percent of the total population. In my 43 years on this Earth, I've known only three individuals I would classify as true Loners. When you consider that I've had cause to deal with tens of thousands of people, then three is a startling number. More prevalent is that many individuals will have a subordinate trait in their Personality that is a high degree of the Loner Personality.

There is also a cross-over correlation many times between the Eccentric Dominant and the Loner Dominant. The Loner Dominant Personality is at the opposite end of the spectrum from the Emotional Dominant Personality. The Emotional is a soulful individual who feels everything to an extreme degree. The Loner Dominant Personality is the opposite in that they cannot feel emotion. As an example, something as ordinary as a handshake is viewed by most as a social nicety, or possibly a gesture of emotional significance. To the true Loner, it's just a waste of time, a strange custom or ritual that people engage in. It can be quite upsetting to many individuals to extend their hand in an act of goodwill or friendship only to have it coldly ignored. Just as upsetting is to nod at or smile at an individual and not get any reciprocal acknowledgement.

Some individuals have a deep-seated fear or resentment when they confront another human being who is the total opposite of what they consider to be normal. The cold, empty indifference of the Loner Personality will often disturb others negatively. The Emotional reaction is often a desire to strike out, to hurt, punish or challenge those who are radically different. A good example of this weakness is that many men have a hatred of cats. The cat is cold, indifferent, dispassionate. You call it and it ignores you. It doesn't care what you want. The end result is some Personality types need to strike back. They want to kill or destroy that which is indifferent to their demands or their need to control or dominate. It's easy to be a bully in a truck who swerves off the road to kill a stray, innocent cat. Likewise, it's just as easy to become trapped when you try the same tactics with a human being who can coldly ignore your emotional insecurities.

The first rule in dealing with the Loner Dominant Personality is to realize that if you become emotional, you lose. Go ahead and berate their play. Tell them it was stupid or even call them stupid. It won't affect them. It will affect you, not in the way that the Loner Dominant Personality views you because they can't comprehend what you're viewing as a problem anyway, but it will affect you as the other players at the table start to zero in on you (your weakness). The Loner dominant simply cannot feel what you feel.

As an example, ask yourself how you feel about Das Spulwasser. I'm 95 percent sure that you don't have any feelings about it. You probably don't even know what it is. I'm 99 percent sure that if you do know what it is, you have no emotional intensity about it. However, if you do, I suggest you reread the chapter on the Eccentric Dominant Personality, again as you will probably find an old friend (yourself) lurking there. Because the Loner Dominant Personality does not have the emotional trappings that others have, they have some advantages. Their reasoning capacity is from clear-cut logic. If they get involved in a pot, it's strictly because it's the correct thing to do based on the circumstances before them.

In contrast, a person such as myself might look across the table and see someone in the pot I like or don't like, and provided the hand I hold is reasonable, here I come. This is logic (my cards), and emotions (my opponents). Herein, the Loner has a slight advantage. The advantage is slight because the Loner can't look down at the end of the table and see that Charlie Chump is involved, and therefore ripe for picking. It's a slight advantage because Charlie Chump is a subjective, probably biased, emotional opinion. Another way of understanding the Loner is to realize they process much like a computer does. A computer will always make the correct decision based on what is. Because human beings are emotional, they process not only on what is, but also on what if. Because the game is poker—what if—is a powerful concept. If probability is a god, then possibility is its wings. The real truth, however, is, if you wish to delve into omnipotence you'll have to conclude that possibility, not probability, reigns supreme.

Many Loner Dominant Personalities have a highly specialized knowledge. As an example, they may be the world's foremost or only expert on some topic such as pine cones or lost works of art. Anyone who has specialized knowledge must be considered as someone worthy of respect. However, the respect must be put into the context of how workable and useful the knowledge is.

In the game of poker, knowledge is a formidable foe. But knowledge in and of itself is no guarantee of success. Just as valuable is experience, confidence, intuitiveness, discipline, etc. The downfall of many brilliant individuals who have specialized knowledge, is they lose sight of the purpose it should have. Their downfall is they can't execute (gamble). Knowledge that cannot be used for action is worthless. Instead of using what they know to accomplish something, they become a victim of themselves as their only quest is to continually expand their knowledge for the sake of knowledge. They become like the dog who continually chases its tail to exhaustion. There is always one more piece of the puzzle to be understood, always one more equation to be analyzed.

If you're going to be a poker player, there comes a time when your best and perhaps only course of action is ready, fire, aim. The Loner Dominant Personality becomes too oriented to ready...ready, aim...aim, etc. The Loner is an observer of facts, trends, things, nuts and bolts. They are not, fortunately, great observers of human beings. With most Loner Dominant Personalities you'll notice a machine-like quality to their play. It's a rigid adherence to textbook play. Because they don't function from an emotional level, they are susceptible to opponents who can execute the unusual style of play at the table. As an example, if the Loner Dominant Personality raises before the flop with a pair of Kings, then is re-raised, their rigid rules would cause them to believe that you have a bigger hand (Aces). It would be illogical to assume anyone would re-raise with much less. It's wise to remember that if you're against a textbook opponent, you can increase the value of lesser hands through raising, re-raising, bluffing. As another example, you can often run over a pair of Kings with a lowly pair of threes, if you're willing to raise or re-raise, if you get an ace on the flop, and the opponent is superior.

The Loner Dominant Personality is value-oriented. They often have a perfect understanding of draws, odds, outs and the mathematical complexities of the game. If they miss the draw, they lay the hand down without any regret. How can there be regret when it's the only correct course of action? Many Personality types view risk as a separate component of the hand or of the game. The Loner Dominant Personality doesn't. Risk is simply one part of a many-part formula or equation. In other words, if the value is there, the risk cannot be computed as risk, but rather as part and parcel of the value package. Other personality types can have value, but they devalue it because they are fearful of the risk involved, while others think if they can increase the risk, they can devalue an opponent's hand. This concept is both true and false. It depends on the personality of the opponent you're against. You can steal a lot of money in poker, provided you pick the right opponents to steal from.

The Loner Dominant Personality is almost impossible to manipulate. There is no emotional tilt within them. It's a mistake to try and play games with someone who doesn't play games. To manipulate someone they first have to be susceptible to emotion, greed, ego enhancement, anger, etc. Because the Loner is not led by these characteristics, they are not reactive to emotional impulses. The Loner is encased in their own world. They want to be left alone. However, just because they are emotionless, doesn't mean they can't be irritated. Ask them questions. Keep up an endless, mindless string of conversation. Say something stupid that causes them to point out the error. They can be irritated to the point that they will want to escape you and your senselessness.

The true Loner is hard to find. They migrate away from people and crowds. You simply won't find many, if any, playing poker as it's too much of a public forum. What you need to be aware of, is the individual who has a high degree of the Loner Personality as a subordinate trait to their dominant trait. This type of individual is dangerous, because the lack of emotional baggage from their Loner side gives them a killer instinct. These can be combinations like Aggressive-Loner, Eccentric-Loner, Vigilant-Loner. The biggest downfall of the Loner Personality is they can observe and analyze people but they can't understand people beyond a robotics sense. When the Loner Personality is combined with a Personality trait that can understand or use emotion, they become like a computer that's armed with more than artificial intelligence. The cold fish that can both analyze and be emotionally cognizant of others is probably going to get the money.

When you sit down at any poker game, one of the first priorities you should have is a separation or grouping of the individuals there. As an example, are they there to win money or make money? This is not a play on words. It is a part of a Personality trait that will dictate what and how they play the game.

Another separation is the overall positive or negative position mode of their body carriage. This will have a bearing on their state of aggression. Another separation is emotional temperament or who can do what to whom. If I can detect or suspect that an individual has within their personality a high degree of the Loner trait I'm going to change the playing strategy I would use with another type of personality. As an example, an unemotional personality is more dangerous as a hand progresses. They are still there for a more valid reason than just hope. A bet or raise at the end has to be viewed differently or given more respect than a bet at the end by those who are emotionally driven. Emotionally-driven individuals have difficulty in letting go or giving up. The longer and more involved an Emotional person becomes will often result in a desire to blindly raise the stakes, regardless. The unemotional individual is more prone to cut their losses at any time if the circumstances justify it. There are at least 10 or 12 separations or groupings that you can make through the course of a game that will equate to small edges for you over a period of time.

Like all of the 13 personality types, the Loner is predictable in what they will or will not do a majority of the time. It's important to adjust your style to take advantage of this predictability. The Loner is very predictable because they are rigid. They succeed in this world not because they are rigid, but because they are rigidly correct in what they do most times. Your success against them should be because you can, with a certain degree of confidence, predict beforehand their course of action.

In this book, we talk about personality. It could just as easily be called a handbook on predictability. While we may not like the idea, as it applies to ourselves, we are all predictable, thus susceptible.

I make money betting the totals in sports. There are two reasons. One is all sports have a predictable flow to the game, and the second reason is the predictability of the coaches who make the decisions. In baseball, because of the predictable flow of the game, there are more reasons to bet a game under the total than over. In sports like football, you can look at the Dominant Personality trait of many head coaches and know beforehand how the game is going to be played. The late Vince Lombardi was a rigid Worker Moralist. Mike Ditka is an Aggressive Dominant Personality. Sam Wyche is an Eccentric Dominant Personality. Bill Walsh is an I-Dominant Personality. Jerry Glanville is a Theatrical Dominant Personality.

These individual teams all reflect the coach's personality style. The Bears and Mike Ditka might try a trick play. So what! More than likely, they are going to go with the Aggressive, stick-it-in-your face style of play that Ditka is most comfortable with and receives the greatest pleasure from. If I can't bet the Bears under the total, then I'll pass the game. Likewise, with a coach like Wyche. If I can't bet the game over the total, I prefer not to bet it at all. Both of these coaches have a pattern of decision-making that makes it easier to predict what the final or complete picture will look like. A coach like Wyche may try to grind it out for awhile, but ultimately, he will revert back to that which feels best.

When a personality type deviates drastically from their norm, it's money in the bank that they will swing back to the norm in an even more dramatic fashion, especially so if they lose. If a coach like Ditka allows himself to get too far away from what he perceives to be the correct way, they tend to compensate drastically the next time out, because their internal scolding mechanism has been working overtime. Poker players are no different than football coaches. They always, sooner or later, revert back to the desires of their dominant personality trait. Whether its effective or not doesn't matter. What matters most is its them. When a coach in any sport makes a public comment that he's going to change his style, it should be automatic that you bet against his team. When they make a comment such as we're going to open it up or, we're going to play rock and sock 'em; what you're hearing is doubt, not conviction. Doubt seldom gets the money. Conviction almost always finishes in the money.

With the Loner Dominant Personality, the predictability factor is that their decision-making process is based on cold, hard logic. If they are betting they have a reason. If you can extend the risk beyond the analytical logic that drives their minds, they quite possibly will lay the hand down. However, anytime you constantly pit emotion against logic, you're in danger. The danger comes from a constant tightrope walk on the edge.

When I taught sales management and motivation, my first rule that everyone had to understand was, a confused mind automatically objects. If you want to make a sale, you can't confuse the buyer. They will emotionally stall as the mind goes on automatic self-preservation. In poker the opposite must happen. You want to confuse the mind. You want to create a state of automatic apprehension when the opponent looks at you. Within human beings, the factor that confuses the mind most often is our own tide of emotions. The Loner Dominant Personality possesses the mind that is most difficult to confuse. It cannot object emotionally. Instead, it analyzes objectivity. In the real world or the business world, this is fine. In poker, things are not always so well-defined.

The Loner is driven to discover the imperfection in things and actions. They can often discern the incorrect, but are more interested in the why and how come, rather than being interested in exploiting the weakness. If the Loner's nature was more parasitic than analytical; they would be much more dangerous as poker players. Nevertheless, be careful.

The Loner Dominant Personality as a Buyer

Imagine for one moment the funniest joke you ever heard. Remember your laughter. Perhaps you laughed so much your side hurt. Now remember an event that made you angry or one that made you fearful. All of the above are easy experiences to remember. All of these experiences are rooted in emotion. Humor is an emotion. Anger and fear are emotions. Because you are a human being, emotions are a natural part of your existence. To a large degree, the range of emotion you experience is the vehicle that dictates the decisions you make and the style of life you live.

Now try and understand that if you were a Loner Dominant Personality you wouldn't have experienced the humor in the joke or the anger of a situation. Of the 13 Personality types, it is the Loner who most functions like a robot. The Loner simply doesn't experience the emotions and feelings that other personality types do.

We all know that you can't put a square peg into a round hole. Likewise when dealing with the Loner you have to realize that emotions and feelings will never fit with their personality. Almost all selling agents use some form of emotion when selling. Experience has taught you that emotions are hot buttons that motivate others to take action. If you can create action you can create sales. Many sales agents are successful using nothing more than emotion.

Do not use emotion to sell the Loner. Using emotion with the Loner will do nothing except create needless detours that stall the sales process. The Loner Personality lives in a world controlled by logic and reason. Function and necessity are what causes this type personality to buy.

The Loner type personality looks at the nuts and bolts that causes the world to work. They care less about the color, the excitement of the ride or that their neighbor has two of them. The Loner tends to be mechanical in thought and analytical in mind. The creation process is infinitely more interesting than the created product.

You will not find or have occasion to deal with many true Loner Personality types. They comprise a very small portion of the total population. They are not great buyers. They seldom venture into the marketplace beyond the buying of necessities or to purchase some specialized item of interest.

The Loner is easy to identify because they are so totally different than other people. The first trait you'll notice is they are cold. Not in a haughty, egotistical manner, (emotions), but rather in the sense that you and other people are nothing more, nothing less than a piece of furniture. You are just a thing that they have no feeling toward, either good or bad. The next trait you'll notice is they are direct, to the point. They don't play games, they don't maneuver for position, they don't care about their ego and they care even less about yours. As an example; if they need to purchase a car, they'll walk in and matter-of-factly say, "I want to buy a car."

They don't want to buy a car because it's big, shiny, flashy, fast or for any of the other reasons most people buy automobiles. They are going to buy a car because they need one to get from Point A to Point B. The style, make, model, etc., will only be important in that it fills a function that's a necessary part of their lives. If they buy one with a big trunk, it's because they have to haul something.

If you're a typical sales agent and you have someone walk in and say they want to buy a car, your typical reaction is to say something like, "I've got something over here you'll really like" (your emotions). The typical reaction you'll get from the Loner Personality is a dispassionate empty stare and the question of, "Why?"

You'll soon learn that the Loner will respond to emotion by asking, "Why?" "Why do you think I'd like that?" "Why would I like that?" "Why" is the way the Loner communicates to you that you've taken a needless detour with them. "Why" is their way of saying they don't understand you emotional outpouring.

To successfully sell the Loner, all you have to do is ask and listen. Ask them exactly what they want. They will tell you. Next is listen and learn. When I say listen and learn what I'm really saying is listen to what they say and learn that that's all you're going to sell them. If they say they want a two-bedroom house with a fence in a quiet neighborhood don't try to sell them a three-bedroom home with a swimming pool and screaming kids next door. If you do you'll find yourself back to "why," as the Loner can't understand why you have so much trouble following simple directions. Just because you have good feelings about a swimming pool doesn't mean you can transfer those feelings to a Loner Dominant Personality. Don't even try. The only road map the Loner can comprehend is the one that maps their own mind. Your map is illogical, emotional and something they can't comprehend.

The Loner is not a social animal. They neither need nor want others in their lives. They tend to seek positions that isolate them from excessive contact with others. They experience contentment and satisfaction by dealing heavily in theoretical fields where components other than emotions create the perfect equation.

Many Loner Dominant Personality types have superb control of their minds. They allow their thought process to go only in the direction that they view as most efficient and expeditious. This is also the manner in which they buy. If they abruptly cut you off in mid-sentence, you should consider it as an indication that what you're saying is not the information they need to make a decision. The Loner, more than any of the other 12 personality types, will lead you directly to the route that will make the sale closeable.

The Loner will buy more than they will be sold. When they need or want something, they move quickly and directly to complete the transaction. However, when they are put into the position of being a solicited buyer they are more difficult to deal with. They are not easy individuals to get appointments with, as they tend to move away from direct contact with people. If you succeed in getting an appointment, you'll find they respond to the logical, the analytical and unemotional reasoning almost exclusively as the switch for their motivational mechanism.

If you suspect you're dealing with a Loner Dominant Personality, the fastest way to confirm it is by asking an emotion-based question. The lack of emotional response in the answer should tell you plenty.

Loners tend to be financially stable. More often than not, it will be a cash transaction. Don't expect to get referral business from this type. The probability is that they will have forgotten your name five minutes after you leave and may not even care to remember you the next day.

When closing a Loner Dominant Personality, you should move quickly and directly. Explain the detail and all relevant information, then ask for the signature or approval. If you experience difficulty, simply ask, "Why." They will tell you the problem in a matter-of-fact style. With the Loner, you will always get to the crux of the matter accurately. They do not mentally process the ego as something to protect. You may not like the answer you get, (it will be directed toward your product or service, never against you), but it will be the unvarnished truth. If you can overcome the objection, you will make a sale. If not, You won't.

THE MASOCHIST

CLINICAL NAME: SELF-DEFEATING PERSONALITY DISORDER

Positive:

Kind

Considerate

Generous

Others First

Humility

Loving

Creative

Service-Oriented

Endurance

Energetic

Compassionate

Charitable

Non-Aggressive

Negative:

Naive

Depression Prone

Unmotivated

Self-Destructive Behavior

Lack of Direction

Lack of Goals

Anger

Easily Manipulated

Dependent

Non-Competitive

No Ambition

Easily Frustrated

A Positive Overview

The Masochist Dominant Personality is perhaps the most generous of all the personalities. They are compulsive givers. They are driven by the need to make others more happy than themselves. They live in the same world that you and I do, but unless you are personally involved with someone of this personality trait, you may never have had first-hand experience in dealing with these people. They seldom step forth to let their own light shine. These individuals are loving toward others, extremely kind and sensitive to the feelings of those whom they are involved with. To say that the Masochist Dominant Personality is charitable would be an understatement. Many of these individuals have spent an entire lifetime devoted to the care or betterment of others. Humility is a trademark of this personality. They neither need nor desire to put on any kind of mask, front or show. They are loyal, up-front in their emotions and honest in their endeavors. They have a staggering capacity to endure pain without complaining.

The Negative Side

The Masochist Dominant Personality is truly self-destructive. They have no identity of their own to sustain their life. They are driven by the need to give. This giving will often go to such an extreme that it becomes hurtful to themselves. The Masochist personality is on a seesaw of conflicting emotions. The compulsive self-sacrificing creates a conflict with their own need to find a reason for their being. They will go from one extreme to the next. They can be totally devoted and happy in their martyr role one day, only to become angry, disturbed and deeply depressed the next. At the root of the masochistic behavior is an inability to enjoy or allow themselves pleasure. They have a habit of inflicting guilt upon themselves. They find their meaning through the stringent denial of self.

Identifying The Masochist Dominant Personality

Do not expect to find the Masochist Dominant Personality at the poker table. The make up of this personality is such that they would simply never be involved in an endeavor such as poker. We will include some of the traits and characteristics of this personality type to give the reader a full understanding of all 13 personality types. Also, to give a working knowledge of possible subordinate Masochist traits in other personalities. It is also valuable to have an overall knowledge of each personality type, as it will expand the base knowledge of how each personality type works with, or relates to, another type.

The Masochist Dominant Personality is, in the strictest sense, one who functions for someone else. They realize their being through doing for others. To feel good they must give, not receive. Enduring and suffering creates the pleasure mechanism for the self. They migrate to where they can fulfill the need to render service. They selflessly tend to the poor, the sick, the underprivileged, (I know it sounds like poker players qualify, but they don't). Many times, they have a lifetime of service in a religious order, or if they marry, they work their whole life for the betterment of their children and spouse. Because they totally reject the idea that they should feel good or be concerned for themselves, they seldom venture into a competitive, public forum. The most identifiable trait they have is their self-denial. They will be quick to point out that they don't deserve a new car, a better home, a vacation, etc.. They often become nervous, uncomfortable or embarrassed if you try and commit them to the idea of being deserving of anything. They will use language that is often indicative of their internal processing:

♠ I don't deserve that

♠ I'd feel guilty if. . .

♠ I'm not worth the effort

♠ Don't waste your time on me

A second identifiable trait they possess is their submissive behavior. They are easily led, and in many relationships, are severely manipulated. This may seem cruel to the outsider while feeling quite natural to the Masochist Dominant Personality. This type, if told to do something, will do so without questioning the outcome.

They are devoid of any kind of competitive nature. Their emotional temperament lacks the necessary components to enable them to have a will to win. Winning is not important. Finishing last is just as good as finishing first. They have no aggression. Instead, they bind the wounds of those who suffer from acts of aggression. This is a personality type who lacks the capacity to manipulate, to be guile in their actions or to contemplate jeopardizing another human being's position. In many ways, this personality type gives the impression of going through the motions of life as a gray, formless shadow in a technicolor world. They often appear vague, abstract, out of focus; attuned only to the harsher realities of the darker side of life. By now, you should be able to see why this personality type doesn't play poker.

On the surface, it may appear that this personality type is noble, angelic, even divine. There is, however, a dark side. This dark side is often seen in episodes of guilt, anger, depression and dark, empty despair. At times, the inability to take, ask or receive will bow even the stiffest of necks and create conflict within. When the self can see only the dark side of human nature (sickness, suffering, anguish), it results in a serious devaluation of the spiritual side of the human race.

If this personality type is severe in its masochistic tendencies, they will deliberately seek out or expose themselves to situations or individuals who will willingly inflict pain, suffering or misery. At the same time, the individual will reject those who could or would help. Within the self, there becomes a constant need for pain and humiliation just to verify the existence of the self as being worthy.

In some respects, all 13 personality types have a masochistic streak. How it manifests itself in the different personalities is, (should be), of interest to all poker players. In reality, these masochistic streaks or tendencies are the result of a need to punish the self for the self's behavior. If you play enough poker, you'll soon hear the word tilt. What it really means is a deviation from a normal emotional plateau to a tilted emotional state of being. An individual in a tilted state is interesting because in one form or another, the end result is masochistic behavior, (the inflicting of pain on oneself). The tilted individual confuses their own mind because of a desire to get, or the need to experience revenge, spite, anger, despair, desperation, insecurity, etc., against their own self.

When we make a mistake or do something that's detrimental to our well being our internal warning system tells us we're in error, in order to prevent further destruction. The correct state of being is to accept the warning and use it to straighten the ship or correct the course. The tilted individual, however, doesn't say, "Okay. I love myself. I won't do things that harm me." Instead, they say, "Damn me! I'm a stupid jerk. I can't do anything right!" They can only straighten out their course of action after they have sufficiently punished or whipped themselves enough to experience the pain in its most severe form.

It may appear on the surface that an individual on emotional tilt is upset or angry at another individual. This is a superficial anger, as the real objective of their anger and desire is to inflict punishment on the self. In another sense, it's the way those who lack discipline try to acquire an artificial state of discipline. Additionally, a state of tilt is not caused by a single act, mistake or error. It's a cumulative series of events that finally reaches the point of exploding. Sometimes, it builds up over a course of days, weeks or even months before it becomes a public whipping of the self. There are always telltale signs in individuals as they edge closer to this state of emotional punishment. There are subtle shifts in the voice. Tension in the lips that doesn't go away. Stress in the fingers, a negative position in the body carriage when the situation is positive. A fluctuation between emotional states of flat, then anger, then flat again. There are subtle tells on how the individual handles money or chips and especially telling are the shifts in how the bet is placed on the table.

Finally, and most telling of all in the individual, is winning a pot or even pots and processing it mentally as a negative accomplishment. The lips show disdain and the eyes betray the victory. You can play a different, and most time, profitable style of poker against any individual when they are in the process of heading for tilt. They assist you because they have already resigned themselves to the fact that it's coming. The shrewd player is more attuned to the period of time leading up to the tilting than with trying to take advantage after the tilt happens. The main reason to be attuned to this process is you'll have less competition. When someone goes on tilt in public, then suddenly the whole table is transformed into world-class wolves.

Furthermore, the public explosion is near the end of the cycle, and therefore, not nearly as profitable as most people think. A good example is to imagine throwing a delicate china cup at a brick wall 100 feet from you. Once the cup leaves the hand, the action is irreversible. The advantage is in the 100 feet as it travels to its shattering, not in the shattering itself. Different personality types show different emotional reactions to their tilted state. Some deliberately try to inflict pain upon themselves by rushing to lose more. Some refuse to play hands that could win. Some will resort to an intense, incriminating inner dialogue that mentally shreds the ego. Some will attack those who are closest to them, (wife, friend). In the worst case scenario, some will inflict self wounds or seek out another form of addiction (alcohol or drugs).

Another deadly trap of emotional tilt is, when in this state of mind, the individual forms associations with those who will abuse willingly. It's a sad commentary when a normally strong, vibrant individual slips to this level. In their despair and need to punish the self, they slip further because they become Co-Dependent in a relationship. A non Co-Dependent in the role of a Co-Dependent in a relationship is in a constant fight. First, they are fighting (they think), just for their survival. Secondly, they are involved in a fierce struggle to regain their self-identity. The relationship is a constant battle as the false Co-Dependent submits then rebels at the repulsiveness of this degrading state.

In poker, the central issue in usually money with the contributing factors being ego and pride. Any gambler who loses their money is most dangerous to themselves. If it's a long, losing cycle, they often have to put up ego and pride as collateral to another in order to continue playing. It can become a vicious cycle, because when self-esteem, pride or ego is hocked, the player is disadvantaged. A normally strong game is weakened as self-esteem, a healthy dose of pride and properly functioning ego are strong allies at the poker table.

The desperate search for money and the need to play doesn't just affect bad players or degenerate gamblers. There are many world class players who become trapped because of this. To the outsider, it may seem to be a contradiction to state that a need to play and being a degenerate are not one and the same. It's not. This is nothing more than a superficial moral judgement by another kind of tilted individual.

I come from the hills of Missouri. Most of the people who live in that area are dirt farmers. From sun up to sun down they plant their crops and farm their land. If you took some of these individuals and forced them to live in the city, forced them to go to work in factories, they would literally die. Maybe not immediately, but each day they would suffer a long, slow, torturous march toward death. They need to farm, they need to feel the dirt with their hands. They need to scan the sky and worry about the lack of rain. They need to feel the open spaces. Does this very real, life-sustaining need make them degenerate farmers? I don't think so! But if it does, then so what? An individual's life, their dreams, their purpose, their hope is more valuable than pious-oriented opinions.

Am I condoning gambling? Maybe! Am I championing the individuals right to self-determination? Absolutely!

If you're trapped you need to stop. You need to stop for at least a week or even a day. It's ten times more difficult to see what's wrong, what's trapping you, when you're still in the middle of the battle. Self-examination, not self-punishment, provides answers.

The second thing you have to do is admit that:

A. You're doing something wrong

B. You can do things differently

C. If it's wrong (not working), then why not do it differently?

The purest, most effective form of self-examination is when you can step back and see yourself involved, but not actually be involved. I often have wished I could videotape myself at the table playing poker, then take it home and watch it the next day. The single biggest trap that people fall into is, they keep doing over and over the action that produces the failure while expecting that the results will be different.

If you're trapped, tilted, punishing yourself, or co-dependent to others, you can break free instantly. You have to stop being a yo-yo on the end of someone's finger or a yo-yo to a situation, or circumstance. As I said, you can do it instantly. Most individuals won't or can't believe you can create change instantaneously. They want to believe that change is synonymous with suffering, struggle or a torturous wrestling match. All you have to do is take a pair of scissors and cut the string to the yo-yo. When you do this a wonderful and great thing is going to happen to you. You're going to crash! Does it sound like an ugly, repulsive word? It's not. When you crash there is only one way you can go, and that is up! When you are on a yo-yo, you're being jerked, teased, you can't go up because you're the puppet to the puppetmaster and their whims or amusements. You can't control, because you're out of control. You can't control, because you are being controlled.

Will you cut the string? My experience has been that champions cut the string and that the mediocre simply choose to die on the string. However, know this: It's a simple, undiluted truth about the capacity of human beings to accomplish. We all have the capacity for the infinite acquiring of skill. The human brain and its capacity dwarfs our ability to even comprehend its abilities, let alone even using it. You and I have only two enemies. Ourselves and time. Perhaps tomorrow you will choose to only have one.

The Masochist Dominant Personality as a Buyer

If you were to rank the personality types by buying ability, the Masochist would be at the bottom of the list followed by the Co-Dependent, Loner, Eccentric. At the top of the list would be the Worker-Moralist, Aggressive and I-Dominant. The Masochist Dominant Personality is simply not a buyer. They buy only out of sheer necessity or in the role of a giver to someone else.

The Masochist is a giver of themselves. They are not materialistic in any sense of the word. They are the disciples to the masses. Many of them live an entire lifetime without accumulating anything. They are the Mother Teresas of this world.

As a group, they are kind, generous people who find fulfillment by giving of themselves in service to others. They have no ego and no sense of a self-image that needs to be fulfilled. The driving force of their personality is self-denial.

About the only time they venture into the buying marketplace is in the role of purchasing something for someone else. In all probability you, as a selling agent, will never deal with this type. If you happen, by chance, to deal with one, don't expect to earn a living by selling to this type of individuals. The best advice I can give you is to treat them with kindness and consideration and give them the best deal possible. The world is a better place to live in because of the service these individuals have given to others. Perhaps if you're fortunate you'll have the opportunity to repay some of their kindness with kindnesses of your own. When I taught sales management I stressed a three-step process that was fail proof. This process would not only make you a better selling agent, it would also make you a better person. The three-step process was, Service, Sales, Service.

Many Masochist Dominant Personality types will live an entire lifetime without owning anything. Many of them will never even establish credit. Many of these individuals spend their entire life under the protection of a service organization or behind the walls of a convent. Their meager needs are supplied by the organization they render service to.

THE REFLECTIVE

THE CLINICAL NAME:
AVOIDANT PERSONALITY DISORDER

Positive:	*Negative:*
Forthright	Fearful
Honest	Anxiety
Dependable	Socially Removed
Kind	Low Self-Esteem
Considerate	Uninvolvement
Strong Work Ethic	Shy
Creative	Self-Doubt
Predictable	Loner
Sensitive	Distorted Reality
Caring	Excessive Worry
Detail-Oriented	Negative Internal Programming
Familiarity	Easily Stressed
Routine-Oriented	A Hidden Life
Passionate	Brilliant Minds

A Positive Overview

The Reflective Dominant Personality is a trait that often has enormous potential. The problem is that it is seldom allowed to shine forth. This type of personality has real and severe problems in dealing with other human beings. They are internally directed and motivated. They are limited because they are painfully aware of and concerned with the opinions of others. Overall, this grouping has high intellect and can be brilliant conceptual thinkers. They are dependable, honest, forthright individuals who are generally principled, moral, law-abiding citizens. These individuals are also predictable in their behavior and in their dealing with others. Their work ethic is strong, as they are conscientious with the property and time of others. They don't play games with the feelings of another human being and it is totally beyond their realm to be intentionally manipulative.

The Negative Side

High anxiety would best describe this personality type. They simply have difficulty in dealing with other members of the human race. They are gripped by fear. It is fear that holds sway over them and produces the emotional problems of anxiety, rejection and withdrawal. The very crux of the problem is one of self-esteem. The Reflective Dominant Personality cannot find their self-worth through their own opinion. They constantly worry about acceptance from others. Even when they are unequivocally accepted by another, they automatically find a reason not to believe the actuality of the acceptance. Their loneliness becomes self-induced as they withdraw further into themselves. They set a standard for being accepted that is so unrealistic that even the slightest hint of disapproval would equate to a disaster and perceived rejection of themselves. Involvement with others is often a painful, traumatic experience. Their shyness and self-doubt is like a festering wound that drives would-be friends and acquaintances away.

Identifying And Playing With The Reflective Dominant Personality

The Reflective Dominant Personality is what I call "The hidden personality." To deal with this person, you need to get to know them on a more personal basis. They are often a contradiction, because there is a huge difference in the person the public sees and deals with and the truer, intensely private individual who the public never sees or deals with. There are two kinds of Reflective Dominant Personalities. One kind shows high anxiety in public, while the other kind exhibits a counterphobic style when in public. The counterphobic is more dangerous, because they have mastered or managed to hide their feeling and insecurities and actually use a negative as a positive. We'll deal with the more prevalent type first, then merge in the counterphobic type.

They are easy to identify. They always appear to be tense or nervous when they are with a new person or in an unfamiliar situation. They exhibit a high degree of outright uncomfortableness. They shun the spotlight. They fidget with their clothing. Their eyes dart from position mode to position mode while avoiding anything but the slightest eye contact. If they are wearing a tie, they will give the distinct impression that they are always on the verge of choking. Women will clutch their purse tightly and hold it to their chests, much like a shielding device. They will stammer over simple words and oftentimes blush beet-red. Their heads will often nod vigorously while you are talking to them. This nodding is often totally out of synchronization with the conversation. When you shake hands with an individual of this personality trait, you may notice excess perspiration and wet clamminess to the palm. They will laugh nervously and at inappropriate times. There is a tendency for muscle tenseness in the face and in some situations, they unconsciously pull on their fingers.

In dealing with these reflective individuals, it is important to always keep in mind a couple of things. First, they are extremely uncomfortable, both physically and emotionally, in any unfamiliar situation with any stranger. You must allow them time to accept you. Their acceptance time is longer than most people, because they are so self-conscious. Not only are they going through an acceptance check as it relates to you, but also, they are running an acceptance check on how your are accepting them. They always look for and need emotional verification. (Do you like them? How do you really feel about them?)

Once you get through the acceptance check, get on a first-name basis. Proceed slowly and be sure that you force them to become involved. The involvement that you need is the weight of their own opinion. If you don't get them involved, you will often find that they seem to be agreeing, when in reality, they are totally out of sequence with what you are saying. An example of this is someone who nods their head with affirmation to everything that you say or who says constantly, "Yes, yes," or "Sure." If you were to suddenly say that the moon was made out of cheese, they would probably say, "Yes."

By demanding their involvement, you are ensuring yourself that their decision-making process in engaged. Their decision-making process is both emotional and logical. They constantly verify internally what is happening externally. Their eyes will move rapidly from neutral to the lower left mode (internal dialogue). Sometimes this will happen as often as a dozen times. They are habitual in playing the scene over and over in their mind as they try and find the proper direction in which to proceed. This constant checking with themselves is a form of protection and caution. They are extremely sensitive to doing the right thing. To ensure that they do this in a safe manner, they seldom make bold moves or take drastic chances without good reason. In many ways, they are creatures of habit. They need the safety net of familiarity.

You will not find many Reflective Dominant Personalities playing poker, unless they have developed a counterphobic trait to their personality. Counterphobic means to run head long into and face squarely that which you fear. You will find this type of Reflective Personalities playing poker, and most of them are highly skilled. From this point on, we will concentrate on the counterphobic Reflective Dominant Personality.

I've been fortunate in my lifetime, because I've had the privilege of knowing intimately several of these individuals. Not only are they a hidden personality, but they often seem to combine a mixture of other personality traits to form their unique personality. They have parts of the Loner, the Emotional, the Eccentric, the I-Dominant and the Adventurer. The five individuals I've known on an intimate basis all shared some strikingly similar characteristics. It may have been purely coincidental, but I don't think so. The characteristics were:

♠ A tight, wry, high strung physical build with an almost total absence of body fat

♠ Multiple ulcers

♠ Would blush when embarrassed

♠ An uproarious sense of humor in private

♠ A creative nature separate from their profession (e.g., writing, music, art)

♠ A combative ego that created the counterphobic self

♠ A sarcastic, biting tongue when pushed, or black humor muttered under their breath

♠ Extreme social graces that gives the impression of belonging in another era

♠ An intense private passion

♠ A dispassionate view of death

♠ A keen understanding of manageable risk and a willingness to engage in it

♠ A low tolerance for stupidity in people

♠ An appearance of being susceptible, naive or fragile when in public

♠ A strong capacity to ignore pain

♠ Long periods of total isolation

♠ A constant creation of fantasy, that eventually played out into reality over a long period of time

♠ An ability to detect a bluff and extract ample payment for it

♠ Extreme stubbornness, being hard-headed to the point of eventual confrontation

♠ Loyalty to those they care about to an extreme degree. A willingness to write it in blood if necessary

The first Reflective Dominant Personality I knew personally, was a man in his late 40s. His father died and left him $50 million. He quickly turned it into 150 million in a high-profile position. He was required to make speeches before thousands of people. It was a disaster. He stammered, lost his place, blushed red, was light years ahead of the audience in knowledge and rambled for two hours. At the end of one speech, he was doubled in pain from ulcers. On the ride to the airport he angrily slammed his hand on the steering wheel. For the next two weeks he stayed in his office behind closed doors. Two weeks later, he was back in front of thousands suffering the same torment.

In private, he was totally different. His private life was walled, guarded, comfortable, secure. it was behind the walls that his genius shined bright. After years of rushing head-long into what he feared. . .what caused him anxiety, he became like a wind-up toy. A remote controlled public person, yet a totally different person in private. I once asked him why he put himself in such situations. He looked me square in the eye and said, "I intend to get $100 million for every ulcer I've got."

His wife once told me in private, he was determined to become a polished speech maker. He never became a polished speech maker, but he did become the best robotic speech maker I know.

He had a combative ego that drove him to master that which made him so uncomfortable; namely crowds, strangers and high insecurity about his own abilities.

When the Reflective Dominant Personality forcefully push themselves into a public arena, they do so in an unobtrusive manner. They are quiet, reserved, more likely to be at the edge of the crowd rather than in the middle of it. They often have a cool, detached demeanor. Behind this cool demeanor is an individual who is watchful. A prolific observer of people and their activities. Their preference is to function alone, and their aloofness is often an attractive feature to the more hard-driven, domineering personality type such as the Adventurer, Aggressive and I-Dominant types. This personality type thinks they are detecting a vulnerability, a person susceptible to scam or weak in temperament. This is a mistake. This is hardly the case, as the Reflective Dominant Personality is accustomed to protecting themselves quite well. As you move in, the Reflective Personality simply starts remote controlling you. You're never getting the real person. True, there's conversation, interaction and the physical presence, but the real person is not available. The real person is the one who functions in private, the one behind the wall.

At the poker table, the Reflective style is one of patience. They understand value. They are highly selective of the hands they play. They are quiet, reserved. They are more likely drawn into conversation, than to be the one who initiates it. Though they are an emotional being, they play poker in a cold, logical manner. It takes a lot more than a poker game to expose the Reflective's emotion.

Many Reflective Dominant Personalities have a subtle tell. Their head nods in a certain rhythm as they start to perceive the situation confronting them. As an example, they bet, you raise, they study the flop intently. If they develop a strong suspicion to what you hold in your hand, the movement of their head verifies what they are feeling internally. The more certain they are of the accuracy of what they have determined, plus the validity of the raise, will almost always result in a call and never a re-raise. This personality type is extremely accurate at putting an opponent on a hand. They undermine this accuracy many times, because they should throw the hand away instead of calling. This is especially true if there are still players to act after the raiser or a player between the raiser and the Reflective. The danger is getting caught between the raiser then a re-raiser later in the hand. Many times, the call means they still have a possible out through a draw.

This type will seldom bluff at the pot late in the hand or as a last attempt to salvage something. A strong asset of this personality, is they are uncanny at detecting your bluff. Watch their eyes. When they suspect you're bluffing, their tell mechanism changes. Instead of staring at the board and externalizing their feelings through head movement, they engage in an engrossing debate with themselves. A human being's eye position mode reveals the current state of how they are functioning. As an example, if I ask you what the color of the first car you ever drove was, you will almost always look up and to the right. When the eyes look up and to the right they are functioning as a pathway switch to the part of the brain that stores and accesses memory. When a human being is engaged in a debate with themselves, their eyes look down and to the left. When the Reflective Dominant Personality suspects you're bluffing, they quickly engage themselves in an internal conversation that is playing out the possibilities. This internal conversation is just as real as if it were a verbal conversation between two people sitting at the table.

Because the Reflective Dominant Personality is an inner-directed emotional personality, they have a constant need to come into contact with the inner voice. The inner voice directs and stabilizes the person when in a public forum. When a Reflective Dominant Personality is losing, they have a tendency to engage in too much internal dialogue. They become lost in long periods of internalization. The poker game is still going on, but the Reflective personality is split. When in this state they are not nearly as effective, because they are more concerned with the inner voice. In this state of mind, they will often lose track of what is happening at the table. To emerge into the public light, the Counterphobic

Reflective will almost always have developed a combative ego. It's what drives them to expose the self. If they didn't have the ego, they would have to avoid the public. In a sense, their combative ego dominates them more than their avoidant nature pulls them back. The I-Dominant individual is ego-driven because they act, feel and assume they are superior. The combative ego needs to prove superiority. The need to prove will always translate into risk-taking.

The Reflective is dangerous because they engage in a well-thought-out type of risk-taking. It's not risk for the sake of risk. It is what one could call manageable risk or controlled risk where the objective is to win within acceptable cost boundaries. I've played a lot of poker with Reflective dominant personalities in private games. I lost a lot of money because I constantly underestimated the risk they were willing to take. Compounding the problem was, I confused the risk they took with the risk that players such as an Adventurer or Aggressive Personality would throw at me. Our favorite game was jacks or better, progressive. This game would result in some huge pots and we added a twist to the game where pay and play or fold and lose increased the pot dramatically each round. If the game taught me one thing, it was never get into a pissing contest with a Reflective Dominant Personality while thinking they wouldn't back me to the wall. What made it worse, was they wouldn't negotiate for a percentage of the pot.

Another strong issue with the Reflective Dominant Personality is control. They simply don't lose control in public. They hide their emotions extremely well. Sometimes to the degree that they will rival the I-Dominant in the stone-cold indifference they display when losing. A difference is the I-Dominant will almost always, at some point, steal a glance at the opponent who beat him. The Reflective will choose to stare at the table instead and engage themselves in conversation. The Reflective and I-Dominant share another trait which is a susceptibility to stinging criticism. The I-Dominant reacts with internal rage at the criticism. The Reflective reacts with self-doubt and the need to protect the self by withdrawing.

Like the Loner Personality, the Reflective Dominant Personality is not easily manipulated. They tend to be too-keen observers of people and of the activities that people engage in to become prone to the tactics of manipulation. If they have a weakness, it is that they have a trust and loyalty to those few people who are close to them. It borders on a maniacal obsession to love and protect those precious few individuals who are inside their walled life.

The Reflective prefers the familiar. They have a detail and routine orientation to that which feels comfortable through experience. As an example, they may have a favorite stream that they return to continuously, as opposed to seeking out one that is unfamiliar.

Because of certain characteristics strengths, they would be better suited to play no-limit games or games where opponents have a greater possibility of hands to play. Because they are on remote control so often, it's an asset when the stakes are higher or the possibilities of the game are more hidden or intricate. While hold'em is a great game, its structure had a diluting effect on players with higher skill levels, especially in limit games.

The Reflective is a disappearing personality at the poker table. They may play for 20 straight days, then not show up again for six months. The reason is, that while they may be highly skilled at the game, it's not an emotional obsession in their life. I once employed a Reflective individual who could play poker with the best of us, if he were in the mood. However, he was seldom in the mood as his real passion was classical music.

It's difficult to create tilt in a Reflective Dominant Personality. Tilt is an emotional outpouring. When the Reflective Personality experiences strong emotional feeling, either negative or positive, they start withdrawing. They withdraw because they need to try to understand what they are feeling and why they are feeling it. Tilt is an exploitable advantage in poker only if it stays around. Unlike the Loner who doesn't experience feelings, the Reflective is afraid to feel. If they feel, their defense is lessened. If they feel, there is a conflict with their need for isolation and the emotional need that will cause them to migrate toward that which incites the feeling. All their lives they have told themselves that there is safety and sureness in being alone. When feelings enter the picture, they have to doubt one of the two as being the traitor.

Reflective's win money at poker because they are difficult for others to figure out. In contrast, the Aggressive is a dangerous, shrewd player, but there is no mystery about an Aggressive Dominant Personality. You soon learn what to expect and what to give back. Oftentimes with the Reflective personality, other players are unsure, they vacillate over the Reflective style, and in turn, what their style should be.

The best advice I can give you is, if it seems every time you zig someone else zags, then quit zigging. But once you've quit zigging, don't make the mistake of fools and start zagging. The fastest way to confront the enemy, whether it be you or someone else, is to turn directly into the fire. It's like confronting fear. The fear may be great; however, I guarantee you that the "fear of" is the greater element that limits and constricts you.

One of the great difficulties I had when playing with the Reflective Personality was determining what, exactly, they wanted. It was easy to determine what personality types such as the Aggressive or Emotional wanted. With the Reflective, I had to constantly ask myself what, why, how come they did that? In retrospect, they enforced caution on me. I never liked that. I finally decided if I lost, then it would be on my terms, not theirs. One day I decided the reason I couldn't figure them out was because maybe they were just smarter than me. The next day, I thought maybe the reason I couldn't figure them out was because I was one of 'em. The next day I decided to put that old country rocker, Ernest Tubb, on the tape player and go fishing in Oklahoma. There is a great truth in life—When the fish are biting, it's hard to worry.

The Reflective Dominant Personality as a Buyer

The Reflective Dominant Personality is somewhat of a contradiction. The other twelve personality types are easily identified and easy to put into a specific category. The Reflective is not. This type of individuals often have characteristics that mimic other traits. I often refer to them as the rainbow personality, as they have the most varied facets of any of the personality types.

The Reflective is an intensely private individual who values their privacy. They tend to shine the brightest behind the walls of their own castle. The Reflective often has two lives, the one that's available for public scrutiny and their private life which is often totally different.

The Reflective is a driven individual with ambition, ego and talent. They are highly intelligent individuals who usually have a vast range of interests. They are often multi-talented in the respect that they are accomplished in more than one field.

The Reflective is also at conflict with themselves. They are uncomfortable in crowds and among strangers. Yet they force themselves to be competitors by using sheer will power to do that which they are not comfortable with. Reflective's are tightly-spun individuals. They wear their high anxiety as an outer garment. They will often have a tension-filled, stress-induced appearance. They are highly guarded people in both speech and mannerisms when they are uncomfortable. Beyond their uncomfortableness with people and situations, you will find an intense, competitive individual with a strong will to win.

Of all the 13 personality types, it is the Reflective Dominant Personality who needs the longest warm-up before a sales presentation. Never say anything important, never ask for commitments or make alarming statements in the first three or four minutes of conversation with these people. To successfully communicate with the Reflective Personality, they must be given time to do an internal acceptance check of you. A worried, anxious mind is a closed mind. A closed mind is an automatic objection that cannot be overcome.

The Reflective is a good buyer. They are also a shrewd, specialized buyer. The Reflective buys services and products that fit comfortably with their personality. Many Reflective Personalities surround themselves with objects that they identify with. These are objects such as art, antiques, unique decor, etc. Many Reflective Personalities have careers in unique fields such as writing, painting, specialized fields of medicine, environment studies and behind-the-scene professions in the entertainment field.

The Reflective is quiet, cautious and most comfortable with the familiar. They tend to come alive behind the walls of their home and within the company of a few select friends. They have a high degree of intelligence and they do their homework before they buy. It's the quiet, reserved nature of the Reflective that causes many sales agents problems. The Reflective is not the type of individual upon whom you can force your will. They buy and they buy well, but it's to their standard, not to yours. Of all the personality types, you'll find it's the Reflective who will be the most demanding about quality, workmanship, fair value and requiring an exacting standard from the product or service. Don't be fooled by the reflective's reserved demeanor or sometimes anxious nature. Beneath that surface you will find a very stubborn, determined individual.

The Reflective is keenly attuned to you. They are highly perceptive individuals who are aware of the behavioral aspects of others. The best way to sell a Reflective is in an honest, straightforward, professional manner. The Reflective is a very good listener with the capacity to analyze a lot of information in a short period of time. Likewise, as a selling agent, you need to pay attention to what the Reflective says. The Reflective will often stall over a seemingly small or insignificant detail. Many sales agents try to brush aside or ignore the little objections. While it may seem insignificant to you, it can be monumental to the Reflective Personality. They will stubbornly refuse to move forward until

their mind is assured of the point in question. It's critically important that if you're on page five that the Reflective also be on page
five. The Reflective is perhaps the most stubborn of the 13 personalities. The worst part is it is not a verbalized stubbornness; so
therefore, it's more difficult to deal with. To successfully sell, you
must have both a buyer and a seller.

Some personality types are easily led. The Reflective is not.
Their mind set doesn't respond well to suggestions that are out of
the realm of their reality. It's important that you find out their
beliefs and desires and fit your product or service within that
framework. The Reflective is quiet and courteous, they will let you
speak for an hour, yet if it's not what they are interested in, you've
done nothing more than waste their time and yours. While they
are polite and courteous, the flip side of their personality is one of
impatience and a low tolerance for ignorance. If you and your presentation is out of step with these individuals, you will not get a
second chance to redeem yourself. The Reflective will politely say
"no" and refuse future contact with you. The Reflective will not
respond to the glib, suede-shoed hype that is the style of many
unprofessional sales agent.

The Reflective moves slowly and cautiously. Their personality
style is to get all the information and details that are pertinent,
then to make a decision later. If your offer is a push, shove, now
or never, take it or leave it proposition, you can forget about
making a sale to these individuals. They simply cannot be pushed
into a hurried decision. They respond much better if you make the
presentation, give all the pertinent information, then ask them
to set a reasonable time frame in which you can get back with
them for a decision. An excellent way of following up with
this type is to also include a written proposal of what was
discussed. Almost all Reflective Personalities I know respond
positively to professionalism.

Silent, unspoken objections are a sales agent's worst nightmare.
As a selling agent, you want all objections to be out in the open, to
be verbalized by the buyer. If you know what objections are stum-

bling the buyer you then have the opportunity to overcome them. Some personality types will object loudly and clearly, other types, like the Reflective, won't. In selling to this type you need to ask for the objections by soliciting their opinion and by asking often for their input. If you fail to get involved with the mind of the Reflective, you may get run over by objections that you neither saw or heard. When the Reflective is objecting silently, they nod their head out of sequence, fidget and look uncomfortable and stare downward or dart their eyes. At times like these, you need to stop presenting and start asking for their help and input.

The Reflective Personality is often a partnership buyer. Most often, this partner is their spouse or business associate. There is often a very powerful, deep bond between the two. The Reflective cares and is concerned about the opinion of this other party. Oftentimes, they will not make a decision until after they have thoroughly discussed all possible ramifications with the spouse/partner in private. The Reflective Personality allows very few people to get close to them in their lifetime. However, the ones who are close have a profound impact on the Reflective's life and the decisions they make.

The most powerful positive for a selling agent is an objection that has been satisfied. An objection is not a deadly poison if you handle it. It's only when you fail to satisfy the buyer's concern that it becomes fatal. When you answer the objection, the objection itself becomes like money in the bank to the selling process. When you turn the objection from a reason why they couldn't buy into values that state why they can, then the objection has lost its power to hold the buyer as a prisoner. Once the buyer's mind is set free to see and accept the values of the product/service, they have in essence taken possession of it. When they agree, it then becomes their idea, not yours. You may choose not to believe it, but buyers buy because of their ideas, while yours run a distant, almost inconsequential second.

The most important aspect of a sales presentation is the opening. When you open right it's much easier to close the sale. More sales are lost not because sales agents can't close, but because they don't open correctly. The only sure-fire way to open correctly is by allowing the buyer to set the initial style and pace. This is easy to master when you pay close attention to the buyer's persona, mannerisms and unconscious behavior. It is of critical importance with the Reflective Personality. You need to break into the walls they build to protect themselves. A chisel works better than a bulldozer. Behind the wall you will often find a wonderful individual and buyer. With the Reflective, your main objective should be to understand that they deal with the world-at-arms distance and gaining their confidence and trust is a big first step toward getting their business.

If and when the Reflective does business with you, it's good business. Most of these individuals are good money managers. They value the dollar and have respect for its importance. They are not good individuals for giving referrals immediately. However, as their confidence in you grows, they will refer many friends and acquaintances to you.

THE THEATRICAL

CLINICAL NAME:
HISTRIONIC PERSONALITY DISORDER

Positive:	*Negative:*
Emotional	Self-Centered
Impulsive	Egoist
Entertaining	Never Enough Applause
Responsive	Disloyal
Sexual and Sensuous	Not a Team Player
Ego Driven	Excess Exaggeration
Reactive	Easily Frustrated
Intense	Exploitative
Dessert First	Manipulative
Outgoing	Unable to Handle Stress
Warm	Sense of Reality
Action-Oriented	Lack of Self-Identity
Feeling	Showmanship
Determination	Passion for Life
Flamboyance	

A Positive Overview

The Theatrical Dominant Personality is the life of the party. A social being that needs and enjoys people. They are highly emotional with a constant orientation toward what they are feeling, and more importantly, how they are inducing others to feel. While the Theatrical and Emotional personalities are similar in many aspects, there are differences. The Emotional Personality is attuned to how they feel toward others, whereas the Theatrical Personality is more conscious of how others are reacting toward them. The Theatrical Personality is creative, energized, a highly visible person. Many times this creativeness, this powerful energy is so intense, that it overshadows the very thing that they are trying to accomplish.

With the Theatrical Personality, there are no strangers. They are bold, dramatic, center stage people. They draw others into their lives easily and effortlessly. Many show business personalities are of this vein. They are often spoken of as being charismatic, magnetic personalities. The Theatrical Personality thrives on excitement, challenge, spur of the moment, go for it endeavors.

They are endowed with a special type of radar or inner sense that allows them to gauge how they are impacting those around them. They are ultra responsive to applause, ego stroking, and will rise to the occasion with superior performance. Many politicians, lawyers, executives, and entrepreneur types are of the dominant Theatrical mode. Many top-selling agents and sales managers are dominated by the Theatrical trait. They are expert actors and actresses whose stage is the selling arena. They thrive on making the dramatic presentation, on making impacts no one else could, and on reaching for the stars.

The Negative Side

Where's the spotlight? Look at me! I did this! I did that! The Theatrical Personality is self-centered. They are, at their core, plagued by self-doubt. It could be said that there is never enough applause. Because their self-identity so very often comes from and through what others are saying about them or what others are thinking about them, they will often have a flawed sense of reality. If they can't influence you to their side, they will have trouble relating to you. They are easily frustrated with hot tempers and an "If I don't get my way, I'll walk out the door" attitude. They, along with the I-Dominant Personality, are the most manipulative of all the 13 Personality types. They can be petty, contentious individuals who will go to extreme lengths to prove a point, (you were wrong...I was right). They are often demanding upon others, and will excessively exaggerate a story or situation to get what they want.

Identifying And Playing With The Theatrical Personality

They dress with style, imagination, flair. They will attempt to sell you, (about themselves). They are warm, bright and personable. They love to take the lead in every venture. They need your involvement toward them. They are extremely conscious of their sexual being. They are, in many instances, a sexual tease, using their sexuality as a lure to attract others. They are always trying to project outward to draw you into their world. They move dramatically and often have the power to dominate an entire room. They don't wait for you to shake hands, they walk up and immediately introduce themselves. They will immediately be on a first-name basis with you, (call me Dick, Susan, Carol, etc.) In the first three minutes of conversation, they may call you by your first name six or seven times. (They are selling you). They move closer, they lean forward, they compliment you. They make it a habit to touch you physically, they touch your arm, they put their hand on your shoulder. They are masterful conversationalists and storytellers.

The key to dealing with these individuals is to reverse the story line. Simply ask the following: "Dick, tell me about yourself." Now, sit back. All along they have been waiting for you to cue them. With only the slightest prompting, they will tell you everything. Ask them about a personal matter and they will often revert to third party ego enhancing stories, ("I've been told...", "People say that I'm. . .," and "Many others feel that I'm. . ."). The Theatrical Personality is a deeply dependent individual. They need you in order to find themselves. They are not logical, reasoning individuals. They run on and are motivated by emotion. They see themselves involved in some way and then start feeling the results. (I saw a beautiful convertible going down the street, and then suddenly I knew that it was made just for me.)

The Theatrical Dominant Personality is, in a sense, someone who has been hijacked by their self-created image. There are two selves within the person. The one that was, and that has since been, fashioned into the fantasy or desire of the person that now exist.

This personality finds itself through the admiration they can receive from others. They must hear the applause. They need unending attention. The stroking of the ego is the drive and fuel of their being.

It's important to realize that the primary way they operate in every facet of their life is: Give in order to seduce. Within this realm, they are masters. They give in order to break your resistance. The giving takes many forms. Compliments, favors, unending attention and so forth. They seduce you by drawing you in. After an endless stream of seemingly sincere flattery, compliments and ego boosting, most heads will start to turn. Suddenly, you're part of their entourage. The King and his court, the Queen and those in waiting. Once the seduction is complete, the subtle endless manipulation begins. The ability to inflict guilt on others is a primary weapon the Theatrical Dominant Personality uses:

♠ After all I've done for you. . .

♠ You're the last person I would have thought would betray me. . .

♠ I'm such a fool. I thought we were so close.

Next comes a devaluing of your importance. You soon begin to sense that, even when they are talking to you, they are scanning the room looking for someone more important. Manipulators always have a shallow quality that is eventually revealed.

Their style of play mirrors their lifestyle. The Theatrical has passion, and the hot throbbing ego drives them endlessly. They are not good players. However, they are dangerous players. They are dangerous because they are willing to play a style that can be extremely costly to an opponent, when things are going their way. Anyone who is willing to stretch the limits of risk will occasionally reap the rewards for doing so. The problem they have is they are superb actors and actresses. This is wonderful, if the audience you're performing before are fans, or even bored patrons of the arts. The Theatrical, however, sits at a table where all the participants are actors or actresses. Each opponent has a varying degree of skill in the theater called poker. There are no fans at the table. There is no oohing and ahhing. If there is a curtain call, it will be born out of your opponent's malicious desire to see you fall flat, again.

If the theatrical streak within the personality is mild or con-trolled, this type player can be above average, as they are constantly attuned to seeking and knowing how other players are reacting. It's been my experience, though, that the Theatrical Dominant Personality is seldom controlled in their quest for ego gratification. The Theatrical Dominant Personality wants to make a statement when playing poker. To their thinking, it's dramatic to draw out on an opponent. They love to pounce from nowhere to make a grand finale play at the end. Within their mind there is the need, not just to win, but to win spectacularly. They want to have a straight flush while the opponent has four of a kind. A win with two pair is not nearly as gratifying to the ego.

The Theatrical Dominant Personality likes to attempt cutesy maneuvers at the poker table. The desire to be cute, (attract atten-tion), seldom works more than once. Other players quickly see through the cuteness once it's exposed. The second time around, it's not as effective. The Theatrical Dominant Personality is the personality type most prone to engage in verbal baiting of opponents at the table. They love to talk, to constantly challenge other players to take or resist their action.

The Theatrical Dominant Personality is out of touch with the reality that exists at most poker tables. The individuals who sit at these tables are, as a group, superior individuals who are not easily swayed or dazzled by anyone or anything. They are tough-minded, merciless individuals who make their living by cutting through the crap and getting to the heart of the matter quickly.

The Theatrical Dominant Personality often overlooks the subtle intricacies of the game in their rush to overtake the game. They are prone to bluff; however, they overlook the fact that bluffing and its effectiveness is often predicated on other factors such as position, number of players, exposed cards, etc. The Theatrical has a low tolerance for detail and an outright inability to deal with the mundane or ordinary. They have great difficulty hiding disappointment, and in extreme cases, make no attempt to do so. They are often temperamental and prone to throwing temper tantrums if things go wrong or if attention is diverted from them for too long.

They are extremely conscious of the rank and order of a situation. They can quickly zero in on the powers to be in almost any situation. At the poker table, they are attracted to, and often try to form alliances with the more dominating personality types. This is a no win scenario, as personality types such as the Aggressive or I-Dominant will quickly use, then crash the personality types who lead, live and die by the ego. Like a boxer who leads with the chin, the Theatrical who leads with the ego is going to suffer greatly in an arena as tough as the poker world. They are deeply affected by rejection, criticism and indifference. Compounding the problem is, when they encounter these traits, they have a desire to create a confrontation. This just adds fuel to the fire of the personality like the I-Dominant who will twist the knife with more delight.

Many highly dominant theatrical personalities will, over the course of time, develop a fairy tale sense of reality to use as a protective mechanism. If they are rejected, they quickly reject the rejector or tell themselves it really didn't make any difference. In this way, every negative is ignored. Everything is kept positive by simply readjusting a few facts to keep the ongoing fairy tale afloat. It's this creation of fuel for optimism that enables many Theatrical Dominant Personalities to keep on struggling for success in fields such as the entertainment business where rejection is the norm.

Of all the personality types, the Theatrical is most prone to develop a series of serious tells at the poker table. This happens because they are superb observers of the wrong things at the poker table. They are constantly watching others, not to learn from the other person, but to observe how the other person is feeling about or viewing them. They then tend to act and play accordingly. If you watch closely, many Theatrical Dominant Personalities are like bad actors in bad science fiction movies. They overact the part or they underact the role and win less money than what's appropriate for the cards they hold. As their playing hand shifts in value, they often mimic it through subtle shifts in their motor rate, (movement).

They will often change slightly how they make or place a bet in correspondence to hand value. They are highly visual types who often look up both left and right as they formulate a strategy. They constantly rearrange their chips in ways that make the stacks look bigger. As the chips start disappearing, they start rearranging. At the crux of all this is the simple fact that poker is not a rehearsable form of art. You have to be reactive. You can sit at home all day and rehearse how your are going to play a hand, but then the damnedest things happen when you arrive at the poker theater. You suddenly discover that all of your rehearsing is for not because all the other actors are ad-libbing, walking all over your lines and stealing your juiciest parts.

The success that a Theatrical Dominant Personality enjoys at the poker table is going to depend in a large degree on you. They are powerful, magnetic, sexual personalities. They are artful seducers of types who are attracted to this type magnetism. In many respects, they are like the spider who spins an innocent-looking web. The spider survives because many plunge headlong into the web. Additionally, there are many personality types who mistakenly believe they can flirt with the fire, but never get burned. To believe this is folly. The overpowering need and desire of the theatrical to have itself fed, can trap even those who think they will just enjoy the warmth, and still avoid the flame. A magnetic personality is just as it implies, a magnet.

The difference in winning or losing is often imperceptible. Many individuals spend a lifetime of frustration chasing success with the mistaken belief that it's one big break that eludes them; this is seldom the case. The width of a single human hair cannot be measured unless you have specially designed equipment. Yet that same human hair, if it accidentally gets into your eye or mouth, can seem like a boulder in its capacity to irritate. Most football games are decided by an inch, a ball thrown an inch too high that results in an interception, a tackle that was missed by an inch, a ball that missed being tipped by an inch, and thus, becomes a winning touchdown pass. . .I could give you 100 other examples of how the game and the winning or losing of it is affected by this mere inch. Yet before the game begins, the one inch seems insignificant. Out of the total length of the playing field, it accounts for only a minuscule .0002 percent of the total. It's not the big things that determine success. It's the attention to and mastering of the small details that so very often decide success.

An emotional crack or flaw smaller than the width of a hair can be fatal in poker. They are fatal because they become as obvious to your opponent as a hair in your eye is noticeable to you. They are fatal because we have trouble recognizing the flaw within ourselves. If you can't recognize it, you cannot correct it. Recognition comes through rigid self-examination of the self and the actions of the self. Of the 13 personality types, it is almost always emotion that is the determining factor in their behavior that begets actions that determine success or failure.

The Theatrical Dominant Personality is an enormously talented type individual. Their success is limited in many fields because of an inability to handle the emotional cracks that develop. If you are likewise emotionally flawed, you cannot take advantage of the weaknesses that others have. Sure, you might be able to pick off the Vigilant, but just as surely the Eccentric will pick you off, then in turn be picked off by the Aggressive. It's like being in a game (life, poker) where the wheels move but the ultimate destination remains forever elusive. If you want to be the worlds greatest poker player, you must do one thing. Master yourself. In doing so, you give your opponents the ultimate bad beat. You deny them mastery over you.

The Theatrical Dominant Personality wants to be the centerpiece at the poker table. Oblige them. A centerpiece is large, it makes a good target, plus it's a willing target. When the driving emotions are impulses, hunches and a highly exposed ego, the target is not elusive; more or less it tends to stumble over itself in its desire to get to you.

The Theatrical Dominant Personality plays poker in a style that looks outward only. It says, "This is what I have (their hand), and this is what I'm going to do with it." In contrast, there is another way to play poker that is more damaging to your opponent on a long-term psychological basis. This style of play says, "What I have and what I want to do is important, but it's secondary to figuring out what my opponent wants me to do, then not doing it."

When you have mastery of this, your opponent can't beat you up in ratio to the frustration you cause him. It's a form of offense that has its roots in defense. The most dominating football team in recent years has been the San Francisco 49ers. The public thinks this team won because of offense. They won because they had a defense that took away offensive options from the opponent. The Theatrical Dominant Personality is one-dimensional in playing style. It's easy to defense one-dimensional offenses.

The Theatrical Dominant Personality is always looking for a shoot out. That's fine! Just make sure you do it on your terms, not theirs. When the Theatrical Personality can't have things his way, he becomes ineffective, careless, and often forgets the risks involved. No, it's at these points of time they are susceptible, easy prey.

The Theatrical Dominant Personality as a Buyer

The Theatrical Dominant Personality is exactly as the name implies. The world is a stage. They are the actors and actresses, the shining stars within their own world. They are ego-driven, almost as much as the I-Dominant Personality. The difference between the two is the I-Dominant is driven by ego to build and acquire an empire to verify the self while the Theatrical is ego-driven to enhance the personal self by receiving admiration from others.

The Theatrical is a tremendous buyer within a certain framework. They buy flash, the ornate, objects that draw attention to the self. The Theatrical not only is obsessed with keeping up with the Jones's, but also with surpassing the Jones's. They buy in direct relationship to how they feel about a product or service, or more accurately how others would feel about them if they owned the item.

The Theatrical is a highly charged emotional being. If their senses are stimulated, they react accordingly. Their primary mental process is visual. They are attracted to things that have visual impact, things that stand out and things that cause others to be visually stimulated. Working hand-in-hand with their visual orientation is a vivid imagination. They see the product or service, they imagine how they would feel if they owned it and then the ego steps in and starts enhancing the desire to such an extent that many times the desire becomes overwhelming.

The Theatrical responds to attention. They want to be noticed, admired, talked about. As a buyer they want center stage. They expect and demand that their selling agent give them preferred status. As a selling agent, you are a most important influence in whether the Theatrical does or doesn't buy your product or service. The Theatrical gets their self-confidence from and through others.

Your words, your praise, your actions are the fuel that sustains their state of self-confidence. The I-Dominant has true inner self-confidence. The Theatrical has false self-confidence; it's only as good as the reflection in the mirror. The mirror is you, the selling agent. The Theatrical is very skilled at sensing how you feel about them. If you are responding to them, they in turn, begin to respond to you.

The Theatrical lives in a world of color and a world that must have excitement. They need to feel, to be involved in the action. To successfully sell this type of individual, you need a presentation that's heavy on sensation and light on detail. The Theatrical cannot stand the mundane, the plain, the routine or the grind. The Theatrical Personality will often develop a Scarlet O'Hara, "I'll worry about it tomorrow," reality in order to avoid responsibilities. Their mental process is if they feel good about the product or service and if they feel good about you, then everything else will get taken care of. Unfortunately, many sales transactions require a lot of grind in order to be completed. It can sometimes be difficult to find enough responsibility in this type of individual to complete the sale.

Because the Theatrical Personality is dominated by their heart or their feelings, their mood and temperament changes frequently. They can run from hot to cold in the same moment. When this happens, they blame you. They will become resentful, raging, melodramatic, etc. As a sales, agent you need to stick to your guns. Don't be afraid to call a spade a spade. A verbal spat will often clear the air and jerk them back to reality. These types seldom have the ability to hide what they're feeling and often need to vent their frustrations verbally. As a selling agent, you can also do the same. The Theatrical is not a grudge bearer indefinitely; therefore, they are not going to resent your passion.

The Theatrical Personality is a mental drifter. If they are hot today, they are just as likely to be cold tomorrow. You should always consider this type of personality as a one-call close. You want to close the deal as soon as possible. If you don't get the

Theatrical when they are hot, you will run into an endless series of absent procrastination. To make a "yes" decision a buyer needs to realize four things:

1. They have to be convinced that your product or service will do the job, fulfill the need, and solve the problem.

2. That the value they are receiving exceeds the money that they are spending.

3. That their decision will be accepted by associates and co-workers as smart, shrewd, prudent, needed, etc. In other words, they will need ego-enhancement from those who are peripherally involved with the use.

4. Instant gratification! Have to realize that they will receive immediate benefits and satisfaction from the purchase of, and the expenditures of, their hard-earned money.

In selling to the Theatrical, No. 4 is the most important, followed closely by No. 3. When any personality type lives and dies for instant gratification, you have within your means a powerful selling tool. This tool is called negative selling. It is a process of taking it away in order to make them want it even more. As an example, "That car will be gone tomorrow," is a negative statement. If you made that statement to an Aggressive, Vigilant or I-Dominant Personality, they would simply screw you down another notch. If you make the same statement to a personality type like the Theatrical, it tends to push the right motivational buttons. Any personality type that is ruled by their emotions can be led in the selling process. The Theatrical is highly susceptible to suggestion and sensory impulses. If the individual is highly Theatrical in nature it's almost impossible for them to resist the lure and temptation of instant gratification.

Sometimes a major problem with the Theatrical Dominant Personality is they are very shallow people. They sometimes live in such a make-believe world that they are no longer acquainted with facts or with the truth. In some cases, they are out-and-out pathological liars. The real them has been hijacked by the performer in them, their alter ego. They tend to visualize a role for themselves, then live that part. The problem with this is it's a fairy tale. It's not rooted in actual experience. A fairy tale sense of reality translates itself into real-life nightmares for those trying to deal with this type personality. Commitments are easily broken or ignored, dependability is nothing more than a one-way street. The only time that is valuable is their own. As a selling agent, you need to both commit and enforce agreements with this type personality. If they want to perform, that's fine; just make sure you're not one of the extras. If you are, you'll find the pay lousy.

A key component in understanding and dealing with the Theatrical Personality is to listen closely to the questions they ask you. So many times the questions will have their root value in vanity or insecurity. They are not questions about value, performance or dependability. They are questions about the individual's need to have their ego pumped. When you hear questions like these, you should immediately realize that if they need your approval to find self-esteem, they will also pay plenty to have objects that will silently praise them to others.

The Theatrical Dominant Personality is often a financial disaster. They can't hold on to money. As soon as they acquire it, they spend it. Often these types earn a lot of money. It's the management aspect of financial transactions that keep them living from paycheck to paycheck. Many of the best sales agents I've trained were of the Theatrical Dominant mold. These were individuals who earned hundreds of thousands of dollars per year. They were superb selling agents, masters of performing for others; yet, in the end, they always allowed their ego to walk with their money.

When vanity, ego, insecurity and a false sense of self-confidence are dominating facets of a personality, you are often going to find a person out of control. If you don't have control of yourself, then it's only a matter of time until a sharp selling agent is running the ink on a contract that has your name on the bottom of it.

The Theatrical Personality is a fantasy waiting to happen. As a selling agent, you will have great success if you take the time to get inside these individuals' heads. The great thing about fantasies is they have no border. They are ever-expanding. Therein, you will find that there is always room for your product or service, provided you can use wrapping paper called ego and tie it with ribbon called vanity.

THE UNDERACHIEVER

CLINICAL NAME:
PASSIVE AGGRESSIVE PERSONALITY DISORDER

Positive:

Individualist

Creative

Spontaneous

Opportunist

Self-Belief

Fun-Loving

Positive

Loyal

Sensitive

Yes or No

Security-Oriented

Freedom-Loving

Negative:

Demotivated

Lazy

Vague

Lack of Direction

Not a Team Player

Condescending

Self-Destructive

Selfish

Malcontent

Stubborn

Resentful

Procrastination

Anger

Argumentative

Passive

Submissive

A Positive Overview

The Underachiever Dominant Personality must be viewed in the context of what values are important, and to whom they are important. To the Worker Moralist or I-Dominant Personality types, the Underachiever is just that, an underachiever. Others with less drive and burning ambition would probably be prone to say the Underachiever is an individual who enjoys life and lives it in the style that they see fit.

The Underachiever Dominant Personality has their own agenda. The music they hear and the drummer they march to, is only what they choose. They have a live and let live attitude that dominates every facet of their lives. They can be creative people who have insight and intuitiveness. They are spontaneous, fun-loving people, who are often more content to enjoy what they have rather than being obsessed with acquiring more. They are people-oriented and enjoy the company of others. They are usually sensitive to the feelings of others, and can show heart-felt empathy. They seldom prejudge others, instead they prefer to hold to the philosophy that there is room enough for every style. They will often have a positive attitude that takes the form of "If it's not all right, today, then there is always tomorrow." They are highly independent personalities who value their freedom above and beyond everything else.

The Negative Side

If this personality trait is severe in an individual, the problems are immense. This then becomes a self-destructive personality. They view the world as a place, where someone is denying them their "due right." There is an attitude of "you owe me." These individuals cannot accept the fact that they are responsible for themselves, and that no one owes them anything. They can be and are mal-contents in the truest sense:

- ♠ The boss is wrong
- ♠ The government owes me

♠ It's not my fault

♠ I'm being singled out

♠ They pick on me

These individuals are fast to point the finger toward everyone except themselves. They want it their way, but don't want to pay the price necessary to have it that way. When they feel that they are being infringed upon or that excessive demands are being made of them, they become stubborn, obstinate, and will pout for days. They often feel that they are overworked and underpaid.

Many of the Underachiever Dominant Personalities are resentful of authority. They feel that rules are there for the purpose of denying them the right to be individuals, and will, if given the right opportunity, sabotage or undermine those in positions of authority. They often have trouble holding a job for more than a few months before a blowup occurs. Many times they are rabid and passionate members and supporters of labor unions and will be the first ones on the picket line.

Identifying And Playing With The Underachiever Dominant Personality

In many ways, the Underachiever is the opposite of the Worker Moralist personality. These two distinct personalities are both driven, but in totally different directions. The Underachiever is primarily interested in themselves and how it will benefit them. They are most easily identified by their attitude:

♠ Lighten up man

♠ No big deal

♠ Who needs the rat race

♠ 9 to 5 is enough

♠ These big companies are just out for a buck

In one sense, it could be said that they have a chip on their shoulder. They will often have ambition; however, if they can't succeed, it's your fault not theirs. All too often they will view you as part of the establishment, and therefore, a part of the problem. Their decision making process is emotional, sometimes impulsive, many times illogical, and often backed up by reasoning to create justification:

♠ I deserve a new car

♠ It's my right to have a vacation

♠ I'm entitled to have. . .

Walk into any sports book, bar or poker room on a payday and you will find this type individuals by the dozens. They are difficult to ignore. They all have an opinion on gambling (who's going to win), and become relentless self-styled experts.

The clinical name for this personality type is Passive-Aggressive Personality Disorder. As the name implies, they fluctuate between passively "existing" then aggressively "seeking." Along with the Worker Moralist personality, this personality type comprises a good percentage of the population. If the Passive-Aggressive trait of personality is mild, these individuals adapt well to life and blend in to form a high percentage of that great unidentifiable middle class (or other classes). They go to work in the morning, come home in the evening, eat dinner and pile up on the couch with a beer. When the weekend comes, they engage in whatever activity they most enjoy. They are willing to do their part, but in exchange they want to be able to drop out once they've punched the time clock.

In many respects, this type seems to be blank faces, not blank faces in the crowd, but rather the blank faces that make up the crowd. As the trait of personality becomes more pronounced, they start to have more identifiable characteristics. The swing between alternating Passive-Aggressive behavior is accelerated.

The Underachiever Dominant Personality is at conflict with themselves. Their mental process is the dog-eat-dog world is not for me, then they suddenly switch gears and decide to wade into the thick of the fight as the aggressive side of their nature kicks in. It is in this mode that they are most likely to show up in a competitive endeavor such as poker.

The Underachiever often has a deep-seated anger. First, at themselves for being just another face in the crowd, then at the world in general which rides roughshod over the faceless individuals. Along with the anger are several other characteristics that are identifiable:

A. The need to find fault and blame others. Things don't always go as we would like them to. Often life is three steps forward and two backward. A normal being will accept this as a part of life and adjust accordingly. The Underachiever Dominant Personality chooses to assign blame. It's often a part of a greater prevailing attitude of total negativity. The Underachiever Dominant Personality will often pick out the negative possibilities in a situation as the point of concentration. Once they have found the fault within the situation, they automatically reduce their accountability to controlling the outcome by assigning blame. In conversation, their speech is dominated by "yes, "but" and "if."

B. An inability to have concrete purpose. An Underachiever Dominant Personality will often give you the mental impression of being like the ball in a pin ball machine. They are always bouncing off the walls, ricocheting back and forth. The lack of sureness of purpose makes any individual susceptible to quitting. A trademark of this personality is an inability to stay the course. They start, stop, start, stop, quit, change projects, stall and procrastinate. The lack of conviction about purpose causes them to follow the leader while being both resentful and distrustful of the course. When they revolt, they do so both in manner and actions that often reveal no semblance of a plan.

C. The low road. The action that almost always comes when there is a lack of commitment or purpose, is the need to take short cuts. The constant searching for, or the belief that there is an easy way out, always undermines the individual's position severely. Mentally tougher individuals make a living by doing nothing more than always attacking the compromised position of others. Once a position is compromised, there is no defense. There is nothing to negotiate, there is only a dictating and following of others terms. As surely as the borrower is a slave to the lender, then likewise, the Underachiever's compromised attitude is prey to the steadfast resolve of the committed.

If the Underachiever Dominant Personality plays enough poker over a long period of time, some or all of the above characteristics will eventually surface in their play. The best way to attack this individual is to simply wait. You really don't have to do anything except to make sure your play is not marked with the characteristics of this personality type. When I owned sales management companies, there was one eventuality I could always count on. It was that sooner or later the Underachiever Dominant Personality would trap themselves or fall into their own pit. The next eventuality was they had to come to me, hat in hand, and I, not them, was going to dictate the rules and terms from that point on. The last eventuality, (and the most fateful), was they would repeat the same trap again and again, thus further compromising themselves.

The central issue and the real heart of the matter is the failure to understand and adhere to the one fundamental and unalterable rule of both life and poker. It's not a pretty rule. It's unglamorous. It's looked on with disdain by the majority of gamblers. Yet the failure to adhere to it or the unwillingness to believe it, cost most the chance to ever wear the banner of champions. In poker and sports betting, it's the single greatest asset that a player can bring to the table. Without it, you're going to lose. It may not be today, tomorrow or even next year but eventually you will lose. That single greatest asset is:

"THE COMMITMENT TO GRIND IT."

In poker (and in life) 80 percent of the time you're digging ditches, 20 percent of this time you're building sky scrapers. Digging ditches is dirty, mundane work. It takes will power and commitment to dig a ditch. In poker, it's easy to say, "I'm the boss, let the workers dig the ditches, I'll build the sky scrapers." In poker it's true, you're the "boss." But you are also the dishwasher, the ditch digger, the lowly peasant. You are in fact "everything." A nation of "one." You are not a link in the chain, you are every link in the chain. It therefore becomes even more imperative that you understand and be willing to do the ordinary and mundane in order to insure your survival.

The best player I never played with, was Mason Malmuth. Quiet, reserved, always watchful. He sat down at the same table where I was. After 20 minutes he led and I popped it. He threw his hand away. Fifteen minutes later he leads, I re-pop it, he calls, the flop comes, he checks, I bet, he throws his hand away. He won't play with me. An hour later he leaves, up $500. I played with him two or three other times, same results. Once he sat down for 30 minutes, never made a bet, then called it a night. After that, I began to appreciate his ability to dig ditches.

This commitment to grind it is not to be construed as an endorsement of greatness to those whose personalities are such that all they can do is grind it. We'll get to those types in the last section of this book. We are, however, ever mindful that the ratio is 80 percent-20 percent. The real point is, you have to have the 80 percent to be able to use the 20 percent effectively. In many ways the title gambler is a misnomer. A title for the ego. Every other taxi driver and bartender in Las Vegas calls himself a gambler, or in moments of reality, part-time gamblers. I've yet to meet anyone who says "I'm a grinder." I don't know who the best poker player is. However I'm sure of one thing, he/she, is a superb grinder. So much so that they effectively make the 20 percent look so large that they put fear in the hearts of many. The best gamblers are those who understand the necessity of grinding it.

Action and risk-taking for their own sake is the pathway to ruin taken by fools. No lasting building can be constructed without first building the foundation. The Underachiever Dominant

Personality despises the foundation. They are always trying to build a house that won't support the weight of its own concepts.

The Underachiever Dominant Personality lacks the commitment to grind it. The may do so for an hour or a day or a week but they still don't have the commitment. When you don't have the commitment to grind, there is another rule that is in the shadow of the first rule we gave. It's consequences are deadly. The second rule is:

"WHEN YOU DON'T HAVE THE COMMITMENT TO GRIND, YOU WILL ALWAYS HAVE TO FIGHT THE URGE TO CHASE."

Most gamblers, if they have to fight the urge to chase money or losses, will eventually lose this fight. It's too big an opponent. Their mind becomes the enemy because it demands their participation in the rush to ruin. The mind, in anger, helplessness, despair and desperation says, "To hell with it." Discipline disappears and it's overpowered by the need and desire to strike out, to blindly fight back. The Underachiever Dominant Personality is the most likely of all the personality types to wildly chase their money. When the mind of a gambler enters into this "rush to ruin" state, they are doomed.

An amazing thing happens. It can't be explained scientifically, yet it happens with deadly accuracy and frequency. A gambler who is chasing will always make decisions that are wrong the majority of time. Murphy's Law becomes supreme law. I think the mind has overloaded, and in its confusion, it deliberately crashes the individual as an act of self-preservation. It's a tragic sight to observe a gambler desperately chasing in a last-ditch effort to survive. The frightening part is to watch how every decision they make takes them to a lower and lower level. This phenomena is the No. 1 cause of casualties in sports betting. It also happens frequently in poker.

One of the reasons, the Underachiever Dominant Personality lacks a commitment to grinding, is because they are always in a quest to make the big score. The constant urge to score big, means you have to constantly challenge the laws of probability while engaging in extended risk-taking. One of the ways the Underachiever attempts this is, when in one of their angry aggressive states, they seek out and play in games where they are over-matched. This over-matching is in both class of players and the limits of the game. Almost always, their first playing tactic is an angry attempt to run over the game. It's about as effective as spitting into the wind.

In many respects, the Underachiever Dominant Personality is always on emotional tilt. When in their passive state, they are sullen, uncommunicative and constantly surrendering without a fight. When they are in the angry, aggressive state, they are set on edge. They become argumentative over everything. With little reason to back them up, they pick fights with the dealer, floor people or other players. If they win a pot, they are quick to point out the superior moves they made, while at the same time they have to tell the opponent all the mistakes they made while playing the hand. Making it more irritating, is the fact that it's more likely to be a commentary than a comment.

When the Underachiever is running good, catching cards and winning pots, they teach poker at the table. No one is spared. They tell you exactly why and how come they are so good. When they are losing, they become poker critics. Even if they are not involved in the hand, they are apt to tell you and everyone else how you should have played the hand and gotten more money. The central issue is self-esteem, they don't have any. They try to create self-esteem in their ongoing moment-to-moment reality. Self-esteem cannot be created in a moment; however, any individual who lacks it can be attacked every moment of the day.

The Underachiever is highly susceptible to the strengths of other, differing personality types. Against the Aggressive Dominant Personality they are disadvantaged because there is a mismatching of aggressions. Against the I-Dominant, they are susceptible to walking into deadly traps as the I-Dominant has ways of turning up the Underachiever's angry aggression. Against the

Vigilant Dominant Personality, they are susceptible because the Vigilant perceives both their passive and Aggressive state of mind, and is forever one step in front of their next move. The final insult is the Reflective will often steal the pot at the end, because the Underachiever has been leading with nothing, and at the end, the Reflective suddenly ups the stakes.

The Underachiever doesn't believe in luck. They do believe in bad luck. Any endeavor is enhanced by a positive state of mind. The Underachiever's mind looks on the negative possibilities and won't let go. A constant expectation that something is going to go wrong makes it difficult to make correct decisions. The Underachiever style of play is often marked by vacillation, caused by apprehension. This is then followed by a move designed to protect a position, rather than enhance it. The Underachiever too often checks when checked to or makes endless calls. The next illogical move they make is an ill-fated attempt to suddenly counteract this asleep-at-the-wheel style by making radical moves.

Another fatal characteristic of the Underachiever is they constantly underestimate the ability of opponents. You may be superior. However, it's inferiority on your part to not recognize that the superiority you have, is in part, because you are always cognizant that any opponent is worthy. Time after time, I've witnessed big time business people hit the skids because they refused to concede that a seemingly unworthy competitor could do anything that would jeopardize their position.

Any player who constantly downgrades the possible hands an opponent could have because of who the opponent is, will, at some time, be bombed into oblivion. Many of the problems (economically), in this country today were caused by our inability to believe that the North Vietnamese were worthy opponents, that they were capable of playing hard ball with us. Billions of dollars and thousands of lives later, we are still paying the bitter price. We would have been better off fighting the Russians, at least then we wouldn't have misjudged the potential of the opponent. Part of the problem the Underachiever Personality has is they become so focused on one single possibility that they become unfocused.

As an example, in sports betting they focus on one possibility as being the determining factor in the eventual outcome. They say, "Well it's a revenge game, or a coaching mismatch, or they cite some compelling technical trend or statistical aberration." It's dangerous to hang your bankroll on one possibility. On his best day, an ordinary quarterback like Jack Kemp will be better than a great quarterback like Montana will be on his worst day. In poker, excluding possibilities is dangerous. An ordinary flop like 10-9-3 has many hidden possibilities besides an obvious draw. It's wise to remember that in poker, the very best and very worst players will often play unordinary hands, but for different reasons in different situations and in a strikingly different manner.

If I wanted to, I could make a pretty compelling case that if it's going to come down to you, from a late position, and the players in the blinds, then you should always raise, regardless. This is not so much to eliminate possibilities, but rather to clarify possibilities later in the hand. I think I could make just as compelling a case that in the same situation, if the individuals in the blinds are either vastly superior or vastly inferior, you should never raise. The Underachiever loves to limp and trap, especially those they perceive as inferior and those who they know are clearly superior. While they have this love affair with limping and trapping, they are often ignorant of the more intricate traps that are there because of the structure of the game. Many times it's difficult to run a bad player out of the blind simply because they have an investment in it. The great player will often defend the blind because they understand the possibilities and the positions of those leading into the blind better than other players grasp the situation. Many times you can play free poker by just stealing the blinds. The down side though is, many times the hand of the player in the blinds is the most difficult to figure out and therein lies many deadly, costly traps.

The Underachiever often can't determine what is essential in the game and what is not important. When the behavior has been to follow, then it's difficult to suddenly assume a position of leadership. On a long-term basis, it would always be more correct than incorrect to aggressively challenge this personality type when they attempt to lead. They most often have no internal reference point for leadership, because they have focused their energy and mental process on the right/wrong actions of others. The debating of the position of others will never be a viable substitute for personal action, tested and honed by fire.

Many times the Underachiever Personality will have a fine grasp of the technical side of the game such as knowing the correct odds or outs in a situation. The usefulness of this knowledge to them is debatable, as they tend to dilute its effectiveness by believing it to be the solution to problems instead of using it as a tool toward the problem.

The shifting between passive-aggressive emotional states indicates confusion in the mind of the individual. Therein, a primary weapon against this opponent should be to create more confusion. Often the best weapon in attacking any extreme in personality is to amplify or push to the limit the dominating force of the personality. In other words, when attacking, you want to use the aggression of the Aggressive as a weapon against them, or you want to make the Vigilant paranoid of your actions. When being attacked, you want the opponent not to be able to use the dominant force of their personality as effectively.

The last question on the Underachiever has to be this, "What exactly is the dominating force of their personality?" The force of the Aggressive is aggression. The force of the Vigilant is their ability to detect. The force of the Adventurer is their warrior capabilities. The inability to provide an answer to the above question should give you all the insight you'll ever need to engage this personality type successfully.

The Underachiever Dominant Personality as a Buyer

The Underachiever Personality is named such only because they have the tendency to be the type that constantly starts then stops projects. There is a large number of this personality type. In many respects, they form part of that large group known as the middle class, although they can be found in all classes and professions.

The Underachiever tends to exist in, and to except whatever circumstances are at hand. Their primary mental process is, "Well that's the way things are and there isn't anything I can do to change it." It is this personality type who is most prone to view the world in abstract terms. When an individual views things in abstract terms, they have a tendency to develop a feeling of being powerless and, therefore, helpless.

The Underachiever tends to be sold more than they buy. Because they live a life that often lacks upward direction, they need to be supplied the direction. As a selling agent, you are a most important individual to this personality type. They need leaders. They need individuals who will take charge from beginning to end. Your sales presentation needs to be fully-loaded and always directed toward accomplishing a specific result for the Underachiever. You must supply initiative, motivation, enthusiasm and will power when the other individual doesn't have it. A stereotypical example of an Underachiever Personality would be the Archie Bunker television character.

If you can have a basic understanding of how each of the 13 personality types think, act, react, are motivated or unmotivated and what their response mechanism is, then the job of selling them is much easier. With the Underachiever, you need to understand that to a very large extent they process everything from a negative viewpoint. They see what won't work instead of what does work. They assign blame as opposed to finding something to praise. They look at the possible loss in a situation while ignoring or overlooking the fact that risk is often the equation for large gain.

In selling to these individuals, you will soon observe that they object often, loudly and negatively. Their form of objecting will often have as its reference point the reality of someone else. As an example you'll hear them say:

♠ I heard

♠ Someone said

♠ Everyone knows

This is a form of a mass hysterical mentality. More often than not, this type of cattle-herd mentality will translate itself into negative thinking that results in negative action. When there is a constant barrage of negativity running through the mind, the eventuality is that the individual will flat out get stuck in mud.

When an individual becomes stuck from lack of action their next mental process is to become angry, frustrated and to develop a dependency on surviving by blaming others. The final step is to develop a deadly form of mental procrastination that assures they stay in the same position forever.

As a buyer, the Underachiever buys a lot and they buy frequently. This is more of a testimony to the skill of the selling agent than it is a statement about the drive of this personality. They can often be persuaded to buy impulsively something that they hadn't even previously considered. In the business world, you will not find this type in position of authority or leadership. Seldom will you even find them in the position of owning their own business. They are followers, not leaders. They work for others and take orders as given. They are the rank and file, yet many times they are the angry, frustrated rank and file.

The vast majority of selling to these individuals comes in the field of retail sales and in-home residential sales. They are generally easy individuals to get appointments with, and if they are handled in the right manner, they can be profitable individuals to sell to.

First and foremost, the selling agent has to break through the wall of their constant negative thinking. People who think negatively have a gray, colorless, ill-defined picture in their heads. When there is no clear image, the individual has no road map for the future. They can only act or react as victims to the circumstances that befall them on a particular day. Whether an individual is negative or positive depends on the value labels they place on events. The events themselves have no meaning beyond the mind's assignment of a label such as good, bad, right, wrong, etc. The event has already happened, it's over, it's history. What remains and what counts is the labeling your mind assigns to it.

When presenting and selling to individuals who process negatively, you have to constantly work with them to assign positive labels. The best way to do this is to individualize the Underachiever Personality. For too long these types have allowed themselves to become part of the masses. They don't see their uniqueness. They don't allow themselves to feel their specialness. To separate individuals from the masses you need to emphasize the "I" and the "you" to them. When their mind goes into the negative state you have to turn "I can't" into "you can," "they say," into "what do you really believe," "the world is screwed up" into "courage and heart to make a difference is just one life...their own." "What's the use" into "because you're important."

The next thing you have to do is refuse to let the Underachiever quit. Giving up and accepting the status quo is the way this personality type finds security. The two greatest statements you can make to prevent this is, "I want to help you" and "I'll work with you." Then you have to be prepared to back up the statement. You'll find that to sell many of these individuals, you will have to do the work for both yourself and them.

When selling and presenting to this type, you need to find specific wants, needs and desires. You have to have a concrete base to work from. Next you have to hammer home the fact that these specific needs, wants and desires are something that can be accomplished. Next you have to give them a specific and precise way to get them. The Underachiever lacks confidence and self-esteem. They don't really believe in their own wants, needs and desires as being important enough to pursue, as they often lack any kind of goals.

When the individual lacks a functional, sustaining self-image, they will develop a life style that lacks any kind of urgency or necessity. They then become life-long procrastinators. When one allows themselves to procrastinate, life becomes an endless excuse for delaying, putting off or quitting. You have to mentally slap procrastinators. You have to give them your fire, determination and zeal. To do this, you have to use whatever specific need, want or desire you can find within them and fan it into a bigger fire. Enthusiasm will move the world. The Underachiever Personality runs hot and cold, sometimes from moment to moment. Become keenly aware of the moments when they are hot and enthused and use those moments as building blocks. As a selling agent, you need to always be perceptually aware of mood shifts in this personality. As they alternate between passive and aggressive states, their mental state will likewise fluctuate rapidly between yes and no. By monitoring their body carriage position you can easily detect these mental shifts. Human beings use their fingers and hands in an unconscious manner that reveals their current conscious state of being or mind. When the mind becomes stressed, concerned or objects silently, it reveals these thoughts neurologically through the eyes, forehead, lips and especially the hands and fingers. We unconsciously tense, close, fidget or move as a response to our concern and uncomfortableness. The human brain cannot store anger, frustration, despair, etc. When our neuro system sends these impulses to the brain, it automatically sends them back to our physical body where it's stored as aches, pains, tension, etc. We deal with and alleviate these responses through movement. As a selling agent, you want to detect and deal with these responses immediately because these are the silent objections that prevent the completion of a sale. A silent objection in the mind of the buyer is so loud that they cannot hear anything else you're saying, because their mind is screaming that something is wrong, be careful.

In selling the Underachiever, you must close as early and as often as possible. There is no mystery about closing a sale. The only time you can close and the only time you should close is when the buyer tells you they are ready to be closed. When the buyer comes forward in body position or carriage they are silently saying "I'm sold, close me." Forward and open means "close;" Back and withdrawn into themselves means they need more information, more values, more reason to make a decision. If you try to close when an individual is in a negative position mode, all that you will accomplish is the creation of another objection that says, "Sorry, but you don't understand me or my special needs."

The Underachiever Personality is a false negotiator. They cannot negotiate anything. Yet they will attempt to do so. They do so because of ego or because they kind of think it's something a sophisticated buyer would do. They don't negotiate to get a better price or terms. If you need to, you can always give up something insignificant just to soothe their mind.

From a financial standpoint, you need to work out all the details for this personality type. Being creative is not a strong point of this personality type. From beginning to end, this type needs leadership, direction and motivation supplied to them. You must overcome their inner frustration with themselves and block their negative thought patterns. If you do these things, you will find they can be very good buyers, more so in numbers than as individual buyers.

THE VIGILANT

CLINICAL NAME:
PARANOID

Positive:	*Negative:*
Self-Reliant	Paranoid
Intuitive	Spiteful
Reserved	Carries the Long-Term Grudge
Loyal	Easily Threatened
Instinctive	Quick to Fault Others
Survival-Oriented	Abusive
Powerful Self-Identity	Emotionally Empty to Others
Cautious	Withdrawn
Protective	Aloof
Strong	Lack of Empathy
Quick Decision-Making	A Council of One
Control	Inflexible
Willing to Listen	

A Positive Overview

The Vigilant Dominant Personality is an individual of unique abilities. They are blessed with the kind of perceptiveness that most people can only wish for. They have the most learned (acquired) intuitiveness of all the 13 personality types. This is the most black and white of all the personality types. The Aggressive is a very black and white personality by their actions and reflexes, the Vigilant becomes this way through incessant demands on the self to produce evidence to prove the black/white reality of the situation. There is a constant demand on the self to eliminate the possibility of gray areas or to allow the birth of wishy-washy processing. The Vigilant Personality marches to the music of their own beliefs.

First and foremost, they depend on themselves. They seldom, if ever, ally themselves with others for the purpose of reinforcement. The judgements they arrive at are the only proof they need. There is a survival-oriented intensity that lays below the surface of this individual. It can come to the rescue in a flash, if the necessity arises. The Vigilant has a deep-seated sense of justice. This right/wrong orientation is toward themselves, others and to various causes. They are principled individuals with definite ideas about what is right and what is wrong. They are willing to defend this position, particularly if it involves what they perceive as an injustice or an infringement of freedom.

The Vigilant Personality can be found in many different marketplaces, both public and private. Many top executives and CEOs are Vigilant individuals. Often these individuals can be found in high-ranking positions of governmental oversight, and not surprisingly, many banking (money) official's personalities are dominated by a strong vigilant streak. From personal observation, it is quite easy to say that this is a personality trait that is more prevalent in the male species than that of the female. They are valued employees whose sense of fair play, loyalty, and perceptiveness, makes them worthy in the eyes of many employers.

The Negative Side

Depending on the degree of vigilance in the personality, these individuals can be downright difficult. When the vigilance goes to the extreme it becomes a paranoid personality. Once they perceive any injustice, either real or imagined, they become spiteful, grudge-bearing individuals. They are easily threatened and overly cautious. They have the ability to take a normal conversation and turn it in their mind into a "They are out to get me" vendetta. These individuals are driven by an overwhelming need to be suspicious of the motives of someone else.

This form of paranoid behavior induces the individual to become withdrawn, tense, stressed, and inflexible in their beliefs and in their dealings with others. They become emotionally empty in feelings to others. They stand at a distance and emotionally keep everyone else at arm's length. These individuals are often spoken of as cold, aloof, and possessing a steel demeanor. If the vigilance in the personality is severe, they will, and can, revert to abuse and violence to correct the injustices, be they real or simply imagined paranoia. At its nightmarish worst, this type individual become cult leaders who prey on the fears of others in order to form alliances that impact society negatively. The Hitlers, Charles Mansons and Jim Jones of this world were all Vigilant Dominant Personalities that went over the line that separates sanity from insanity. At the root of this destructive behavior is their inability to accept or to believe others at face value. They are compulsively driven to go beyond the surface to find ulterior motives, (e.g., they are out to take advantage of me).

Identifying And Playing With The Vigilant

Remember Clint Eastwood and the type of character he played when he was making the western movies or the tough cop character, Dirty Harry? In the westerns, he played the lone cowboy, with hat pulled low and eyes of steel that surveyed the situation, constantly looking for or expecting danger. In movies such as

POKER, SEX & DYING

Hang'em High, A Fistful of Dollars or Dirty Harry the central part was of a vigilant individual. Now, picture in your mind, a mousy little person who wears horn rimmed glasses, wears a visor and pours over the accounts and books of a company while stuck off in an office somewhere in the back. Both of these characterizations are stereotypical examples of a Vigilant Dominant Personality. Both are correct; however, the Vigilant individual can come in many other sizes, shapes or forms.

Many individuals, especially poker players, will have a degree of vigilance in their personality make up. Vigilance is a state of watchfulness. It's the cop, the detective, the guard that looks out for the self. I doubt that there are few, if any, world-class poker players who don't have the trait of vigilance in their personality, at least as a strong subordinate trait. There are many who think they are vigilant; yet it's safe to say that less then 5 percent of the population is of the Vigilant Dominant Personality mold. If you think you are a Vigilant Dominant Personality, all you have to do to test it is tell yourself what the page number is at the bottom without looking down. A highly Vigilant individual knows what page they are on. Very little escapes their senses. The Vigilant is different. They see and hear things that other individuals miss or ignore. From this ability to see and hear, they acquire an intuitiveness to get a feel on the situation at hand. The Vigilant does not have the natural intuitive feel that an I-Dominant, Adventurer, Emotional or Reflective Dominant Personality has. They compensate for this by putting their keen ability to see and hear together to formulate a sense of strategic feel.

If the degree of vigilance within the personality is controlled, it is one of the best assets a player can bring to the table. The player who possesses it has a distinct edge over rivals who don't. Many good players who don't possess the trait of vigilance will try to compensate by imposing upon themselves a state of concentration, a degree of watchfulness through sheer discipline. This is good. Even more than good, it's necessary in poker.

The single biggest observation I ever made in poker as it pertained to skill level or the ability to compete, had to do with the degree of concentration that was put into the game. The best players were superior at concentration, observation and watchfulness, especially when they were not involved in the playing of a hand. Many players who had a natural instinctive feel for the game sabotaged their abilities because they couldn't concentrate unless they were in the hand or else they concentrated on the wrong things and became trapped later because they misjudged what they were observing. Being able, through discipline, to concentrate is good; however, the forced watchfulness is not nearly as effective as true vigilance.

If I had to choose one ingredient that keeps good players from stepping up one class to greatness, it would be because they don't have a state of natural vigilance. The good player will watch, observe, concentrate, but they will still miss what the Vigilant so easily sees and hears.

The Vigilant Dominant Personality is dangerous because they see and hear differently. They see and hear the shifts, distortions, contradictions and transformations within speech, actions motivations, etc. I'll give you a couple examples, have you ever heard a cricket? That funny little insect that makes screeching sounds. Most people have heard one, but do you really know what its cadence sounds like? Most individuals would say it's like this (_____=cadence). _____. It's not! It's like _____ _ _ ____ __ _____ __ _____. It doesn't make one continuous unbroken sound. The Vigilant not only hears the cricket, he also hears the shifts and patterns of the sound. Another example. Player A asks player B to bum a cigarette. Player B gives player A the cigarette. If you were watching what did you see? Most individuals will see player B give player A the cigarette. The Vigilant Dominant Personality sees much more. He sees the mannerisms and style, the subtle shades of expression and variations, and most of all, discrepancies in messages, be they verbal or silent. The Vigilant Dominant Personality may have noted as many as 20 or 25 different points to use as future references. I won't go through the whole list but will give a few to highlight the Vigilant's processing mechanism:

- ♠ Was it the first time or one of many times on the part of player A?

- ♠ Did player B check the pack either before or after he gave the cigarette?

- ♠ Did player B avoid looking directly at player A when he gave him the cigarette?

- ♠ Did player B decide to have a cigarette also?

- ♠ Did player A light up immediately?

- ♠ How deep is player A inhaling?

- ♠ Does player A roll the cigarette between his fingers when he holds it?

- ♠ Did either player change their position from the waist up after the act?

- ♠ Is player B concentrating more on the game now than before?

- ♠ Did player B touch, look at, or move his chips sometime after the exchange?

All of the above have a significance to the Vigilant Dominant Personality. The Vigilant constantly measures the slightest shifts that take place within individuals and situations. Deviations from the norm are a Vigilant's way of accessing and understanding both causes of action and probably course of action.

The highly Vigilant individual is deadly at detecting inconsistencies in an individual. I'll give you another kind of example. In the 40-80 Hold'em game at the Bicycle Club, a guy walks by and is pulled into the game by a friend of his. He sits down, but expresses reluctance. He speaks softly to his friend for awhile. He hasn't been running good, but he has been playing good.

He doesn't feel comfortable with the 40-80 limit as he prefers the 15-30 game. He has tension in the eyebrows, constant shifting and movement in his lips, and his hand reaches out to form a barrier to the front side of his stacks, obviously a player in over his head in this particular game, because of his current circumstances.

That particular night it's a ram and jam game. The action is heavy, the chips are flying in all directions and there is a big turnover in players. Most of the players sitting at the table heard or observed little, if any, of the above when this player was pulled into the game. He almost immediately got involved in pots. The betting starts and he says, "I raise." The flop comes, someone bets, someone else says, "I raise." he says, "I raise." He loses the pot to two pair. Next time he's involved, he leads and says, "I raise." The flop comes. He gets a bet in front and says, "I'm gonna raise." The other player says, "I'll re-raise." It's a decent pot now. It's rag, rag, showdown. He wins the pot. He plays for three hours, re-buys at least four times and can't catch anything. He wins maybe three pots and loses close to $3,000.

He was a good player, but he never listened to himself. He shouldn't have volunteered so much information. Were there two players at that table who heard the discrepancies in what he was saying and what it really meant? Have you figured out what it was that cost him so dearly? I've already told you. If you haven't figured it out, I'll put it at the end of this section.

There are many characteristics which give clues in identifying the Vigilant Dominant Personality. In many respects, they are the opposite of the Theatrical Personality in temperament and their processing mechanism, and strikingly different from the Emotional Dominant Personality as it relates to what and how they feel.

A. **Codes of Honor.** The Vigilant Individuals pride themselves on their code of honor. They have a high regard for honor in others. The handshake is just as good as the written document. They are extremely conscious of their personal freedom and have a willingness to fight for it. The Vigilant is loyal, trustworthy and highly protective of those who are fortunate enough to get inside their circle. If push comes to shove, don't bet against the Vigilant. In crisis situations, they are fearless. They can, and will, endure for a cause they believe in above and beyond any of the other personality types.

B. **Physicality.** The Vigilant is self-contained. They seemingly occupy less space. They make no moves that are not necessary. They often give the impression of sitting in the same position for hours without moving. Highly Vigilant individuals often give the impression of being tightly bound, like a spring that has too much tension. When they move through a crowd, it's not in a helter-skelter manner, but rather with a certain pureness of purpose. When they are listening, which is always, their eyes move left and right, sideways. If they detect a contradiction, their eyes will quickly look left or right then back to the center mode position. The quick looking left or right is the way they process, sort and make distinctions on what they have just heard. In a poker game, the Vigilant can often watch and hear everything without having to move anything more than their eyes. This is easy to detect when you contrast it with how other individuals often have to turn, or tilt, their head to follow the flow of the game.

C. **Primary Mental Process.** The Vigilant Dominant Personality is cautious. They don't move headlong into any situation. The caution exhibits itself in many forms such as:

- ♠ Extremely reserved

- ♠ Being excessively quiet

- ♠ Communication through gesture instead of verbal exchanges. (nodding the head instead of saying yes or no).

♠ Being present, but not participating in the social flow of the situation.

♠ Being unwilling to participate in the situation at hand immediately.

The constant caution is a form of protection. It allows the wary individual avenues of escape if they detect, or even suspect, that which they are uncomfortable with is present. There is nothing wrong with being cautious. However, when the caution becomes excessive, the mind will almost automatically fixate on the worst possible scenario while ignoring other, more probable possibilities. As an example, suppose before the flop there are two players involved with no raises. The flop comes K-Q-7. Now, there is raise, raise, re-raise, etc. If the mind is so overly trained to be cautious it will automatically start saying, "Uh Oh! Three Kings." To the point that it can't comprehend the other, more likely possibilities. In poker, when the individual becomes too cautious they get run over with the greatest of ease. . .often by a hand holding little more than an attitude.

D. The Primary Motivation. Just plain old suspicion. It's the primary inducer that causes the caution. At the very core of their being, the Vigilant individual cannot accept things at face value. To their way of thinking, there has to be an underlying motive for what people say or do. The more Vigilant (paranoid) they are, the more convinced they become of the darker, sinister side of possibility. More than one individual has had hell on Earth because they were married to a paranoid personality. It becomes endless after awhile. If the individual comes home late, the only possible explanation is that they are having an affair. If the phone rings and it's the wrong number, it's really some kind of code or signal, etc.

When there is a constant focusing on suspicions, the mind tends to look at or seek out that which lends credence to the suspicion. You can falsely confirm many things by just looking at a part of the total scene, or by taking things out of their proper context. When the mind misinforms itself, the outcome is often worse than misinformation from another source.

E. The Internal View. The Vigilant Dominant Personality views themselves as the underdog. Even if they didn't hold this view of themselves, they would soon develop it as constant suspicion, undue caution and the searching for injustice would automatically tilt the mind in that direction. The underdog role means they view life and its various endeavors as a tough place to survive. This mind set tends to limit rather than expand the reality of an individual. There is a very real danger in focusing only on what one knows and not being capable of extending the boundaries of possibility. This rut regimentation makes the glass always half empty, and never half full. If you bring a limited perspective to the poker table it, means you are probably going to have to "grind it" exclusively, as you are unable to see any different, possibly expanded roles for the self.

On the positive side, the underdog viewpoint tends to make an individual keenly aware of what's necessary to survive. The Vigilant will not be inclined to underestimate the potential of any opponent. If anything, they give too much credit, especially to those who are successful leaders at the poker table.

F. The Mind Of God. As with all the personality types, the critical issue with the Vigilant has to be the degree of vigilance within the personality. If it's vigilant and not paranoid, this personality is a vicious foe. As the personality stretches toward the paranoid side, other problems surface which tend to hinder the playing style of the individual.

It's been my experience that the Adventurer Dominant Personality and the Vigilant Dominant Personality were the two personalities most likely to tilt to the extreme side of the personality scale. Of these two, it was the Vigilant that walked the tightest rope over the fine line that defined mental order vs. mental disorder. When this personality type becomes too vigilant, they become paranoid. Once they have entered this state, they lose the ability to take direct action. They are overpowered by the all consuming need to know everything. They can never detect enough information. There is an unending trail of clues that torment the mind. At it's maddening extreme, they become involved in a quest that is the same thing as trying to figure out the mind of God. The simple truth is, there are some things that we cannot figure out. If you think about it, the probable reason God didn't give us the capacity to know what is going to happen tomorrow was to ensure that we enjoy and appreciate today.

At its best, the game of poker is a game of incomplete information. At its worst, it's a game of misinformation or just plain wrong information. At some point, the mind has to put aside the hunger to know and take action in order to really know. When the individual is paranoid, they lose sight of the distinction between thought and action. The consuming thought replaces the taking of action. In all creation there is a three-step process that is both sequential and unalterable. It is: Thought fathers action which begets results. Poker, like everything else, is ruled by the above. It's the ability to take action with incomplete information that distinguishes personality types such as the Adventurer, Aggressive and I-Dominant at the poker table.

One of the marked characteristics of a paranoid's style of play is waiting to see what the other player does first. The downfall here is that this style of play means you are always shooting at a moving target. One of the most valuable lessons I was taught in sales management was that it's important to remember that in a team of huskies pulling a dog sled, the only perspective that ever changed was that of the lead dog. In poker, the ability to take the lead and be willing to back it up with the necessary action, creates in the mind of opponents either consciously or unconsciously several elements, such as:

♠ Respect

♠ Fear

POKER, SEX & DYING

♠ Uneasiness

♠ Wariness

♠ Caution

♠ Mental Russian Roulette

It's the last one that is the bank roll buster. If you're not leading, you are relegated to a guessing game of trying to figure out
what is going on in the leader's mind (God's mind). The part that
most conveniently forget to observe is, you're not just one step
behind, because in reality, it take two steps to overtake the leader,
(one to pull even, one to go ahead). In many respects, it's like
betting that a streak will end. It's a losing proposition. If you
want to see a bookmaker's eyes glaze over, all you have to do is
walk up and start betting that the team won't win their eighth in
a row. The issue is not whether you win or lose; the issue is
you have already lost. First, you're not on the streak (leading);
second, you're sticking your finger into the buzz saw after the
fact (following).

When you lead, you take the burden of guessing from your
shoulders and place it squarely on the shoulders of your opponents. It's a heavy burden that often weighs the individual down
with fear, caution and uneasiness. Hand in hand with the burden
of guessing comes "the burden of leadership." Have you heard
that statement? It's a statement that is incorrect. Not only is it
incorrect, it's a statement of manipulation. It's one of the more
subtle manipulations that is fostered on the unsuspecting. There is
no burden of leadership. The burden is on all those who have to
blindly follow and hope for the best.

Leaders perpetuate the manipulation. It's the leaders who
moan and groan about the so-called "burden." Yet, ask any leader
to change places with you, the follower, and you'll be greeted
with an icy stare. The crocodile tears being shed about the
so-called "burden" is a manipulation that has its design in

protecting the leaders position by discouraging followers from
]the idea of assuming a leadership role. It's an effective way of
discouraging competition.

If you want to really lighten your burden at the poker table,
start leading and stop following. If you want to go to the top of
IBM, you are not going to get there by first attacking the janitor,
then moving up to take on the mail room clerk, then going head
to head with the delivery boy. At that rate you'd have to live 800
years just to get to junior vice-president. The hierarchy in poker is
an open forum. Seniority, reputations and positions have little to
do with whether you get to the top. The willingness to lead instead
of follow, is a sure first step for you.

If the personality is not paranoid, but fully functional in the
vigilant capacity, they are dangerous at all times. They have,
through keen perspective, the ability to put you on a hand with a
high degree of accuracy. Additionally, they may know what your
next move is going to be before you do. They zero in on the
minute discrepancies. They see the slightest hesitations, they
understand the slightest shifts in signals given by the physical
carriage. The worst thing you can do is talk while involved in a
hand with the Vigilant Dominant Personality. Their ability to
detect discrepancies and inconsistencies in speech is frightening.
They hear the contradictions and immediately start zeroing in on
the hidden agenda that is serving as the real vehicle that's fueling
its perpetuation. The Vigilant is keenly attuned to hearing words
like always, must, forever, can't, everybody, nobody, never, etc. . .
words that convey a concrete absoluteness are just as likely, upon
close examination, to be rooted in shifting sand as they are to be
embedded in the concrete of truth or conviction. As an example,
suppose someone says to you:

"You must move to Los Angeles. To succeed you have to live
in Los Angeles. Everyone who succeeds lives in Los Angeles." You
say "But I'm not moving to Los Angeles." He says, "You don't
understand, there is no other way, you have to. Nobody will give
you the opportunity unless you live there." You say, "But I don't

want to live there." He says, "But when you see it you'll want to live there."

First you can bet against words like:

♠ Nobody

♠ Must

♠ Everyone
(and you can bet more than 15 percent)

Or you can put them into the proper context by adding the correct punctuation:

♠ Nobody?

♠ Must?

♠ Everyone?

The real importance is the shift and contradictions in what is being said. There is a huge difference between the beginning, you must, you have to and the end, you'll want to. Is the real truth because of nobody, must, everyone, or is it rooted in the word want? If so, whose want is at the top of whose agenda? It's an outright contradiction to stand on the necessity of must and have to, then bastardize the argument with a shift toward want to.

The Vigilant Dominant Personality is going to note the discrepancies and ask themselves a couple of questions. The first question is, "Is it because I have to or because I want to?" Once that question is answered the next question will be, "I want to or you want me to?" Once they have determined the answer to the second question, their next probable action is to move it all in on you, be it in the game of life or the game of poker. Remember: The naive believe, the foolish become trapped by the senselessness of their own words and the Vigilant hears. However, it's only the Vigilant who lays awake at night pondering what was said.

The Vigilant hears the contradictions in speech and measure it against their understanding of reality. For instance, if someone says "I'm going fishing someday" the Vigilant devalues "I'm going" and assigns the real value to "someday," or if someone walks up to you in a sports book and says "I'm betting the Oilers today, what do you think?" The Vigilant devalues the fact that you're betting the Oilers and assigns great value to your contradiction of saying one thing while the reality is you're really seeking an opinion to support your lack of sureness. What you're saying and the contradictions you're revealing are miles apart. If you are going to bet a team then solicit another opinion about the game, you have verbalized an internal conflict. Your best course of action is either bet the other side or don't bet the game at all.

There is nothing wrong with getting another opinion or viewpoint before making a decision. There is a lot wrong with saying you're going to bet a team and still need to solicit opinions. Whatever opinions you receive will only serve to reinforce the bias you already hold. The same type of contradictions and inconsistencies happen in poker games when players speak. The Vigilant, more than any other personality type, understands and bets against the contradictions that are revealed.

Perhaps it's an observation of the inconsequential, but it's hard not to notice that you see a lot of players wearing sunglasses, but you don't ever see a player with a piece of tape over their mouth. Perhaps it might be because if someone said, "I check," it might sound like they said, "I sic(K)." Can't have that discrepancy, you wouldn't know whether you were going to get bitten or puked on.

Another dangerous facet of the Vigilant Dominant Personality is that they have a powerful capacity to immediately reference to past experiences and use them for a comparative analysis to understand a current situation they are facing. Experience is a huge edge in any endeavor, so much so that the only proof you need is that those who don't have it often downplay its importance; therein, their lack of experience is speaking loudly. Experience in and of itself is no guarantee for success. It simply means you've been there before. How you use it is the determining factor. Experience is valuable because it tells you what won't work as much as it tells you what will work.

The Vigilant is superb at finding references points from their past experiences that warn them of traps and dangers in current situations. It's like they push a button in their heads and have immediate access to a full playback of the same situation, even though it may have happened ten years ago.

Experience can't be taught, it has to be acquired. Personality types such as the Vigilant, I-Dominant and Loner use it with deadly expertise. Other personality types with the same experience tend to ignore their past experience, because there is a bigger fix in creating a new experience.

If a Vigilant lays down or gets out of a hand when it appears there was no good reason, you can bet money it was because they used a reference point from past experience that warned them. Just this one asset makes it difficult to trap a Vigilant, and increases your risk of being trapped. If the game is no-limit, the danger is more pronounced because it's difficult to protect your ass in increments in a no-limit game, which is what the lack of experience tries to do. The other telling sign is the mind flip-flops and tries to compensate the lack of experience by increasing the risk. Nevertheless, the Vigilant's reference library usually has a book on both plays.

The Vigilant is unemotional in playing style. When they lose they have a tendency to mentally play the hand back as a self-correcting procedure. If an incident occurs at the table the Vigilant has a sharp, caustic tongue. They can have a short, violent temper if pushed in an argument. The Vigilant Dominant Personality will often exhibit a playing style that prefers to capitalize on existing advantages (players errors), rather than trying to create advantages. They are adroit at moving in behind the unsuspecting player. They are respectful of money and usually have a tight reign over its use.

Like the Reflective Dominant Personality, the Vigilant will sometimes recognize their weakness and develop a counterphobic attacking style. They recognize that they are too concerned with knowing, at the expense of taking action. In the counterphobic state, they are extremely dangerous because they usually have more than enough information to start with and are only lacking in action. The Vigilant doesn't attack blindly, their style is often to test, probe, test for the weakness. If they don't find it, they will lay the hand down. Ego is not a controlling factor in this personality, as they are willing to let results speak for themselves.

If you want to tilt the Vigilant Dominant Personality, you have to give them cause to doubt you and your actions. Oftentimes the simplest things will raise the Vigilant's level of suspicion to the paranoid classification. A highly Vigilant Personality will look at the opponent to his left and right before daring to look at his hand. The reason again is caution, caused by suspicion. You create problems in the mind of the Vigilant if he thinks you're watching him examine his hand. A simple act like smiling at the Vigilant creates problems in their minds, as they view themselves as being outside the circle and naturally suspect any attempt by those in the circle to seduce them.

The simplest way to set the wheels spinning in the mind of the Vigilant is to reverse the roles. When the observer is observed they become paranoid. A whisper causes alarm, sit next to the Vigilant and engage them in an endless, mindless conversation and they become agitated. Telling them you thought they flopped a straight after they've exposed it as fact creates another kind of doubt in their mind. It is against the Vigilant where the ability to alter playing style is most important. If you fail to do so, the Vigilant will, in a short period of time, become highly accurate in shadowing your play and extracting a price from you. You want doubt, not action, from the mind of the Vigilant.

The Vigilant Dominant Personality is definitely better equipped to play certain games. A game such as 7-Card Stud, where observation is a necessity, would be one game. Games where drawing and bluffing are the major components would be well-suited to this temperament. No-limit is definitely better than limit. The Vigilant is a superior player in a head-up situation. In limit games, they defuse their skills as there are often too many players involved in a pot and too many observations to be made that serve to distract rather than enhance. This temperament would be superior at no-limit because as the risks increase, the Vigilant's survival orientation is then forced to respond with action. As another kind of example, a Vigilant Dominant Personality would be better on the S.W.A.T. team than being in charge of supplies and wasting his talent wondering who's stealing bullets. The Vigilant needs to fire bullets, not guard them.

In the truest sense, the Vigilant is the parasite of the poker table. Their capability is to find the cracks and flaws within another player's style. It's probable to assume they could grind a living by just moving in behind the mistakes that other players reveal. Their real potential for success is realized if they can combine the vigilance with aggression.

It's my personal opinion that the best poker players are the ones who combine the personality traits of Aggressive/Vigilant, Vigilant/Aggressive or I-Dominant/Vigilant. When there is a compensating trait to accompany the Vigilant streak, this personality type is loosened from the constant mental process of weighing information and being immobilized between hazard/risk vs. detection and sure gain. There is no sure gain in poker. Hazard and risk are necessary components to the game. If you're Vigilant, fire away. If you're not Vigilant wear protective clothing and become a master at creating doubt. Doubt is an invitation to caution. An overly cautious Vigilant always knows where the cookie jar is, but he can't put his hand into it because he's sure someone has poisoned one of the cookies. It's a special torment when you crave Oreos but are fearful of the consequences of indulgence.

♠ The individual at the Bicycle Club revealed his hand through his language. When he was drawing, up against over cards or just plain bluffing he would always say, "I raise." When he had the top pair, pairs, the nuts, etc., he would always say, "I'm gonna raise."

The Vigilant Dominant Personality as a Buyer

Eat your Cheerios and put on your spurs when you start dealing with this personality type. You'll need both. The Vigilant
Personality is dominated by their mind. It's a powerful, consuming
mind that can be either brilliant or a tyrant or a combination
thereof. Selling the Vigilant is a challenge. Any average sales agent
can sell the Emotional, Theatrical or the Underachiever types.
When you start moving up to the Aggressive, I-Dominant and
Vigilant types, your ability as it relates to skill and execution
becomes important factors. With the Vigilant you need to be able
to execute. Skill is essentially knowledge. Many individuals have
skill as it relates to knowledge. It's the ability to execute with the
skills that you have that determines success.

When you're dealing with the Vigilant, you have to use a two-
step selling process. Furthermore, the process has to be sequential
in its order. The first step is you have to sell yourself to the
Vigilant. If you are successful in that endeavor, you must then sell
your product or service to the individual. Understand that initially, your produce or service means nothing to the Vigilant. The
Vigilant will not buy one thing from one individual until they feel
that they can trust you. Execution is important in that it allows
you to use skills in multiple ways. The more adaptable you are at
using your skills to match the differing needs of each personality
type, results in more sales more easily made. Many of the best-sell-
ing agents in this country are of the Theatrical Dominant
Personality mode. They often have enormous selling skills, yet
they fail miserably when selling certain personality types such as
the Vigilant because they don't understand or adapt to what the
Vigilant needs. Remember: two automobiles traveling in different
directions on a one-way street will either collide or wind up at an
impasse. When selling to the Vigilant, either a collision or an
impasse is a losing proposition.

The Vigilant values trust and loyalty above all else. Until these
two factors are established, the Vigilant cannot function as a buyer
because their mind is an objection-creating mechanism. The

Vigilant's mind automatically distrusts everyone until the mind is proven different. When one's mind is distrustful, caution becomes the primary mode of operation. When one's mind is cautious there is a constant looking and searching for the danger in a situation. It's easy to put the Vigilant's mind into overdrive as it relates to caution and suspicion. What you say, how you say it, what you do and how you do it is what the Vigilant judges and reacts to.

The Vigilant traps others because they are superb listeners. They are cool, detached individuals who sit back and let you come forward with the information. Their ability to listen tends to serve as an encouragement for others to talk excessively. The Vigilant listens for inconsistencies in what is being said. If, and when, they detect something that is inconsistent, they store it for a later use. It will at some time become like a scalpel that's used to shred you, your presentation and your product or service. The mind of the Vigilant is the ultimate detective. All they need is one clue that rings untrue. If they find it, they use it as a cornerstone to build an entire case of never-ending distrust.

In many respects, the Vigilant is the most difficult of all personality types to sell. They buy, but they are not great buyers, per se. The true Vigilant Personality is probably less than 5 percent of the total population, so you will never deal with these individuals in large numbers. However, as a professional selling agent, you should realize that it's the tough sales that make you better. Steel, not marshmallows, sharpens steel.

In selling the Vigilant, the one thing that is necessary is the truth. It must be the plain unvarnished truth. It can't be colored, stretched, watered or altered. You can never re-route the Vigilant's mind when it finds a valid objection to you. Any lie or distortion of the truth means an automatic rejection of you forever. The Vigilant has an us vs. them mentality. In their minds "us" is the pure truth, "them" is the lie or the distortion. "Us" is the crusader, "them" is the perpetrator of injustice.

It's no secret that many selling agents stretch the truth about a product or service. Likewise, it's no secret that buyers do the same when dealing with the seller. You can be a completely honest sales agent, but because of the Vigilant's demeanor, find yourself anxious in an unconscious way. When this happens you start distorting your presentation with words like "if," "maybe" and "perhaps." This distortion or conceding happens because you think what you're saying is not penetrating the distance between you and the Vigilant. This is an incorrect assumption on your part. What you are saying is making a huge impact. The question, though, is it negative or positive? If you want to assure that it's positive you must do one thing, stand your ground. If the roof leaks, say so. If the motor needs overhauling, say so. You can negotiate the good, bad and ugly later, you can never negotiate yourself later. Never, never compromise yourself or your position with the Vigilant. If you do, you will never get yourself into a position to sell the product or service.

In selling yourself and your product or service, you need to come straight at the Vigilant. Don't try to be slick, coy, cute, seductive or suede-shoed. The devil's advocate resides full time in the mind of the Vigilant. There is a constant measuring and testing in their mind of what you say and an almost unconscious matching of it to your physical position and movements. The devil's advocate is a voice in their head that dissects and guides the Vigilant's actions. It's a powerful voice that's always on guard, always ready to point out the dark shadows lurking in the hallway.

The Vigilant believes that they are going to be taken advantage of. They keenly remember events from the past that were unfavorable. Therefore, they protect themselves by keeping you at a distance and by being non-committal. In the beginning, the Vigilant speaks in non-committal language. "I don't know," I'm not sure, I haven't thought about it, maybe," etc. This is not a stalling process, but the actual mental process that they feel. When you hear this type of language, you can be fairly certain that they are still in the mental process of accepting or rejecting you personally.

Successfully selling the Vigilant is mainly accomplished by a series of questions and answers. Initially, you will have to do most of the talking, because the Vigilant needs and prefers to listen. It's best to start with a simple introduction of yourself and a reasonable outline of your product or service. In the beginning, ask for one simple commitment. Ask if they are willing to listen to what you have to say about your product or service and then give you their opinion or decision. You'll find this type of individual will be willing to do this, because it's exactly what they needed to hear.

In making a presentation to this type, it's very helpful to watch their eyes. The Vigilant's primary way of accessing information is through hearing. When they hear something that makes an impact they will move their eyes directly to the left or right, then back to center all in a split second. If the eyes move left or right then down, it means you've said something that has probably caused an objection or a question in their mind. Very quick eye movement to the left or right then back to center, will almost always be a signal of an objection, doubt or suspicion. These are objections that won't be verbalized until later. In the present time, the devil's advocate voice is busy laying out all the possibilities to the mind of the Vigilant.

Be prepared to repeat the sales presentation to the Vigilant. During the first presentation, they are busy gathering, sorting and storing objections. They are not hearing the values of your product or service. When you cover the same points in the presentation a second or third time, they will be more prone to verbalize their feelings and to having their mind turned in a direction that frees it to make a decision about the merits of a product or service.

The Vigilant moves slowly and cautiously when making decisions. When they become interested, the devil's advocate part of their mind moves from a silent position to a position of asking verbal questions. The Vigilant tends to ask questions that are serial in nature. The first question is designed to get them into a position to ask a second question that's designed to get them to the third question, which was the question they really wanted to ask in the first place. The first two questions were simply set up or trapping questions.

By listening intently to the questions that the Vigilant asks you can develop an accurate road map to where their mind is. Being paranoid is a form of fear. Fear is the second strongest emotion that human beings can experience. It is also the most crippling human emotion as it relates to taking action. If the individual is highly paranoid, you'll find a mind that is crippled, unable to take direct action. Most Vigilant individuals will take action as it relates to buying only after they've asked sufficient questions that alleviate their fears and suspicions.

The Vigilant is emotionally unemotional. They are afraid to reveal their feelings. However, beneath their cool, detached exterior there lurks an individual who has strong emotions, passions and ideas. As a selling agent, it's difficult to use these emotions to sell this type because they use their emotions as a stifling device instead of a creative mechanism. They can never quite trust their self with their emotions, so they seek logic and reason as the substitute. This substituting only serves to create a conflict that results in further inaction. By listening closely to the questions they ask, you can sometimes detect where their emotions are.

Vigilant individuals value the security of their home, family and friends. They are very protective of these individuals and have a strong desire to provide for their welfare. You can often appeal to these virtues within these individuals to get them to take action.

Closing the Vigilant can be difficult. They are naturally suspicious of contracts. They will often need a detailed explanation of each part of the contract, especially the fine print. In selling a product or service, we almost always work off of the concept of agreeing through contractual agreement and also of binding the parties, with penalty, through the signing of a contract.

Proof of the sale is through the seller obtaining the agreement and signature of the client. This is crunch time, will they or won't they. More importantly, if they don't, what must you do to ensure that they will?

♠ Always use the "contract" as a barometer to determine exactly what you must do next.

♠ Don't slide the contract across the desk.

♠ Always, always, hand it to the buyer. Force them to physically take it in their hands.

♠ Force them to come forward to meet you at least half way in the distance that separates the two of you.

♠ Always tell them "exactly" what you expect them to do.

"John, this is the agreement, look it over then sign at the bottom where your signature is required."

♠ Shut up and pay attention to what the buyer does.

The buyer will reveal two things to you through the action and behavior they show:

1) Exactly what their thoughts and feelings are.

2) The course of action you (the seller) need to take to most effectively correct their behavior.

The buyer will always do one of four things with the contract:

1) Sign the agreement.

2) They do not sign, but keep the agreement in their immediate possession. They will keep it in their hands, fumble with it, lay it down, pick it up, read it again, etc.

3) They do not sign. They read the agreement, then lay it on the desk/table in front of them.

4) They do not sign the agreement. They may or may not read the agreement. They then lay the agreement down and push it away from themselves.

By watching the buyer's behavior with the contract, you receive insight into exactly what they are thinking and feeling. You also have the correct course of action you need to take to counteract their behavior.

A. They sign the agreement. Congratulations, the deal is completed.

B. They don't sign, but keep the agreement in their immediate possession. This behavior is saying, "I really want to do this. . .but." "But" means they need to be reassured. Go over the details once more. Clarify the important points. Emphasize the benefits. Confirm their needs. Explain how the agreement fulfills their needs, then tell them again the behavior you expect from them (I'll need your signature at the bottom, etc.).

C. They don't sign after reading the agreement. They place it in front of themselves, but do not push it away. This behavior indicates that in order to make the sale, there are points that have to be "renegotiated." Find out exactly what issues are causing the problem. Get a commitment that, if these issues can be resolved, the agreement will be signed. Do not renegotiate the issues without first getting the commitment.

D. They don't sign the agreement. They push the agreement away from themselves. The troublesome part is not that they didn't sign the agreement. Many buyers will initially stall when it comes to signing their name. This stalling can almost always be overcome through offering assurance and/or renegotiation of a few sticking points. The trouble arises when the client deliberately pushes the agreement away from their physical self. Often the buyers themselves are unaware of this behavior. What they are doing is rejecting both the deal and the seller. They are completely turned off. Their whole body position mode becomes negative. As a seller, you are put into the most difficult position of having to salvage the deal. You have created the major part of the problem yourself by allowing the objection(s) to rear its ugly head at the worst time (the time of the close). You will not get into this position if you realize, detect and handle the objections during the presentation. Because they have entered into the negative body position mode, your only recourse is this: Don't close, instead, you must resell.

Successful selling of the Vigilant Personality type is more easily accomplished when they feel that you can identify and understand them. The Vigilant has a strong underdog mentality and will deal more easily with those whom they feel are similarly inclined. A sincere interest in their welfare always impacts these individuals positively. The Vigilant will seldom close a deal the first time around. Don't push them. If you do, you will lose them and the sale forever. If you can't close the deal the first time, simply put the burden of proof on them. Ask how and when they want to proceed and use their own comfort level as your guideline.

Money and value are important to the Vigilant. They are tight with money and don't easily part with it. Always show the value of a product or service clearly. Stress dependability, performance, savings, etc. Use logic and reason in a non-threatening manner. As these individuals start to trust and accept you, ask for their input and ideas. To get them to take action, you need their involvement. The Vigilant is not good at giving referrals as they are too much of the lone-wolf type. However, if you're successful at initially getting their business, they tend to give you all of their repeat business. They are much more secure in dealing with you, as a known factor, than having to deal with an unknown stranger. Just make sure that whatever you sell, whatever you promise, is what these individuals receive. If crossed, they are unforgiving and can carry deadly grudges forever.

THE WORKER MORALIST

CLINICAL NAME: OBSESSIVE COMPULSIVE PERSONALITY DISORDER

Positive:	*Negative:*
Work	Workaholic
Hard Worker	Stingy
Principled	Caustic
Moral	Rude
Commitment	Pushy
Team Player	Perfectionist
Strong Character	Emotionally Empty
Detail-Oriented	Overly Concerned with Details
Strong Values	Rigid
Decision Maker	Strict
Dependable	Stubborn
Order	My Way Only
Intense	Narrow-Minded
Loyal	Procrastination
Devoted	Harsh
Systematic	

A Positive Overview

Welcome to the front lines of the American work place. It is this personality type that forms the largest segment of the 13 personalities. In whatever endeavor you choose, you will find many of this personality type. They are outstanding men and women who, more than any of the other 13 personality types, have built this country. They are the driving and sustaining force behind capitalism. They are the building blocks and support system within our society. They are also the majority in family, church, and social endeavors. They are highly principled individuals who have a belief about what is right and what is wrong. They are law-abiding, tax-paying citizens. They are concerned with justice and fair play. They truly believe that mankind functions and fulfills their calling through their work. They are precise in their outlook. There are seldom any areas of gray in their life. They strive to be efficient. They are precise, disciplined and are willing to sacrifice in order to accomplish their goals. They pride themselves on being very good judges of character. Their style is one of steadiness with a disdain for the spectacular. They are dedicated to their families, to the organizations of which they belong, and always to those who employ them.

The Negative Side

They can be overbearing, demanding of others, and severe taskmasters who will berate someone for making a mistake. They are workaholics who are often consumed by the need to do more. Often the doing of more is not enough. If they show up for work by 7:00 a.m. they, likewise, expect you to be there. No task, including those that they do, is ever completed to their satisfaction. They are perfectionists. The quest to do it better often stymies the project. The Worker Moralist views the world through a very narrow tunnel. Everything is black or white, clear cut. Reality is "The" truth, not "A" truth. This stringent outlook will often cause conflict between co-workers or other family members who possess a different dominant personality trait.

Further complicating the situation beyond the black/white syndrome, is that they tend to view everything in the context of right or wrong. They have strong convictions and beliefs. If you are like them, you're okay. If your beliefs and convictions are different, then it can be a sore spot. The Worker Moralist sometimes appears to be rude, uncaring, and unsympathetic to the needs of others. Their brusk, business-like manner is often intimidating. They are often described by others as being stone-faced, empty or unemotional. Often they give the appearance of being unaffected by anything, simply content to try and maintain the status quo.

Identifying And Playing With The Worker Moralist Dominant Personality

These individuals are distinct in many ways. They, of all the 13 personality traits, are the most predictable. They are the most comfortable with the familiar, with the routine. To the Worker Moralist viewpoint, the world is a very tough place to exist in. Life is harsh. The only way to survive and succeed in such an environment is to be willing to put your nose to the grindstone and keep it there. They view work and accomplishment as the separating factor between right and wrong, good and bad.

Immediately after the work ethic is their belief about moral ethics. The Worker Moralist Dominant Personality believes they are superior individuals. It doesn't matter what the beliefs entail or the doctrines that give cause to the assumed moral superiority. This supposed superiority doesn't even have to have its roots in religion. They simply believe their guiding principles and the beliefs they adhere to, along with the character they possess, makes them a class above all others. Naturally, the next step is a separating of people into classes. They are quick to internally catalogue individuals into an us vs. them, right vs. wrong, superior vs. inferior designation. The more rigid the personality type becomes, results in more stringent classifications. It suddenly goes beyond good/bad to good/evil, or right/wrong to right/heathen.

The rigid Worker Moralist Dominant Personality has a severe problem with pleasure. They don't want to allow themselves any more than the bare minimum, while they are morally outraged at anyone who dares to live a lifestyle that ignores their viewpoint while freely indulging in a lifestyle that says "pleasure is good, even a divine gift." Morally superior people earn pleasure, inferior individuals seek pleasure. At its rigid worst, the Worker Moralist will try to enact rules, laws or regulations that hinder or prohibit others in a pursuit or endeavor.

The driving force within the Worker Moralist Personality is the need for perfection. After all, if the individual believes they are superior, then perfection is the barometer that provides proof. The quest for perfection is a conflict-creating mechanism. The inability to attain it results in an even more desperate attempt to reach it. The quest for perfection is not some haphazard, shotgun approach. It has to be sought for in a very precise, detailed, thought-out manner.

We will list some of the identifiable characteristics of this personality type. They are more easily identified by their actions and reactions than by any physical characteristics. They come in all sizes, shapes and forms. They could be your doctor, an engineer, your next door neighbor, your husband or the poker player sitting next to you.

A. The Compulsion For Details. The Worker Moralist Dominant Personality elevates the need to know details to the classification of deity status. They have an overriding compulsion to take care of the details. To be spontaneous is to be inferior. Everything has to be planned. They don't just jump in their car and take a trip. The trip has to be planned, the car has to be thoroughly checked, the calendar has to be cleared, a list has to be prepared. The packing has to be done in a very specific fashion. The itinerary has to be carefully thought out, e.g., eat breakfast at 7:00 a.m., drive 200 miles, take a break, eat dinner at 6:00 p.m., be in bed at 9:00 p.m., up at 6:00 a.m., etc. Then there has to be a contingency list of "what if." At some point, the destination becomes secondary to the details of getting there. The mental process is, "Ready, ready, ready, aim, aim, aim, fire." If they miss the target, they don't just fire away again, instead the whole detailed process must be examined in even greater detail to discover what went wrong.

B. The Lecture Of Intolerance. God help you if you're one of those creatures who is different. If you're going on the trip also, and your idea of fun is to throw something in a bag, toss it in the trunk and fly by the seat of your pants, then beware. You have created a conflict for yourself and for the rigidly programmed Worker Moralist. The first tactic of the Worker Moralist is to point out the error of your way. If that fails to cause sufficient repentance, the next tactic is to lecture you on your inferiority. Next comes outright criticism. You're wrong, this is not the way to do things, you should, you shouldn't. The final tactic is rejection and a cold indifference to you, your feelings and a determination to prove you wrong (punishment), and to affirm their superiority (reward). The Worker Moralist has a low tolerance for that which is different and cannot be reformed.

C. Restricted Feelings. The Worker Moralist has difficulty with feelings or revealing emotions. They can often relate how they feel about "things" or "situations" much better than they can understand their feelings toward people. Their feelings are often relegated to providing the essentials and using that as proof of feelings. In other words, they make the house payment, pay the insurance, mow the grass. That is their proof that they care. However, to have a hot, throbbing passion, or to have to declare emotional intensities is often processed as something that's not necessary, or it's something they prefer not to experience. They may have some vague idea that they should feel more, but the end result is they seldom experience it as it is not something they are comfortable with.

They understand the world differently. It's black and white, order and disorder, nuts and bolts make more sense than roses and hearts. This is not to say they won't bring roses. They will if they sense an obligation or if they can see through a detailed analysis of how it might enhance an objective they have. "Things," "nuts and bolts" and "inanimate objects" are preferable because they are easier to understand. There is no anarchy in "things," no chance for unmanageable chaos to disturb the 2+2=4 equation that neatly explains life and how it should work.

D. The Guiding Light. The Worker Moralist Dominant Personality has an inner voice that is a severe taskmaster. It is a constant critic. Every move, impulse, thought or reaction is done with one ear attuned to what this internal critic is saying. This inner voice is what keeps the Worker Moralist on the straight and narrow. When they deviate from the proper course, the critic is harsh, judgmental and scornful of the actions. We all, as human beings, have this internal critic. Most times it functions as friend and keeper. With the Worker Moralist, it tends to become the dictator. It assumes a dictatorial position, because the individual gives too much credence to what should have been done or what could have been done better.

By listening to this internal critic, the Worker Moralist loses sight of a very significant concept which is: In an imperfect world, imperfection works better than perfection. There is no one perfectly correct way to accomplish everything. However, the need to hide behind the apron of perfection provides the perfect vehicle for accomplishing very little. Justification becomes easy when you can explain to the self that the reason you're not in the middle of the battle is because the battle is imperfect. The worst critics are those who criticize from the sidelines. Their commentary is invariably, "What I would have done." It stinks to high heaven as it's impotent in the face of "What I have done."

The Worker Moralist Dominant Personality is a textbook gambler. That is not only a misnomer, but also the problem this personality type has with realizing success at poker. It's sorta like saying you performed a mercy killing on your neighbor because he had a sore throat. Mercy killing is a misnomer. Textbook gamblers cannot win because the textbook cannot provide the essence of the gambler or the spirit that creates, thus enables or empowers, the "gamble" that's inherently necessary. The textbook is a part of the whole. With the Worker Moralist, it becomes the whole, plus it's the mechanism for replacing the gambler and the gamble (risk). Gambling by the textbook causes several problems. It's sorta like a catch 22 situation. Often the Worker Moralist does everything so correct it becomes incorrect. They bring several assets to the table that are good, necessary to beat the game. It's the style with which they use these assets that creates the catch 22. We'll cover some of these next.

A. Discipline. The Worker Moralist has a God-called discipline. It dominates every facet of their lives. At the poker table, they practice this discipline to the highest degree. Q-10 off suit never looks like a monster hand to this personality type. They are programmed to wait for the right hand, the right situation and then make the right decision. All of this is fine: however, every other player at the table is aware of what they are doing and the end result becomes ineffectiveness.

The Worker Moralist form of discipline creates a glaring predictability. This predictability exposes their hand and their probable course of action. Some of these individuals are so programmed in their style of play that they might as well play with their hands exposed. As the other player, all you have to do to win is stay out of their way when it's obvious. In a Hold'em game where they come in from an early position without raising, always gives me cause to suspect a big hand. It's a trait of this personality to try and sneak in early with a big pair. They do this because experience has taught them that if they raise they lose opponents faster than Hussein loses airplanes. The end result of this predictability is the size of the pots they win is less than the true value of their hands.

B. The Grind To Oblivion. The Worker Moralist is the grinder of the 13 personality types. I strongly believe the commitment to grind is the biggest asset that a poker player can bring to the table. However, I believe just as strongly that the grind is an asset only if you can use it to set up the times in a game where you can bring out a sledgehammer and enforce your will on the table. I use a ratio of 80 percent grind 20 percent sledgehammering. The Worker Moralist eventually falters at the game of poker because the only ratio they can comprehend is 100 percent grind.

It's not going to get any better, because they can't change what they are. I have a head full of gray hair. If it weren't for knowing better, I would tell you it's because of their inability to change how they operate and view the world. At one time, I had sales organizations that comprised hundreds of individuals. These types of organizations break down into components of thirds. The top third is comprised of the high-flying personality types such as the I-Dominant, the Adventurer, the Aggressive, the Theatrical, the Emotional, etc. The top third produces 50 percent of the business and creates 90 percent of the problems. The middle third is comprised almost exclusively of the Worker Moralist personality type. They create 40 percent of the business and cause about 2 percent of the client/company problems. The bottom third is comprised of the specialty type personalities that are in the process of either moving up or moving out the door. It is the middle third who were valuable. They wrote good business, caused little trouble, and most of all, they were dependable. The top third was the most talented, caused the most problems, and were the least dependable.

I valued the Worker Moralist because they were the most cost-efficient. Their liability was they couldn't be spectacular. I couldn't move them into the top third to replace the Prima Donnas, thereby reducing my cost, because they were limited in what they could produce. They could grind until the cows came home, but they could never take the bull by the horns and accomplish the extraordinary. For years, I labored under the false belief that I could change them. I tried encouragement, intensive training, role playing, threats, etc. Nothing worked. You can't give pizzazz to those that don't have it. You can't give boldness or daring to those who don't understand it. I finally accepted the fact that the only thing they could do, because it was the only thing they felt comfortable with, was grind it out day after day. I never changed one Worker Moralist. If anything, I made them worse as they fell flat on their faces when they tried to be jet fighter pilots, while their personality traits kept screaming to them, "you're a foot soldier."

The Worker Moralist grinds because it's how he finds his security in this world. In the real world, and in the world of poker, a central issue with the Worker Moralist is they need, crave, must have, security. The Worker Moralist loves money. It's the reward. It's proof of security and protection that their world will not be torn asunder. The next logical question then has to be, "If the above is so, then why do they gamble?" It's a good question, but the answer is even better, "They don't gamble." No Worker Moralist ever sat down at a poker table to win money. The sit down to earn some money. They look across the table at those sitting there to win money and categorize them as fools. Poker is a job, not a game, and the only way they can understand it is the way they understand everything else. . .the nose to the grindstone.

C. The Issue Of Risk. To a Worker Moralist Dominant Personality, a bird in the hand is worth more than any 100 birds in the bush. In fact, they don't even want to stick their hand in the bush. To say that the Worker Moralist is tight is a linguistic kindness. They are stingy. Their mental process is to hold on to what they have. They process risk differently than any of the other 13 personality types. Risk is viewed in the context of,"what I could lose," never in the context of "what I could gain." I used to do some very serious, intensive, training with this type. I wanted them to become more bold, to take more chances. Their resistance came in the form of a common thread that held them all together. Their ultimate response was, "Yes, but what if I lose, I'd rather have a sure three sales out of ten than take a chance of getting six out of ten and maybe losing the three."

I really became aware of how serious this issue was with them when some of them confided to me in private that they were worried about me. They were afraid I would head the company in a direction that involved too much risk, and therefore, jeopardize their position.

D. A Confused Mind Automatically Stalls. The desire to not lose through the taking of risks creates another problem. The only way you can gamble without risk is to always be right. If you make the correct decision at all times, the risk is nullified by the correct decision. If you have the A-K of hearts and the flop comes Q-J-10 of hearts, there is no risk and the correct decision is easily arrived at. However, most decisions in poker are slightly more difficult than the one above.

The Worker Moralist, in a vain struggle to make the most correct decision that most effectively reduces the risk, runs smack into the wall of their own mind. They are suddenly caught in the trap of saying, "Should I do this or should I do that?" "Is this more correct or is that more correct?" "If I do this, would it be better than doing that?", and, "If I did that how much better would it be than doing that?" The ultimate result is the right or wrong, which would be better, debating confuses the mind. When the mind is confused, it stalls. If the mind is being pulled in ten different directions it's unable to go in any direction. When the mind has effectively stalled, the resultant behavior is procrastination and the inability to do anything.

In poker games procrastination is most likely to result in behavior that exhibits itself in the form of checking, checking then calling, surrendering the hand, or in extreme cases, check raising or bluffing. When you match the personality to the maneuver, you can greatly reduce possibilities.

An effective way of understanding and dealing with the different personality types is by asking yourself a couple of questions:

A. "What is it that this personality type wants or needs? e.g., action, ego stroking, safety, etc.?"

B. "How are they most likely to try attaining it?"

C. "Is it to my advantage to supply or deny what they need?"

The Adventurer Dominant Personality wants, needs and craves action. They want to gamble. They are most likely to try and get the action by hard gambling. They will up the stakes, increase the risk factor, etc. Your success depends on whether you make the correct decision on the supplying or denying of what they are wanting. This is true of all the personality types. The Worker Moralist wants you to allow him to play with the least possible risk. His primary objective is to grind you down. In the sales profession, it took the Worker Moralist, on average, 40 percent longer to complete a sale than the other personality types. It took him 40 percent longer because he was a superb grinder. If nothing else, some people would buy from him out of the fear that he might continue to sit there, causing their death to be premature, through boredom. The best rule I can give you in playing with the Worker Moralist is:

"DON'T GRIND THE GRINDER"

You have to increase the risk to a level that is downright uncomfortable. You want to plant the idea in their head that poker is the wrong game for those who want to keep it in their back pocket. When the risk increases to an uncomfortable level, the Worker Moralist will always take steps to cut their losses. That proverbial rainy day is a very real component to their mind; you can't save for a rainy day if you're living on the edge. The grinder succeeds because they are content to get it one nickel at a time. Their strength is to position themselves in such a manner that you, also, have to grind. In the real world, they succeed. The proof is that they own a fairly sizeable chunk of the world.

The Worker Moralist hides their true feelings. You may think they appear unaffected by emotional storms. However, behind that facade or serenity, there are tides of emotions. They keep it hidden, because it's inferior to be a basket case. The two emotions that are most often prevalent are anger and resentment. They often have anger at themselves through the inner realization (although not verbally expressed), that life is more than the hand they deal themselves. The obsessive side (the thought), of their nature comes in conflict with the compulsive side (the action). It's a constant tug of war between giving in to the compulsion and hating and trying to suppress the obsession. Good little boys that want to be bad, but won't let themselves, are going to have large conflicts to wrestle with.

The other emotion, which is resentment, is directed toward others. They resent those who can let their hair down and let the chips fly. All the resentment accomplishes is it makes the upper lip even stiffer. The resentment tends to build and seethe to the point that they develop a hatred and coldness toward those other "kinds" of people. There is often a great desire to punish this behavior. The problem is it's hard to extract enough punishment when it's done a nickel at a time.

The Worker Moralist is not naturally instinctive, intuitive or perceptive. They tend to learn by rote. They often are so preoccupied with the routine they can't comprehend the intricate. They figure out the puzzle, one piece at a time, instead of trying to see how the big picture looks. The failure to look at the possibilities of the bigger picture will often make it more difficult to put the pieces in one piece at a time. Instead of turning the big picture over in their minds, they're left with the exhaustive chore of turning hundreds of small pieces constantly to find the proper fit.

Control is a driving force within this personality. They want and need self-control. Being out of control is weakness. One of the ways they ensure self-control is by utilizing the inner voice as a constant reminder. The inner voice constantly warns them that there are no short cuts, there is no easy way. The Worker Moralist likes to have their ducks in a row. When there is confusion, the road to travel becomes unclear. When the course is unclear, they become guarded, because the fear of mistakes rears its ugly head. Procrastination becomes the enemy. One of the manifestations of procrastination is the spinning wheels effect. It appears to the self and to others that progress is being made, yet it's an illusion. The wheels are turning, yet the self is stuck in mud. When the procrastination is severe, the simplest decisions become difficult. Sometimes at the poker table, it seems like the simplest decision stretches out forever.

The Worker Moralist criticizes the self more harshly than any of the other 13 personality types. Many times, it's an endless dressing down. When the criticism comes from an outside source, it stings the soul, making the individual do a critical self-analysis. In severe cases, the Worker Moralist will go to extreme lengths to avoid the self-criticism. They often become workaholics out of the need to prove themselves worthy to the self.

The Worker Moralist tends to blame themselves when they lose. Because of this, they will often have difficulty playing back to back hands after a severe loss. They need to analyze and correct excessively whatever went wrong during the loss. It's this need to analyze and correct that often gives others the idea that they have tightened up or screwed it down another notch. This self-analysis and correcting procedure is often an exercise in futility. What the Worker Moralist loses sight of in the game of poker is that it's not his technical play or his textbook that is in need of analysis. It's the style that is causing the problem. However, the Worker Moralist rejects that concept out of hand, as they can't see any other style that would be acceptable to their inner self.

The planes land in Las Vegas every day. What often walks off these planes is the counterphobic Worker Moralist. They arrive from far-flung destinations. When they are away from home, away from the role of their self-image, an amazing transformation occurs. They become gamblers. They let the hair down and whoop and holler it up for a few days. The naughty little boy locked inside has escaped. Into the poker rooms of California and Las Vegas they come marching. The chips are flying and there is no draw too big to consider. If they lose, it's okay. After all, this is Las Vegas, or they're at The Bike. If they can give you a bad beat, it's even better. It makes the whole trip worthwhile.

This sudden shift in personality and new-found bravado doesn't last long. The guy sitting at the poker table Saturday night is totally different than the one who will return home and go to work Monday morning. The inner critic will sober his senses and he'll quickly return to the grind.

POKER, SEX & DYING

One of the more interesting facets of this Saturday night Worker Moralist is that they always have to have their buddies or companions with them. It's too much of a deviation from the norm to go it alone. It just goes to show you that three Worker Moralists can have as much fun as one Adventurer. In poker games where these individuals are playing, you have to be willing to step up your own game. If you play too conservatively these guys won't catch the plane home as they are having too much fun. The counterphobic Worker Moralist is even fun to be around at these times. It wouldn't even surprise me if I saw one of them make a field bet on the crap table someday. . .On second thought, though, I doubt it. That would be too much fun.

The Worker Moralist Dominant Personality will often become a better player in a game like Hold'em as the hand progresses. As the information becomes more abundant, they can more easily make the correct decision. The "am I right, am I wrong" debate in their mind is satisfied when details or information is clarified. Conversely, if cards come on or after the flop that complicate the possibilities or increase the chance of a wrong decision, then it's more likely that they will stall. When the Worker Moralist is in this state of mind, a raise, re-raises or outright bluffing are often enough to take the pot. At the worst, their inability to decide will be enough to get you a free card.

This personality type is tenacious. They don't quit. It's a mistake to underestimate the quality of tenaciousness in an individual. To other personality types, these individuals often appear unglamorous, dull, plodding; yet, it's these very qualities that are an intricate part of the game that stumbles many of the other high-flying personality types. Being steady and methodical serves as an anchor in troubled waters. It stays their course, while other less tenacious individuals will be swept aside by impatience, lack of control or the need to grab for satisfaction too many times. The Worker Moralist is a blue collar poker player. They will show up every day to grind the table. Their ability to bring it every day should serve as fair warning that they possess some assets that are both desirable and dangerous in the game of poker.

The Worker Moralist Dominant Personality as a Buyer

The Worker Moralist Personality type is the No. 1 buyer of all the 13 personality types. They come in every shape and size and can be found in every profession. They are business executives, doctors, lawyers, owners of their own business, assembly line workers, housewives, etc. They are the heart, soul and many times, the conscience of our country. They comprise roughly 40 percent of the total population.

This type of individual has a strong moral sense about themselves and about others. They have definite ideas about what constitutes right and wrong and about how one should live. Their mental process is be responsible, be reliable, strive for perfection and work hard to get what you want out of life.

The world they live in is relatively simple. There is a right way and a wrong way of doing things. They have a compulsion that drives them to dot all the i's and cross all the t's. They believe that life is hard, that the mentally tough are the ones who survive and flourish. Work, hard work, long hours, sacrifice and attention to all details are what brings reward.

The Worker Moralist Personality type is easy to sell if you understand a couple of their driving mental forces. First and foremost, they have a compulsion for detail. This type of individual can only deal with and comprehend the big picture by first knowing all the small pieces. Many high-flying sales agents stumble because they try to ram and jam the big picture at these individuals. It just won't work. The Worker Moralist is a frustrated perfectionist. The only way they can get their perfection fix is by carefully examining each part of the puzzle over and over. The Worker Moralist has a powerful need to do the right thing, to make the right decision. The flip side of this need is a fear of being wrong, a fear of making mistakes or the wrong decision.

Over the years, I've trained hundreds of selling agents who would sneeringly refer to these people as engineer types when they couldn't sell them. What the selling agents failed to realize was just because mundane details were not important to them didn't mean it wasn't important to the Worker Moralist. To successfully sell the Worker Moralist you have to adopt their mentality. As a selling agent, you may be full of creative flash, unending enthusiasm and high-flying dreams, but don't think the Worker Moralist is. If you want to sell these individuals, you are going to have to get your fingernails dirty. You are going to have to grind them as hard as they grind you. You are going to have to earn the sale in that old-fashioned way called work. Hard work.

If you go to a social event, walk into their office or just make their casual acquaintance, you'll find one of their first probable questions to be "What do you do?" "What kind of work do you do?" That, in itself, should give you a clue to what is important in their mental process. Worker Moralist Personality types like and are most comfortable with other individuals who have the same values and belief system that they have. To their way of thinking, that means you have earned your spurs exactly as they have. If you're not like them, then it's quite possible that you have a character flaw and must be dealt with in a very cautious manner.

The Worker Moralist needs a structured, very precise presentation. They need to be overwhelmed with details. The Worker Moralist has a very severe critic in their head that judges their every move. It's a stern task master who berates weaknesses and mistakes. These are individuals who are caught between the need to do what's right and the fear of doing anything, because it might be incorrect. Their inner critic is silenced when every possible detail has been covered, in depth.

The Worker Moralist is not entrepreneurial in their outlook. They prefer the tried and true over the unknown. Taking risks makes this type uncomfortable. Foolish, unreliable individuals take risks. Solid, moral individuals do not gamble with their future or their company's future. This type is attracted to products or services that have a proven track record. Reliability, dependability, warranties, guarantees, etc., are components that soothe this personality type's mind.

All of their values are rooted in family, business, friends and organizations. These are the things that give them comfort; these are the things that fulfill their purpose in life. The Worker Moralist is a duty-bound individual. They have a strong need and desire to be good providers. They work hard and their dependability is beyond question. Work always comes before pleasure.

The Worker Moralist does not have a free-flowing creative mind. Their skill is acquired by repetition, by doing something over and over until they have mastered it. They buy in the same manner. Flashy, imaginative presentations do not make an impact on their mind. They want and need substance. They need to have assurances about quality heaped upon them. The Worker Moralist is an organization-type person. They need and seek the security of others who share their opinion. If you can use referrals and testimonials from others as it relates to your product or service, it impacts their mind positively.

When the Worker Moralist is unsure about what to do, they procrastinate. They become trapped by the "am I right, am I wrong" debate in their mind. They are great at saying, "I want to think about it." When this happens, you need to go back to square one with this type. Clarify every possible point to find out what the stumbling block is. Many times, you will find it comes down to dollar value. The Worker Moralist is, at best, tight and, at worst, down-right stingy. They equate money with security. Their world would be a frightful place if it had no security in it. The two objections that most often stall the selling process are:

A. "Money"

and

B. "I want to think about it"

These are objections about value.

The question I'm most often asked is, how to handle the above two objections. There is only one fail-proof way that I know of to handle these objections.

When the service or product being offered has a "value" in the mind of the buyer that exceeds the "cost" by 1 cent, it is automatically bought.

The above statement is one of the most basic statements that I can make about human behavior. It is the first and foremost law of selling or persuading. When you hear money as an objection, what they are really saying is, "Hey! In my mind I don't have enough value to part with my hard-earned money." When you hear, "We'll think about it," they are saying in the politest way that they know, "Sorry, I'm confused, you want my money, but I can't see the value of what you are offering." 90 percent of the time when you dig behind the "I want to think about it" objection, you will find the root problem is money vs. value.

Build the "value" to the point where the buyer is the loser.

When the value is built beyond the cost, the buyer's mind will snap. Their internal programming will make them the loser if they fail to buy. If you take it to the point where it is not a case of whether they will win, but rather, to what they will lose if they don't buy, they start selling themselves. It is much easier to build value than to negotiate price. You are limited on what you can do as it relates to price. You are practically unlimited as to what you can do as it relates to value. Additionally, it is much easier to deal with buyers when discussing value as opposed to money.

Be prepared.

If you can't think of a minimum of 20 value features and/or benefits, you are going to lose sales. The average buyer needs a minimum of 5 concrete values to become interested. If you can only think of five or six, they may not be the values that the buyer needs. By having at least 20 you have the ammunition to deal with the hardest buyers.

If this personality type stalls at a time when the sale should be logically concluded, you may have to ask them to help sell themselves. The Worker Moralist is a team player. They are usually fairminded people. The problem is, they are sometimes not fair with themselves. Many times you can ask these individuals to put themselves in your shoes. Ask what course they would follow to solve a problem. The Worker Moralist is not manipulative, per se. However, they are stubborn in their desire to be right, to be more perfect. Sometimes you have to make these individuals see that the rigidness of their personality is hurting only themselves or the ones they care most about. Self-denial is a way these types sometimes find acceptance within themselves.

In selling to this type, you want to eliminate as much risk as possible. Propositions that are risky causes the voice in their heads to start screaming, thus confusing their decision-making process. Don't pull surprises on this personality type and don't try to be cute. They find their security level in the middle of the road. They respond to honesty, integrity and old-fashioned morals. Common sense, logic and reason are more of a motivating factor than emotional impulses. This type is not overly emotional. They often use and understand responsibility and obligation more than any kind of emotional passion.

From a financial standpoint, this personality type is usually solid. They may not be rich, but they will almost always have money, because they are prudent and thrifty. If they are satisfied with you and the deal they receive, they are excellent at giving referrals. As a selling agent, you want to be able to sell this personality type. If you master them, they are money in the bank. At times, they can be frustrating individuals. A presentation can drag on endlessly sometimes as they become mired down in needing detail and assurances. However, if you understand that they are just wanting to do the right thing and are fearful of anything less, perhaps you will develop the patience and persistence needed to satisfy this personality type.

IN THE END...

THERE IS NO END. When we are dealing with a subject as explosive or difficult as human personality traits, caution becomes necessary. There are no absolutes. All individuals are unique. Every opponent is potentially dangerous. We can, with a certain degree of accuracy, predict actions and reactions; however, we cannot definitively define how any human being will react 100 percent of the time. In many respects, insight, knowledge and understanding creates a Pandora's Box. The more knowledge we acquire, and the more understanding we gain, often only serves to highlight the knowledge and understanding that we don't have. The more we learn simply teaches us that we are always on the tip of the iceberg, and ironically, may never be able to move beyond that point. Expertise, be it given or solicited, is like a jagged piece of glass in that it's best handled with care.

There are many aspects of the human spirit that cannot be predicted or measured. No one is an expert when it comes to predicting the higher qualities of the human experience. Qualities like love, faith, hope and desire cannot be measured nor defined in terms of their limit or their impact. At best, we can only hope that we can possess these qualities for ourselves. If there is one certainty, in life it's that there will always be uncertainty. Acceptance and change are a part of life. Our ability to deal with it is directly related to our success. Success is not a mystery. It's easily defined. If we have happiness and joy, we are successful. If we don't have happiness and joy, then any imagined success we think we have is someday destined to be a bitter pill that's called an awakening. Ultimately, the game you play won't matter. What will matter is you, the individual. Be brave, be kind, be bold, find your happiness. Give it your best at all times. The results will speak. . . in your defense and in your honor. It's the mark of a champion, in life and in poker. I will close with something I wrote many years ago, "The love you give. . . the memories you keep, a mirror that easily measures every man."

RECOMMENDED READING

Bringing Down the House:
The Inside Story of Six MIT Students Who Took Vegas for Millions
By Ben Mezrich

Welcome to the world of an exclusive group of audacious MIT math geniuses who legally took the casinos for over three million dollars -- while still finding time for college keg parties, football games, and final exams. Filled with tense action and incredibly close calls, *Bringing Down the House* is a real-life mix of *Liar's Poker* and *Ocean's Eleven* -- and it's a story Vegas doesn't want you to read.

$24.00   Item #742690

Knock-Out Blackjack:
The Easiest Card-Counting System Ever Devised
By Olaf Vancura

The revolutionary new Knock-Out and card counting system eliminates the mountain of mental arithmetic necessary to win at blackjack. This second edition, revised and expanded, is now easier to use than ever!

$17.95   Item #96803

Guerrilla Gambling:
How to Beat the Casinos at Their Own Games!
By Frank Scoblete

Guerrilla Gambling is the most authoritative, insightful, and complete guide you'll find for taking command of today's games! It's more than just a guide – it is a guided missile that explodes with winning strategies that can help players win their war against the casinos.

$12.95   Item #529625

Find all at the lowest prices – ANYWHERE!

www.superbookdeals.com